MW00985604

Oliver Wendell Holmes Jr., Pragmatism, and the Jurisprudence of Agon

Oliver Wendell Holmes Jr., Pragmatism, and the Jurisprudence of Agon

Aesthetic Dissent and the Common Law

Allen Mendenhall

Lewisburg
BUCKNELL UNIVERSITY PRESS

Published by Bucknell University Press
Copublished by The Rowman & Littlefield Publishing Group, Inc.
4501 Forbes Boulevard, Suite 200, Lanham, Maryland 20706
www.rowman.com

Unit A, Whitacre Mews, 26-34 Stannary Street, London SE11 4AB

British Library Cataloguing in Publication Information Available

Library of Congress Cataloging-in-Publication Data

Names: Mendenhall, Allen, 1983– author.
Title: Oliver Wendell Holmes Jr., pragmatism, and the jurisprudence of Agon :
  aesthetic dissent and the common law / Allen Mendenhall.
Description: Lewisburg, Pa. : Bucknell University Press, 2016. | Includes
  bibliographical references and index.
Identifiers: LCCN 2016043389 (print) | LCCN 2016044223 (ebook) | ISBN
  9781611487916 (cloth : alk. paper) | ISBN 9781611487923 (electronic)
Subjects: LCSH: Holmes, Oliver Wendell, Jr., 1841–1935. | Dissenting
  opinions—United States. | United States. Supreme Court. | Judges—United
  States—Biography. | United States. Supreme Court—Officials and
  employees—Biography.
Classification: LCC KF8745.H6 M36 2016 (print) | LCC KF8745.H6 (ebook) | DDC
  347.73/2634—dc23
LC record available at https://lccn.loc.gov/2016043389

∞™ The paper used in this publication meets the minimum requirements of
American National Standard for Information Sciences—Permanence of Paper
for Printed Library Materials, ANSI/NISO Z39.48-1992.

Printed in the United States of America

For Marc Silverstein

Contents

Tables

Preface

This book argues that Oliver Wendell Holmes Jr. can help us see the law through an Emersonian lens because of the style in which he wrote his judicial dissents. By using an aesthetic approach borrowed from Emerson and carried out by later pragmatists, Holmes not only made it more likely that his judicial dissents would remain alive for future judges or justices (because how they were written was itself memorable, whatever the value of their content), but also shaped our understanding of dissents and, in this, our understanding of the law itself. When different judges or justices on the same case disagree as to the legal reasoning or conclusions that should be applied, the majority's opinion becomes the official ruling, but judges in the minority may compose a "dissent" to influence later rulings in related cases. By opening constitutional precedent to potential change, Holmes's famous dissents made room for future thought, moving our understanding of legal concepts toward pragmatism and away from formalism. This new understanding involved the idea that the "canon" of judicial cases includes oppositional positions that must be sustained if the law is to serve pragmatic purposes.

Chapter 1 begins with preliminary explanations of dissents and the legal system. The remainder of the chapter explores the implications of Richard Poirier's theories of Emersonian superfluity for an analysis Holmes's jurisprudence. Chapter 2 adds to the concept of superfluity another pragmatic theory flowing from Emerson: "the poetics of transition." This theory, articulated by Jonathan Levin, helps us understand the vindication of Holmes's dissents. Chapter 3 considers the implications of Holmes's notions of freedom of speech and expression for the evolution of the legal canon in a common-law system. Chapter 4 suggests that Holmes's Emersonian pragmatism, as expressed through his dissents and his evolutionary paradigm of the common law, represents a synthesis of Emerson and fellow pragmatists C.S. Peirce, William James, and John Dewey.

Mindful that a book of this nature and content will have multiple audiences—legal, philosophical, and literary—I have avoided the kind of disciplinary jargon and specialized subject matter that might divide or distract readers. Holmes demands an interdisciplinary approach. He was a poet who read novels and poetry and felt that the law instantiated the practical effects of philosophy, yet lawyers and judges continue to consult his writings for guidance and authority. It is the distinct merit of the pragmatic method that it appeals to anyone who undertakes to make his or her ideas clear and to facilitate constructive lines of inquiry. I hope that this book serves as a bridge to more study and questioning and enables the conversation about Holmes, dissents, pragmatism, and common-law jurisprudence to continue unabated, expand wider and deeper, and reach more curious minds.

Acknowledgments

I wish to thank the following individuals who read all or portions of this book before its publication: Marc Silverstein, James Emmett Ryan, Kelly Kennington, Theodore L. Becker, Catharine Wells, Aron Ping D'Souza, Alexander "Sasha" Volokh, Anne Richardson Oakes, Wayne Chapman, Mike Reid, and the anonymous peer reviewers selected by Bucknell University Press. I am grateful to Greg Clingham for making this book possible, Pamelia Dailey for guidance, and Sanford Levinson for sharing research. I am also grateful to Zachary Nycum at Rowman and Littlefield for his assistance with the more irritating aspects of transforming an unpublished manuscript into a published book. Peter R. Hanchak, Wallace Stevens's grandson, kindly granted permission for me to reprint his grandfather's work.

I have dedicated this book to Marc Silverstein, who teaches by example how to maintain scholarly objectivity and integrity. He is open to considering all views, no matter how much they differ from his own, and he attempts in good faith to understand the arguments of those with whom he disagrees. I am a libertarian. He is not. Our conversations about law, economics, and politics were always civil and constructive. His influence allowed me to write fairly and impartially about Holmes, whose jurisprudence is often at odds with my own.

I also thank the editors, journals, and organizations that have granted their permission to reprint material that they previously published. Portions of this book first appeared as follows: "Oliver Wendell Holmes Jr. and the Darwinian Common Law Paradigm," *European Journal of Pragmatism and American Philosophy* 7, no. 2 (2015): 129–151; "Pragmatism on the Shoulders of Emerson: Oliver Wendell Holmes Jr.'s Jurisprudence as a Synthesis of Emerson, Peirce, James, and Dewey," *The South Carolina Review* 48, no. 1 (2015): 93–109; "Oliver Wendell Holmes Jr. Is the Use of Calling Emerson a Pragmatist: A Brief and Belated Response to Stanley Cavell," *Faulkner Law Review* 6, no. 1 (2014): 197–230; "Dissent as a Site of Aesthetic Adaptation in the Work of Oliver Wendell Holmes Jr.," *British Journal of American Legal Studies* 1 (2012): 512–550; and "Holmes and Dissent," *The Journal Jurisprudence* 12 (2011): 679–726. Thanks are in order, as well, for Henry Holt and Company, LLC, and Penguin Random House, LLC, for the permissions described at the end of this Acknowledgments section. Wordsworth Editions, Ltd., kindly granted permission for me to reproduce an excerpt from Emily Dickinson's "Void," which appeared in *The Selected Poems of Emily Dickinson* (Hertfordshire, United Kingdom: Wordsworth Editions, 1994).

Finally, I am forever grateful to my wife, Giuliana, and our children, Noah and Gabriela, for their patience and understanding as I worked on this book.

Introduction:
Evolutionary Common Law

This book investigates the dissents of Oliver Wendell Holmes Jr. to understand how they instantiate his evolutionary view of the common-law system. Influenced by Darwinian science and the classical pragmatism of C.S. Peirce, William James, and John Dewey, Holmes forged a paradigm for the common law in which legal principles progress through constructive competition and the selective elimination of unfit theories and practices. He rejected any formulation of the law as static and unchanging. The style and rhetoric of his dissents in particular drew attention to his legal propositions.

Holmes's dissents have been taught, read, and cited in law schools and have enabled his legal arguments to persist in the legal canon and, in some cases, to become the majority position. Holmes thus ensured that the oppositional proposition was retained in the legal canon for future judges and justices to consider and possibly vindicate. He guaranteed that the legal system had some "play in its joints"[1] and remained sufficiently flexible to adapt to changes in culture and technology. This book demonstrates that the literary dimensions of his writing—his rhetorical flair and colorful style—have become an integral part of his legacy and contributed to the vindication of many of his dissents.

Dissenting opinions are by nature agonistic; they compete with majority opinions, push back against established precedents, multiply the range of judicial options, and diversify the franchise in legal theory. Their oppositional nature and function make them productive sites for aesthetic and theoretical experimentation.

In the field of literature, Richard Poirier and Jonathan Levin, drawing from Harold Bloom, have proposed that literary pragmatists in the Emersonian lineage developed their own dissenting tradition by struggling against "the anxiety of influence" and what Poirier and Levin call "linguistic skepticism" to produce original and lasting aesthetics. Despite his focus on the law, Holmes was clearly part of this tradition: Emerson was his mentor, and Holmes was a member of the Metaphysical Club discussions where pragmatism was first developed. By dissenting with a style that demanded attention, Holmes himself struggled against the textual and institutional limitations that were also the sources of his ingenuity. Using his uncommon facility with metaphor, sound, rhythm, and figurative language, Holmes unsettled majority positions and enabled a constructive vagueness in the law that future judges and justices were forced to confront, interpret, and overcome.

THE GREAT DISSENTER

This book examines Holmes's dissents as an aesthetic genre. Most scholarly treatments of Holmes's dissents are written for those who study and shape United States constitutional law and do not interest those who study language, literature, rhetoric, or even pragmatism. As a result, legal scholarship on Holmes lacks a literary and rhetorical perspective that a combination of Emersonian aesthetics and pragmatic philosophy can supply. This is also the first extensive non-biographical work to consider the theoretical relationship between Emerson and Holmes and to focus on their mutually illuminating uses of language and influence. Although the rapport between these men is mentioned in biographies and discussed in essays and articles, no one has adequately drawn out the jurisprudential implications of their relationship through the matrix of literary theory and pragmatism. Holmes is frequently referred to as the Great Dissenter. This book demonstrates that his dissents are significant not for their quantity but for their quality.

To varying degrees and with differing styles, Harold Bloom, Richard Poirier, Louis Menand, Joan Richardson, and Jonathan Levin develop and explore a tradition of pragmatist writers whose work points back to Emerson. By adding Holmes to the mix, we see how this canon is plugged into the practical and administrative machinery of government as manifest in the judicial branch of the United States. Indeed, the influence of Holmes in the law can be traced more clearly than is usually possible for the influence of pragmatists in literature. When writing fiction, authors generally do not acknowledge their influences. In a common-law system, however, each law or legal finding must be linked to some proper authority, either case precedents or statutes or constitutional provisions. We can therefore examine precisely how and when Holmes's dissents have influenced later judges and justices, and through them, the laws of the land.

TWO PARADIGMS FOR THE COMMON LAW

Holmes's evolutionary conception of the common law is at loggerheads with the more august and magisterial conception of the common law as a reflection of divine will written on men's hearts and aligned with sacred scripture and the laws of nature. Dissents support the evolutionary conception of the common law because, by their very nature, they imply that binding rules and principles are always subject to change and adaptation: Why would a judge or justice dissent if not to shape the future of the law? Holmes wrote in one dissent that the "common law is not a brooding omnipotence in the sky."[2] "We do not realize," he remarked on another occasion, "how large a part of our law is open to reconsideration upon a slight change in the habit of the public mind."[3] In *The Common Law* he employed Darwinian terminology to describe how a "rule adapts itself to the new reasons which have been found for it, and enters on a new career" so that the "old form receives new content" and "in time [. . .] modifies itself to fit the meaning which it has received."[4] He maintained in this regard that the law "is forever adopting new principles from life at one end" while "always retain[ing] old ones from history at the other, which have not yet been absorbed or sloughed off."[5] This line echoes Emerson's proposition that "every law [. . .] was a man's expedient to meet a particular case" and that all laws are "imitable" and "alterable."[6] Holmes saw in the common law the embodiment of what Emerson called "the very oldest of thoughts cast into the mould of these new times."[7] He decried proponents of a fixed natural law because he agreed with Emerson that "[t]here are no fixtures in nature" or in a "universe [that] is fluid and volatile."[8] Dissents make possible in reality what Holmes suggested was true in theory, vesting in case precedent the potential for future modifications in light of changed circumstances.

This book positions Holmes's dynamic, fluid jurisprudence in contradistinction to the paradigm of a static and unchanging common-law system most associated with Sir William Blackstone.[9] "[I]n the early days of the Republic," according to one narrative, "there was one dominant worldview that shaped virtually all American jurisprudence: the presupposition that there was a higher law, an unchanging law, which provided the basis for the common law of England as substantially set forth by Sir William Blackstone."[10] It is easy to see to see how this take on Blackstone emerged. Blackstone authored "The Lawyer's Prayer" and described the "general signification of law" as a "rule of action dictated by some superior being," who issued principles that "must be invariably obeyed." Blackstone also spoke of "certain immutable laws of human nature" that corresponded with "the eternal, immutable laws of good and evil."[11]

One author claims that Holmes "shook the little world of lawyers and judges who had been raised on Blackstone's theory that law, given by God Himself, was immutable and eternal and judges had only to discover its contents."[12] "Holmes," she says, "wrested legal history from the aridity of syllogism and abstraction and placed it in the context of human experience, demonstrating that the corpus of the law was neither ukase from God nor derived from Nature, but, like the little toe and the structure of the horse, was a constantly evolving thing, a response to the continually developing social and economic environment."[13] The "immutable principles" of Blackstonian common law suffered from an "inertia" that prevented them "from dealing with the disorder and changefulness and all the other complexities of nineteenth-century life."[14] Holmes believed that the greater scientific knowledge of his day led thinkers away from speculating about an unchanging divine plan, and toward examining laws as the results of past processes of change—likely to be changed again under new circumstances.[15]

A textbook used by one Christian law school pits Blackstone against Holmes, stating that the former "believed that the principles and doctrines underlying the common law of England were unchanging"[16] whereas the latter undermined "the fixed Divine absolutes which have anchored the law in America since her birth."[17] The high stakes at play in this conception of Holmes are evident in the remarks of one professor at Northwestern University School of Law: "Holmes probably was not the Antichrist, but he surely gave the Prince of Darkness a run for the money."[18]

AGONISM

This book suggests that pragmatism influenced Holmes's thinking about the common law and dissents. He saw dissents as an agonistic genre that allowed for literary creativity while enabling growth and improvement in the rules adumbrated by case precedents. Critical to my argument is the literary theory of agon, a mode of influence whereby aesthetic competition generates creativity. This theory of agon resonates in the common-law context, in which all laws are the product of argumentation and suasion and in which judges and justices issue dissenting opinions to counteract or offset rival contentions.

Chapter 1 provides data about Holmes's writings as a justice on the United States Supreme Court to show that Holmes is remembered as the Great Dissenter because of the aesthetic properties of his dissents, not because he was a prolific dissenter. Poirier's theories about literary or rhetorical "superfluity" shed light on Holmes's literary or rhetorical approach to his judicial dissents. The term *superfluity* signifies the creative urge to overcome, outdo, move beyond, facilitate, generate, push forward, transcend, outlast, or surpass. Like genius according to Emerson, superfluity "looks forward" and "creates."[19] Superfluous language "smites and arouses" with its "tones," "breaks up" our "whole chain of habits," and "opens" our eyes to our own "possibilities."[20] It is characterized by an extravagance of style that consists of sound, metaphor, rhythm, and complexity.

Holmes's dissents sought to overcome and surpass the stasis resulting from the institutional restraints imposed by case precedents and majority opinions. The fluidity and vagueness of language problematize the very utterances that obtain as law. Examples arise whenever judges and justices undertake to interpret the meaning of a statute. Holmes explained to this end that "[i]t is not true that in practice [. . .] a given word or even a given collection of words has one meaning and no other."[21] Holmes recognized that a "word is not a crystal, transparent and unchanged" but rather "the skin of a living thought" that "may vary greatly in color and content according to the circumstances and the time in which it is used."[22] There is much at stake when the diction and syntax that constitute the law lack the clarity and consistency on which people base their decisions. In Holmes the tension between stability and uniformity on the one hand and dynamism and transition on the other hand comes to a head. He never completely resolves this tension, which may defy resolution, but he does suggest that "the substance of the law at any given time pretty nearly corresponds, so far as it goes, with what is then understood to be convenient," even though "its form and machinery, and the degree to which it is able to work out desired results, depend very much upon its past."[23] What Holmes calls the "substance of the law" is language itself; all rules and regulations are conveyed in utterances. Language is a system of representation; it never completely corresponds with its referents in the phenomenal world. The manner in which language obtains as law in one time and setting will differ in another time and setting because the meaning of language itself depends upon context and situation. Holmes accordingly saw the need for the law to adapt and adjust. His dissents were colored with superfluity to undermine the clarity and authority of the majority position. And they destabilized prevailing rules by convincing future judges and justices to reconsider the arguments—the language—that did not attain a majority the first time around.

The pragmatic common-law tradition of Holmes and the pragmatic literary tradition of Emerson share a root concern not only with the inheritance of past forms and ideas but also with future forms and ideas that must be anticipated and articulated in the present. Holmes, like Emerson, inaugurated a style that attracted future adherents whose transformative creativity both extended and revised the tradition. Holmes operated on Emerson's dictum that society did not lie "before him in rigid repose" but was "fluid."[24] His common-law paradigm comports with Emerson's premise that the "law is only a memorandum,"[25] a product of our "political institutions" that "are not better" than "any other in history" but rather "fitter for us" and "in coincidence with the spirit of the age."[26] Holmes and his progeny—Louis Brandeis, Benjamin Cardozo, John Paul Stevens, and Antonin Scalia—have struggled against their judicial precursors just as Emerson and his progeny struggled against their literary precursors; both aesthetic camps sought to communicate with and influence future generations with the originality and strength of their language. Judges and justices subvert the settled rules of cumulative majority positions by writing dissents to both validate and give audience to a disorienting and unsettling legal position, one that goes against the grain of precedent.

Chapter 2 examines the reception and legacy of Holmes's dissents to demonstrate that his dissenting views have become vindicated and hence that the common-law system is, in fact, adaptive and meliorative. The theory of the poetics of transition, derived from Poirier and made comprehensive by Levin, can pertain to judicial opinions as much as to poetry and works of imaginative literature. The theory of the poetics of transition is predicated on Emerson's notion that "[p]ower ceases in the instant of repose" and "resides in the moment of transition from a past to a new state."[27] Such a transition can occur when a dissenting opinion is vindicated by a later judge or justice and, thus, transitions from non-law into law, in part because of the rhetorical properties of the dissent.

Holmes's dissents in particular make Poirier's and Levin's theories of influence, as expressed in terms of superfluity and the poetics of transition, both useful and legible beyond the typical pragmatist associations with such authors as William and Henry James, George Santayana, Wallace Stevens, Gertrude Stein, and Robert Frost. This chapter examines Holmes's dissents for evidence of the Emersonian superfluity that brought about the poetics of transition in the form of judicial vindication. These dissents are placed alongside Holmes's letters about sound and language, which demonstrate that his superfluity was deliberate and designed for its lasting effect or ability to survive in the canon. He intentionally resorted to style and sound rather than syllogism. His vindicated dissents show how a state of deliberate vagary and unrest in the law can facilitate judicial adaptation to the social environment and overcome dominant legal trends.

The literary theories of Poirier and Levin involve a type of canon formation that resembles the canon formation of cases within the common-law system. Chapter 3 argues that creative struggles in judicial opinions and dissents in the United States develop into a dynamic canon of legal theories and principles. This canon balances contradictory ideas and sustains multiple dialectics. The dialectics do not solidify as a single compromise; nor do they synthesize. Rather, they preserve competing binaries and gradually wear away theories that are no longer suitable for the social and technological environment. The United States constitutional canon is made up of canonical and anticanonical cases that struggle against each other in a contest for authority; a unique literary or rhetorical quality of an opinion or dissent can enhance the lasting value of that opinion or dissent. The aesthetics and style of Holmes's dissents guaranteed that his legal positions did not, in Emerson's words, "pale" and "dwindle" before "the revelation of a new hour."[28]

Holmes's most canonical dissents involve his First Amendment jurisprudence regarding freedom of speech and expression. His views on the First Amendment evolved, and as he grew more tolerant of dissenting opinions in the social and political sphere he also began to author more dissents from the bench. His First Amendment jurisprudence parallels his agonistic, evolutionary conception of the common law in that it championed the free interplay of competing ideas as the best means for filtering the good from the bad. In his view, ideological competition ensured that contest and disagreement remained rhetorical and discursive and did not degenerate into brute force or physical violence. The case for rhetorical and theoretical struggle is also, according to Holmes, the case for practical and institutional tolerance; agon is paradoxically about neutralizing conflict. Holmes's canonical dissents regarding the First Amendment suggest that his model for the common law is also a pragmatic model for the way in which society itself can adjust to change and to divided opinions among the populace.

Holmes's First Amendment jurisprudence is imbued with peacefulness, despite its couching in martial metaphors and military diction that recall his soldier past. As a student at Harvard, Holmes served as a bodyguard for the abolitionist Wendell Phillips. He later enlisted in the infantry before joining the Twentieth Massachusetts, a regiment that lost five eighths of its men.[29] He was wounded at the Battle of Ball's Bluff in October of 1861, when he took a bullet to his chest; the bullet passed through his body without touching his heart or lungs. In September of 1862 he was wounded at the Battle of Antietam, a bullet having passed through his neck. In May of 1863, at Marye's Hill, close to where the battle of Fredericksburg had taken place six months earlier, Holmes was shot and wounded a third time. This time the bullet struck him in the heel, splintered his bone, and tore his ligaments; his doctors were convinced that he would lose his leg, but he did not. These experiences were philosophical determinants for Holmes, shaping his view that true violence could be curtailed if conflict and competition were limited to discursive and rhetorical struggles and dispersed among distant communities rather than concentrated in one centralized body of powerful actors.

Chapter 4, the final chapter, explores the compatibility of pragmatism with Holmes's evolutionary paradigm of the common law, revealing that Holmes more than anyone integrates the disparate elements of what is now called the "classical pragmatism" of Peirce, William James, and Dewey. Holmes's common-law theory shares with Peirce a consensus-based methodology for ferreting out the rules that govern phenomena, with James a respect for pluralism and variety, and with Dewey an instrumentalist approach to social inquiry. Theories of pragmatism have become so intertwined with theories about the common law as established in the United States that Thomas Grey has insisted that "pragmatism *is* the implicit working theory of most good lawyers."[30] Posner has likewise insisted that "most American judges have been practicing pragmatists."[31] What makes Holmes's pragmatism jurisprudentially unique is its use of Emersonian aesthetics to draw attention to antagonistic arguments, which, by their very antagonism, ensure that competition among ideas continues in the legal canon. Holmes appreciated the common-law system because, unlike a civil code, it comported with his pragmatic cognition whereby critical control is dispersed among authorities and jurisdictions and the law is like a continuous stream without definite boundaries. Judges in this endless flow are, in effect, conduits through which pass the strongest principles that are differentially replicated and selectively retained.

Holmes's evolutionary paradigm for the common law is politically noncommittal. He uses philosophical pragmatism as a mode of knowing or a method of learning rather than as a form of social advocacy or partisan lobbying.[32] Pragmatists have been politically conservative and politically liberal, and pragmatism as a system of thinking does not lead inexorably to a political program or agenda, only to theoretical postulates that answer concrete problems. Acrimonious attempts to assign political labels to Holmes fail because they do not account for his relative indifference to the normative models, simplistic hypotheticals, and general histrionics that characterize popular politics. Allergic to current events and partisan dogma, Holmes did not read newspapers; after the Civil War, he was not active in social causes. He remained aloof from the political arena, preferring simply to ride the wave of evolutionary progression or regression, accepting his role as one jurist in a vast web of inferential and situational legal processes.

AGAINST STASIS

The common law figures in Holmes's writings not as the quasi-divine expression of first principles frozen in time—the Blackstonian view[33] that I have simplified for purposes of differentiation—but as a receptacle for filtered theories or as the latest living product of the relentless workings of natural selection. For Holmes the common law is not a unified, fixed body of rules with determinant applications that contemporary jurists can mine for certain answers and definite resolutions. Law has evolved, and continues to evolve. Such evolution has taken place in the United Kingdom and in the United States within a single framework: the common law. The common-law system therefore is not a statement of what the law is but a designation for the methodology of making, enhancing, repairing, and reformulating the law. The common law is a framework within which the law fluctuates. What is at play is not the formal structure itself—the common-law system—but the binding vocabularies and interpretive claims *within* the formal structure that give direction to our everyday activity. Within the common-law framework the interactions between finite social rules and the concrete circumstances to which those rules apply find expression in judicial opinions and dissents.

Holmes's attempts to effectuate his theory of the common law in the United States were in some ways anachronistic because the United States was not the home of the British common-law system that had emerged from antiquity. The United States had a constitution to which all states and jurists were bound. "Blackstone," on the other hand, "recognized the existence of a constitution in the modern sense [. . . but] did not consider there to be a body of constitutional law strictly separated from other law."[34] The common law in the United States is a system in which judges and justices are constrained to follow precedent within the confines of a constitution. It is distinguishable from the civil law in nations that have rejected the common law and where judges and justices interpret large bodies of legislative code by way of opinions and rulings that do not bind future judges and justices.

Holmes was a scholar of the British common law and authored his only book, *The Common Law*, on that subject to much acclaim. Holmes's understanding of the common law was historically informed and mindful of the numerous legal developments and jurisprudential variants that had emerged in response to political urgencies and complex social conditions throughout British and American history. By comparison, Blackstone's own *Commentaries on the Laws of England* "was not very profound."[35] Blackstone not only "expected little more in history than a plausibility at first sight" but also regarded legal history in particular "as an object of 'temperate curiosity' rather than of exact scholarship."[36] Blackstone's teachings about the common law were "an attempt to explain and justify the common law in the eyes of the laity."[37] The lectures that made up Blackstone's *Commentaries* were not delivered to scholars or lawyers or judges but to young boys considering the study of law at Oxford. One such attendee was sixteen-year old Jeremy Bentham, who was famously unimpressed by Blackstone's primer and gained a reputation by criticizing Blackstone.[38]

Blackstone used the common-law trope to inspire laypeople and the youth and to classify and abridge prevailing legal norms for educational purposes.[39] He was not interested in formulating an exact science or an accurate history, and with few exceptions his compilations and analyses of legal decisions were descriptive rather than prescriptive: he evaluated what the law was and how it came to be. But he was not a consistent activist or a ready polemicist advocating for what the law ought to be.

Despite his humble pedagogical objectives, Blackstone looms large in American history. It has become "part of the accepted wisdom of American history that Sir William Blackstone and his *Commentaries on the Laws of England* [. . .] have exercised a dominant and pervasive influence on America's political thought and legal development."[40] One metanarrative maintains that the American founders' "faith in God and in His revelation in support of their revolutionary cause mirrored Blackstone's faith in God's will as revealed in nature and in the holy Scriptures."[41] According to this story, the "Biblical philosophy that laid the foundation for the common law at the time of America's founding" had met its demise, "occasioned by a late nineteenth century Darwinian revolution"[42] during which "God's revelation as the foundation and framework of the common law came under relentless attack from the pens of Oliver Wendell Holmes, Jr."[43] Holmes thereby marked a "shift from a common law system founded and framed by God's revelation to a common law system determined by judges' opinions."[44] This claim is called into question by the fact that Blackstone's *Commentaries*, "from Bentham on," have been critiqued as "confused and contradictory, based on theoretical foundations which were either irrelevant to [Blackstone's] task, or ignored in practice in the book."[45]

The above praise for Blackstone's paradigm of the common law is even stronger than Sir Edward Coke's apparent reverence for the common law as an expression of "the wisdom of the most excellent men, in many successions of ages, by long and continual experience (the trial of right and truth) fined and refined."[46] Coke's chosen diction suggests that Holmes's conception of the common law as a vessel of experience is more similar to Coke's and Blackstone's conception than caricatures of Blackstone allow. Blackstone himself articulated a version of Holmes's claim that the life of the law was not logic but experience when he declared that the "judges in the several courts of justice" were "the depository of the laws" who "must decide all cases of doubt" because their "knowledge of the law is derived from experience and study."[47] Blackstone's accounts of equity, as well, reveal his dynamic conception of the law. Differentiations between the Blackstonian and the Holmesian common-law paradigms are often exaggerated for ideological purposes, and I have not fully adopted either essentialism. Instead, I recall these essentialized understandings of Blackstone and Holmes, even though I find them problematic, because they clarify the major differences between competing interpretations of the common law in the United States.

Oliver Wendell Holmes Jr. "still evokes strong emotions in people," and "to introduce his name into informed discussion is to risk a fight."[48] David Bernstein's *Rehabilitating Lochner*[49] displays on its front cover a cartoon of Justice Rufus Peckham, the author of the majority opinion in *Lochner v. New York*,[50] punching out Holmes in a boxing ring; both men are clothed in judicial robes and boxing gloves. The image is telling: Holmes's legacy remains disputed. In *Kelo v. City of New London*,[51] Justice Stevens's majority opinion and Justice Thomas's dissent both rely on Holmes for different propositions that lead to different results. Even state appellate courts have wrestled over Holmes's jurisprudence. In 2013 the Supreme Court of Alabama rendered an opinion in *Ex parte Christopher*[52] in which Chief Justice Roy S. Moore overruled a 24-year-old precedent established in *Ex parte Bayliss* (1989).[53] Chief Justice Moore claimed that the author of *Bayliss* had misapplied one of Holmes's hermeneutical metaphors to arrive at an improper conclusion that threatened the separation of powers between the judicial and legislative branches. Having dissented in *Ex parte Tabor* (2002),[54] a case following the *Bayliss* precedent, Chief Justice Moore authored the majority opinion in *Christopher* and now enjoys the unique distinction of having vindicated his own dissent.[55]

Rather than taking sides in any one controversy over Holmes and his approach to judging, I seek to remain objective and to follow the facts where they lead, although I have permitted myself some critical remarks about *Buck v. Bell*[56] in the closing passages of Chapter 4. Nor do I have in mind to defend Holmes or to celebrate or validate his common-law jurisprudence. Holmes does not need my patronage. His legacy will outlast my opinion of it. By pointing out that there is a tradition attributed to Blackstone that treats the common law as immutable and static, I have fashioned a permeable dichotomy to suggest the type of jurisprudence Holmes was writing against, although his true targets were most likely his contemporaries. If we do not understand why Holmes's dissents became canonized—i.e., because of their rhetorical superfluity that enabled the poetics of transition—then we cannot answer the more significant question: Why are Holmes's dissents important? If we do not understand how the principles in Holmes's dissents transitioned from non-law into law, then we cannot know how rules that continue to regulate our everyday activities came to be and so cannot predict how they might change in the future. Holmes's dissents incarnate the increasingly popular notion that "some dissents mattered greatly" to the American legal system because they "shaped the constitutional dialogue and in doing so shaped the type of government we now enjoy."[57]

Posner once said of one of Holmes's canonized dissents that it would not have received a passing grade on a law school examination.[58] Chief Justice Taft reportedly said that Holmes's dissents were unhelpful.[59] If Holmes's dissents lacked logic and citations and other judicial conventions, why were they canonized and vindicated? How could an unconventional legal opinion become the law when it did not start out as the law? Holmes opened *The Common Law* by stating that the "life of the law has *not been logic*" and by explaining that "[t]he felt necessities of the time, the prevalent moral and political theories, intuitions of public policy, avowed or unconscious, even the prejudices which judges share with their fellow-men, have *had a good deal more to do than the syllogism* in determining the rules by which men should be governed."[60] Holmes's dissents prove this to be true by their pragmatic, memorable appeals to culture and experience—and by their ability to transform a rejected argument into the majority position in spite of the fact that they did not present model legal arguments. Instead, Holmes's dissents anticipated cultural change by using language that was meant to connect with future audiences; they were, in this sense, prophetic—not because he purported to know what the law would become but because his views of what constituted the law were vindicated by future jurists.

The field of pragmatism has settled into a condition of repose that is at odds with pragmatism's meliorative nature and function. Since the linguistic turn in philosophy, pragmatists have, broadly speaking, divided into two coherent camps: the neopragmatists (those who have followed in the footsteps of Richard Rorty) and the traditional pragmatists (those who have followed in the footsteps of the classical pragmatists, refusing to dispense with truth as a meaningful category of discourse). Debates about the reconciliation of these pragmatist factions have quieted; practitioners on both sides have carried out their work without reference to their competitors. Colin Koopman's *Pragmatism as Transition*[61] sees the transitional pragmatism of scholars like Poirier and Levin as a way forward and as a mechanism for disrupting the philosophical impasse that now characterizes pragmatism at the expense of pragmatic inquiry. Neopragmatism and classical pragmatism share an understanding of *transition*, a concept central to Emerson and Holmes. Holmes bridges classical and neo-pragmatism and has the potential to free the field of pragmatism from the non-pragmatic stasis in which it is imprisoned. This book marks a shift and a renewal. It provides an interdisciplinary and melioristic resource for future pragmatists who wish to mobilize and reenergize pragmatic reasoning and discourse. Let us move on.

NOTES

1. Bain Peanut Co. of Tex. v. Pinson, 282 U.S. 499 (1931) at 501.
2. Southern Pacific Company v. Jensen, 244 U.S. 205 (1917) at 222.
3. Oliver Wendell Holmes Jr., "The Path of the Law." *Harvard Law Review* 10 (1897): 466.
4. Oliver Wendell Holmes Jr., *The Common Law* (Chicago: American Bar Association, 1881), 4.
5. Oliver Wendell Holmes Jr., *The Common Law* (Chicago: American Bar Association, 1881), 25.
6. Ralph Waldo Emerson, "Politics," in *Emerson: Essays & Poems* (New York: Library of America, 1996), 559.
7. Ralph Waldo Emerson, "The Transcendentalist," in *Emerson: Essays & Poems* (New York: Library of America, 1996), 193.
8. Ralph Waldo Emerson, "Circles," in *Emerson: Essays & Poems* (New York: Library of America, 1996), 403.
9. See, e.g., Albert W. Alschuler, "From Blackstone to Holmes: Revolt against Natural Law," *Pepperdine Law Review* 36 (2000-2001): 491-506. In the latter article, Alschuler states, "Scholars view the *Commentaries* as an illustration of the formal vision of law that Oliver Wendell Holmes and the legal realists condemned" (Albert W. Alschuler, "Rediscovering Blackstone," *University of Pennsylvania Law Review* 145-97 [1996-97]: 1-55, 17).
10. Alan Sears, preface to *Sir William Blackstone and the Common Law: Blackstone's Legacy to America,* by Robert D. Stacey (Eugene, OR: ACW Press, 2003), 7.
11. William Blackstone, *Commentaries on the Laws of England, Book the First* (London: Dawsons of Pall Mall, [1765] 1966), 39-40.
12. Liva Baker, *The Justice from Beacon Hill: The Life and Times of Oliver Wendell Holmes* (New York: HarperCollins, 1991), 257.
13. Baker, *The Justice from Beacon Hill,* 258.
14. Baker, *The Justice from Beacon Hill,* 249.
15. Oliver Wendell Holmes Jr., "Law in Science and Science in Law," *Harvard Law Review* 12 (1899): 443.
16. Herbert W. Titus, *God, Man, and Law: The Biblical Principles* (Oak Brook, IL: Institute in Basic Life Principles, 1994), 4.
17. Titus, *God, Man, and Law,* 6.

18. Stephen B. Presser, "Some Thoughts on Our Present Discontents and Duties: The Cardinal, Oliver Wendell Holmes, Jr., the Unborn, the Senate, and Us," *Ave Maria Law Review* 1 (2003): 118.

19. Ralph Waldo Emerson, "The American Scholar," in *Emerson: Essays & Lectures*, edited by Joel Porte (New York: Library of America, 1983), 58.

20. Emerson, "Circles," 409.

21. Oliver Wendell Holmes Jr., "The Theory of Legal Interpretation," *Harvard Law Review* 12 (1898-99): 419, 417.

22. Towne v. Eisner, 245 U.S. 418 (1918) at 425.

23. Holmes, *Common Law*, 1.

24. Emerson, "Circles," 559.

25. Ibid.

26. Emerson, "Circles," 563.

27. Ralph Waldo Emerson, "Self-Reliance," in *Emerson: Essays & Poems* (New York: Library of America, 1996), 271.

28. Ralph Waldo Emerson, "Art," in *Emerson: Essays & Lectures*, edited by Joel Porte (New York: Library of America, 1983), 405.

29. Max Lerner, *The Mind and Faith of Justice Holmes: His Speeches, Essays, Letters, and Judicial Opinions* (New Brunswick, NJ: Transaction Publishers, 1989), xxiii.

30. Thomas C. Grey, "Hear the Other Side: Wallace Stevens and Pragmatist Legal Theory," *Southern California Law Review* 63 (1990): 1590. Emphasis added.

31. Richard Posner, "What Has Pragmatism to Offer Law?" *Southern California Law Review* 63 (1990): 1666.

32. See generally Seth Vannatta, *Conservatism and Pragmatism in Law, Politics, and Ethics* (New York: Palgrave Macmillan, 2014), in which Holmes figures prominently in chapter seven.

33. This view is essentialized and represents a caricature of Blackstone's thought, which is more like Holmes's than certain commentators realize. Richard Posner characterizes Blackstone's view as compatible with Holmes's: "[W]hat is important and distinctive in Blackstone's method is a view of law which embeds it firmly in the social and political conditions of its time, which sees law responding to the changing needs and circumstances of the social environment[.] [. . .] Law is presented by Blackstone not as a speculative abstraction or a collection of rules but as a functioning social system" (Richard Posner, "Blackstone and Bentham," *Journal of Law & Economics* 19 (1976): 569-606).

34. John W. Cairns, "Blackstone, an English Institutist: Legal Literature and the Rise of the Nation State," *Oxford Journal of Legal Studies* 4, no. 3 (1984): 318-360.

35. Theodore F. T. Plucknett, *A Concise History of the Common Law* (Indianapolis, IN: Liberty Fund, Inc., [1929] 2010), 286.

36. Ibid.

37. Ibid.

38. See Richard Posner, "Blackstone and Bentham," *Journal of Law & Economics* 19 (1976): 569-606, for a criticism of Bentham's attack on Blackstone.

39. "What must be emphasized for Blackstone's treatment is that he wished to set forth a systematic exposition of English law for teaching purposes. For Blackstone, law based purely on cases had no natural or inevitable or proper structure. To make law systematic (and to prevent English law from appearing uncouth) he had to treat substantive law separately from procedure. Blackstone wished to set

English law forth as a system of rights" (Alan Watson, "Structure of Blackstone's *Commentaries,*" *Yale Law Journal* 97 [1988]: 795-822, 810).

40. Dennis R. Nolan, "Sir William Blackstone and the New American Republic: A Study of Intellectual Impact," *New York University Law Review* 51 (1976): 731.

41. Herbert W. Titus, "God's Revelation: Foundation for the Common Law," *Regent University Law Review* 4 (1994b): 4.

42. Ibid.

43. Herbert W. Titus, "God's Revelation: Foundation for the Common Law," *Regent University Law Review* 4 (1994b): 15.

44. Herbert W. Titus, "God's Revelation: Foundation for the Common Law," *Regent University Law Review* 4 (1994b): 16.

45. Michael Lobban, "Blackstone and the Science of Law," *Historical Journal* 30 (1987): 311.

46. Edward Coke, *The Reports of Sir Edward Coke in Thirteen Parts,* 1572-1617 (London: Joseph Butterworth and Son, [1777] 1826), 6.

47. Blackstone, *Commentaries,* 69.

48. Michael F. Duggan, "The Municipal Ideal and the Unknown End: A Resolution of Oliver Wendell Holmes," *North Dakota Law Review* 83 (2007): 471.

49. David E. Bernstein, *Rehabilitating Lochner: Defending Individual Rights against Progressive Reform* (Chicago: University of Chicago Press, 2011).

50. Lochner v. New York, 198 U.S. 45 (1905).

51. Kelo v. City of New London, 545 U.S. 469 (2005).

52. Ex parte Christopher, 145 So. 3d 160 (Ala. 2013).

53. Ex parte Bayliss, 550 So. 2d 986 (Ala. 1989).

54. Ex parte Tabor, 840 So. 2d 115 (Ala. 2002).

55. See also *Julie P. Magee* (Julie P. Magee and Thomas L. White, Jr., in their official capacities as Commissioner of Revenue and Comptroller of the State of Alabama, Respectively, v. Daniel Boyd et al., ___ So. 3d ___ (Ala. 2015)), in which the majority, including Chief Justice Moore, overruled the holding in *Densmore* (Densmore v. Jefferson County, 813 So. 2d 844 (Ala. 2001)), by adopting the position that Chief Justice took in his dissent in *Densmore.*

56. Buck v. Bell, 274 U.S. 200 (1927).

57. Melvin Urofsky's *Dissent and the Supreme Court* echoes my earlier work on dissents by arguing that prophetic or canonical dissents shape our constitutional dialogue and the future of the law. See my review of Urofsky's book: "The Power of Dissent." 2016. *The Alabama Lawyer* 77, no. 3: 170-71; Melvin I. Urofsky, *Dissent and the Supreme Court: Its Role in the Court's History and the Nation's Constitutional Dialogue* (New York: Pantheon Books, 2015), 36.

58. Richard Posner, *Law and Literature* (Cambridge, MA: Harvard University Press, 1998), 271.

59. Former President of the United States and Chief Justice of the United States Supreme Court William Howard Taft reportedly complained that Holmes "gives more attention to [. . .] his dissents than he does to the opinions he writes for the court, which are very short and not very helpful" (quoted in Lerner, *Mind and Faith,* 132).

60. Holmes, *Common Law,* 1. Emphasis added.

61. Colin Koopman, *Pragmatism as Transition: Historicity and Hope in James, Dewey, and Rorty* (New York: Columbia University Press, 2009).

1

Holmes's Dissents and Emersonian Superfluity

"We do not write on a clean slate," wrote Justice Anthony Kennedy in 2007, "for the decision in *Dr. Miles* is almost a century old."[1] The case was *Leegin Creative Leather Products, Inc. v. PSKS, Inc.*,[2] and Justice Kennedy was referring to *Dr. Miles Medical Company v. John D. Park & Sons Company*,[3] a prior decision of the United States Supreme Court. At Justice Kennedy's writing, *Dr. Miles* remained binding precedent. Holmes had dissented in *Dr. Miles*, stating, "I think also that the importance of the question and the popularity of what I deem mistaken notions makes it my duty to express my view in this dissent."[4] Twenty-five years following Holmes's tactical line, Justice Kennedy was born in Sacramento, California, just a year after Holmes's death. Holmes could not have known that a soon-to-be-born child from California would, nearly a century after *Dr. Miles*, overrule *Dr. Miles* with his colleagues. By dissenting, however, Holmes supplied the formal variation that increased the probability of such reversal. Recalling Holmes's evolutionary jurisprudence, Justice Kennedy opined in *Leegin* that "the common law adapts to modern understanding and greater experience."[5] "The case-by-case adjudication contemplated by the rule of reason," Justice Kennedy said, "has implemented this common-law approach."[6] By declining to adhere to the rule announced by the majority in *Dr. Miles*, Justice Kennedy vindicated Holmes's dissent in that case and added yet another mutation to the genetic makeup of case precedents in the American legal canon. Justice Kennedy's opinion in *Leegin* may seem like a minor moment in American constitutional history, but it testifies to the meliorating, elastic aspect of the common law that prompted Holmes to author creative dissents.

Dissents are not the law but may protest what the law is and propose what the law ought to be. The dissent is constitutionally agonistic in that it establishes itself against the dominant trend or rule and subverts the reasoning of the binding opinion. It is possible for a dissent to become binding law if future judges or justices vindicate its reasoning over that of the majority.[7] Dissents are in this sense the state of exception: they are not law but always retain the potential to become law. They await validation and cannot control the population until they receive validation. They can command respect and attention, even though they stand outside the law, because they confirm the validity of the rules that they simultaneously undermine. They reify the principles that they seek to demolish and demolish the principles that they seek to reify. Their disruption of the official, authorized opinion invests them with underdog appeal, especially when they are couched in memorable language that commands attention.

The importance of dissents in the aggregate is not only to overcome some majority opinion; it is to multiply and diversify jurisprudential options for the lawyers, judges, and justices whose arguments about the rules of society obtain to the population writ large. Faced with a set of facts that does not easily comport with the law as expressed in binding precedent, a judge or justice may consult a stock of dissents for clarification or illumination. Finding some dissent that is on point and well-reasoned, the judge or justice might vindicate the dissent and turn what was dead letter into living authority. The most powerful dissents are those that the legal community does not have to look for because they are already well-known. The question for these dissents is not whether they will be cited but when, not whether they will be remembered but whether the memory of them will lead to their vindication. If such dissents were never written, future generations of lawyers, judges, and justices would lack a textual record to consult, revise, and adopt. Only by authoring dissents may judges and justices ensure that their arguments remain preserved in the textual record.

Holmes's dissents achieved their canonical status in part because their literary qualities were memorable and therefore revisited, discussed, taught, and cited. Their greater impact upon the United States is in their vindication and in their graduation from non-law into law. Holmes's talent as a writer enabled his most memorable dissents to become canonized and later vindicated. It is not possible to prove that Holmes's literary aptitude *caused* his dissents to become law, only that it made that possibility more likely.

HOLMES'S DISSENTS

Holmes served on the United States Supreme Court from December 4, 1902, to January 12, 1932. Table 1 lists in chronological order each dissent in which Holmes participated either by writing or by joining the writing of another justice. I have not included cases in which Holmes dissented without a writing or joined other justices who dissented without a writing. Examples of such cases include *Chicago, M. & St. P. R. Co. v. State of Wisconsin*,[8] in which Holmes joined Justice McKenna in dissenting without a writing, and *Williams v. Standard Oil Co. of Louisiana*,[9] in which Holmes dissented without a writing and no other justices dissented. Table 1 also does not include dissents that Holmes never published.[10] It shows that, during his tenure as a United States Supreme Court justice, Holmes authored 73 dissents and joined 25 dissents written by other justices. Of the 25 dissents written by other justices and joined by Holmes, 17 (or 68%) were authored by Justice Brandeis.

Holmes sometimes wrote a dissent and joined a dissent in the same case. Table 1 categorizes Holmes's writings in those cases as both "Dissenting Opinions Authored" and "Dissenting Opinions Joined." Totaling the dissents in each column will not result in the sum of the cases in which Holmes dissented because Table 1 includes only cases in which Holmes dissented with a writing. (As mentioned above, Holmes sometimes dissented without an opinion or joined another dissenting justice who did not write an opinion.) The seven cases that appear in both columns are *Haddock v. Haddock*;[11] *American Column & Lumber Co. v. U.S.*;[12] *U.S. ex rel. Milwaukee Social Democratic Pub. Co. v. Burleson*;[13] *Myers v. U.S.*;[14] *Tyson v. Banton*;[15] *Olmstead v. U.S.*;[16] and *Baldwin v. State of Missouri*.[17]

Some conclusions and reasonable inferences may be drawn from Table 1. For instance, Holmes was more likely to write dissents as a proportion of his writings in his last decade on the United States Supreme Court than during his first two decades there. Sixty-four percent of his authored dissents (47 total) appeared during the latter half of his tenure on the United States Supreme Court. Eighty-eight percent of the dissents that were authored by others and joined by Holmes (22 total) occurred during this same period. These percentages do not necessarily imply that Holmes was more likely to dissent the longer he sat on the United States Supreme Court. The years 1902-32 can be divided into roughly three decades: 1902-12, 1913-22, 1923-32. In the first decide, the numbers in columns one and two of Table 1 are 24 and 3. In the second decade, the numbers in the same columns and table are 22 and 12. In the third decade, the numbers in the same columns and table are 27 and 10. In these same three decades Holmes's majority opinions amount to 327 and 347 and 216 per decade. Therefore, by absolute dissent authorship no trend is apparent. Absolute dissent votes increase from 27 to 34 to 37 by decade, but this rise does not correlate with frequency or proportion. The ratio of dissents authored to majority opinions authored is .073 to .063 to .125 by decade, suggesting a dip in the middle decade but a substantial rise in the last decade. The

Table 1. Holmes's Dissents

Dissenting Opinions Authored	Dissenting Opinions Joined
1. *Northern Securities Co. v. U.S.*, 193 U.S. 197 (1904) (Holmes, J., dissenting).	1. *Board of Directors of Chicago Theological Seminary v. People of State of Illinois* ex rel. *Raymond*, 188 U.S. 662 (1903) (White, J., dissenting).
2. *Kepner v. U.S.*, 195 U.S. 100 (1904) (Holmes, J., dissenting).	
3. *Muhlker v. New York & H.R. Co.*, 197 U.S. 544 (1905) (Holmes, J., dissenting).	2. *Hafemann v. Gross*, 199 U.S. 342 (1905) (White, J., dissenting).
4. *Lochner v. New York*, 198 U.S. 45 (1905) (Holmes, J., dissenting).	3. *Haddock v. Haddock*, 201 U.S. 562 (1906) (Brown, J., dissenting).
5. *Madisonville Traction Co. v. St. Bernard Mining Co.*, 196 U.S. 239 (1905) (Holmes, J., dissenting).	4. *Neilson v. Rhine Shipping Co.*, 248 U.S. 205 (1918) (McKenna, J., dissenting).
6. *Haddock v. Haddock*, 201 U.S. 562 (1906) (Holmes, J., dissenting).	5. *Sandberg v. McDonald*, 248 U.S. 185 (1918) (McKenna, J., dissenting).
7. *Bernheimer v. Converse*, 206 U.S. 516 (1907) (Holmes, J., dissenting).	6. *F.S. Royster Guano Co. v. Commonwealth of Virginia*, 253 U.S. 412 (1920) (Brandeis, J., dissenting).
8. *Travers v. Reinhardt*, 205 U.S. 423 (1907) (Holmes, J., dissenting).	7. *Schaefer v. U.S.*, 251 U.S. 466 (1920) (Brandeis, J., dissenting).
9. *Chanler v. Kelsey*, 205 U.S. 466 (1907) (Holmes, J., dissenting).	8. *U.S. v. Reading Co.*, 253 U.S. 26 (1920) (White, C.J., dissenting).
10. *Raymond v. Chicago Union Traction Co.*, 207 U.S. 20 (1907) (Holmes, J., dissenting).	9. *Burdeau v. McDowell*, 256 U.S. 465 (1921) (Brandeis, J., dissenting).
11. *Howard v. Illinois Cent. R. Co.*, 207 U.S. 463 (1908) (Holmes, J., dissenting).	10. *American Column & Lumber Co. v. U.S.*, 257 U.S. 377 (1921) (Brandeis, J., dissenting).
12. *Adair v. U.S.*, 208 U.S. 161 (1908) (Holmes, J., dissenting).	11. *Duplex Printing Press Co. v. Deering*, 254 U.S. 443 (1921) (Brandeis, J., dissenting).
13. *Chicago, B. & Q. Ry. Co. v. Williams*, 214 U.S. 492 (1909) (per curiam) (Holmes, J., dissenting).	12. *U.S.* ex rel. *Milwaukee Social Democratic Pub. Co. v. Burleson*, 255 U.S. 407 (1921) (Brandeis, J., dissenting).
14. *Keller v. U.S.*, 213 U.S. 138 (1909) (Holmes, J., dissenting).	13. *U.S. v. Moreland*, 258 U.S. 433 (1922) (Brandeis, J., dissenting).
15. *Continental Wall Paper Co. v. Louis Voight & Sons Co.*, 212 U.S. 227 (1909) (Holmes, J., dissenting).	14. *U.S. v. Oregon Lumber Co.*, 260 U.S. 290 (1922) (Brandeis, J., dissenting).
16. *Atchison, T. & S.F. Ry. Co. v. Sowers*, 213 U.S. 55 (1909) (Holmes, J., dissenting).	15. *Lemke v. Farmers' Grain Co. of Embden, N.D.*, 258 U.S. 50 (1922) (Brandeis, J., dissenting).
17. *Southern Ry. Co. v. King*, 217 U.S. 524 (1910) (Holmes, J., dissenting).	16. *Kentucky Finance Corp. v. Paramount Auto Exch. Corp.*, 262 U.S. 544 (1923) (Brandeis, J., dissenting).
18. *Kuhn v. Fairmont Coal Co.*, 215 U.S. 349 (1910) (Holmes, J., dissenting).	17. *Texas Transport & Terminal Co. v. City of New Orleans*, 264 U.S. 150 (1924) (Brandeis, J., dissenting).
19. *Pullman Co. v. State of Kansas* ex rel. *Coleman*, 216 U.S. 56 (1910) (Holmes, J., dissenting).	

Dissenting Opinions Authored	Dissenting Opinions Joined
20. *Western Union Telegraph Co. v. State of Kansas ex rel. Coleman*, 216 U.S. 1 (1910) (Holmes, J., dissenting).	18. *Jay Burns Baking Co. v. Bryan*, 264 U.S. 504 (1924) (Brandeis, J., dissenting).
21. *Dr. Miles Medical Co. v. John D. Park & Sons Co.*, 220 U.S. 373 (1911) (Holmes, J., dissenting).	19. *Myers v. U.S.*, 272 U.S. 52 (1926) (Brandeis, J., dissenting).
22. *Bailey v. State of Alabama*, 219 U.S. 219 (1911) (Holmes, J., dissenting).	20. *Di Santo v. Commonwealth of Pennsylvania*, 273 U.S. 34 (1927) (Brandeis, J., dissenting).
23. *Brown v. Elliott*, 225 U.S. 392 (1912) (Holmes, J., dissenting).	21. *Tyson & Bro.-United Theatre Ticket Offices v. Banton*, 273 U.S. 418 (1927) (Stone, J., dissenting).
24. *Hyde v. U.S.*, 225 U.S. 347 (1912) (Holmes, J., dissenting).	22. *Olmstead v. U.S.*, 277 U.S. 438 (1928) (Brandeis, J., dissenting).
25. *Donnelly v. U.S.*, 228 U.S. 243 (1913) (Holmes, J., dissenting).	23. *Wuchter v. Pizzutti*, 276 U.S. 13 (1928) (Brandeis, J., dissenting).
26. *Coppage v. State of Alabama*, 236 U.S. 1 (1915) (Holmes, J., dissenting).	24. *John P. King Mfg. Co. v. City Council of Augusta*, 277 U.S. 100 (1928) (Brandeis, J., dissenting).
27. *Frank v. Mangum*, 237 U.S. 309 (1915) (Holmes, J., dissenting).	25. *Baldwin v. State of Missouri*, 281 U.S. 586 (1930) (Stone, J., dissenting).
28. *Southern Pac. Co. v. Jensen*, 244 U.S. 205 (1917) (Holmes, J., dissenting).	
29. *Motion Picture Patents Co. v. Universal Film Mfg. Co.*, 243 U.S. 502 (1917) (Holmes, J., dissenting).	
30. *Ruddy v. Rossi*, 248 U.S. 104 (1918) (Holmes, J., dissenting).	
31. *Toledo Newspaper Co. v. U.S.*, 247 U.S. 402 (1918) (Holmes, J., dissenting).	
32. *International News Service v. Associated Press*, 248 U.S. 215 (1918) (Holmes, J., dissenting).	
33. *Hammer v. Dagenhart*, 247 U.S. 251 (1918) (Holmes, J., dissenting).	
34. *City and County of Denver v. Denver Union Water Co.*, 246 U.S. 278 (1918) (Holmes, J., dissenting).	
35. *Abrams v. U.S.*, 250 U.S. 616 (1919) (Holmes, J., dissenting).	
36. *Maxwell v. Bugbee*, 250 U.S. 525 (1919) (Holmes, J., dissenting).	
37. *Evans v. Gore*, 253 U.S. 245 (1920) (Holmes, J., dissenting).	
38. *Knickerbocker Ice Co. v. Stewart*, 253 U.S. 149 (1920) (Holmes, J., dissenting).	
39. *Eisner v. Macomber*, 252 U.S. 189 (1920) (Holmes, J., dissenting).	

(continued)

Table 1. *(continued)*

Dissenting Opinions Authored	Dissenting Opinions Joined
40. *Truax v. Corrigan*, 257 U.S. 312 (1921) (Holmes, J., dissenting).	
41. *American Column & Lumber Co. v. U.S.*, 257 U.S. 377 (1921) (Holmes, J., dissenting).	
42. *Smith v. Kansas City Title & Trust Co.*, 255 U.S. 180 (1921) (Holmes, J., dissenting).	
43. *U.S. ex rel. Milwaukee Social Democratic Pub. Co. v. Burleson*, 255 U.S. 407 (1921) (Holmes, J., dissenting).	
44. *Leach v. Carlile*, 258 U.S. 138 (1922) (Holmes, J., dissenting).	
45. *U.S. v. Behrman*, 258 U.S. 280 (1922) (Holmes, J., dissenting).	
46. *Federal Trade Commission v. Beech-Nut Packing Co.*, 257 U.S. 441 (1922) (Holmes, J., dissenting).	
47. *Adkins v. Children's Hospital of the District of Columbia*, 261 U.S. 525 (1923) (Holmes, J., dissenting).	
48. *Bartels v. State of Iowa*, 262 U.S. 404 (1923) (Holmes, J., dissenting).	
49. *Commonwealth of Pennsylvania v. State of West Virginia*, 262 U.S. 553 (1923) (Holmes, J., dissenting).	
50. *Craig v. Hecht*, 263 U.S. 255 (1923) (Holmes, J., dissenting).	
51. *Panama R. Co. v. Rock*, 266 U.S. 209 (1924) (Holmes, J., dissenting).	
52. *Gitlow v. People of State of New York*, 268 U.S. 652 (1925) (Holmes, J., dissenting).	
53. *Weaver v. Palmer Bros. Co.*, 270 U.S. 402 (1926) (Holmes, J., dissenting).	
54. *Schlesinger v. State of Wisconsin*, 270 U.S. 230 (1926) (Holmes, J., dissenting).	
55. *Myers v. U.S.*, 272 U.S. 52 (1926) (Holmes, J., dissenting).	
56. *Frost v. Railroad Commission of State of Cal.*, 271 U.S. 583 (1926) (Holmes, J., dissenting).	
57. *Power Mfg. Co. v. Sanders*, 274 U.S. 490 (1927) (Holmes, J., dissenting).	

58. *Tyson & Bro.-United Theatre Ticket Offices v. Banton*, 273 U.S. 418 (1927) (Holmes, J., dissenting).
59. *Compania General de Tabacos de Filipinas v. Collector of Internal Revenue*, 275 U.S. 87 (1927) (Holmes, J., dissenting).
60. *Quaker City Cab Co. v. Commonwealth of Pennsylvania*, 277 U.S. 389 (1928) (Holmes, J., dissenting).
61. *Louisville Gas & Electric Co. v. Coleman*, 277 U.S. 32 (1928) (Holmes, J., dissenting).
62. *Panhandle Oil Co. v. State of Mississippi ex rel. Knox*, 277 U.S. 218 (1928) (Holmes, J., dissenting).
63. *Goodyear Tire & Rubber Co. v. U.S.*, 276 U.S. 287 (1928) (Holmes, J., dissenting).
64. *Long v. Rockwood*, 277 U.S. 142 (1928) (Holmes, J., dissenting).
65. *Louis K. Liggett Co. v. Baldridge*, 278 U.S. 105 (1928) (Holmes, J., dissenting).
66. *Olmstead v. U.S.*, 277 U.S. 438 (1928) (Holmes, J., dissenting).
67. *Black & White Taxicab & Transfer Co. v. Brown & Yellow Taxicab & Transfer Co.*, 276 U.S. 518 (1928) (Holmes, J. dissenting).
68. *Springer v. Government of Philippine Islands*, 277 U.S. 189 (1928) (Holmes, J., dissenting).
69. *U.S. v. Schwimmer*, 279 U.S. 644 (1929) (Holmes, J., dissenting).
70. *Farmer's Loan & Trust Co. v. State of Minnesota*, 280 U.S. 204 (1930) (Holmes, J., dissenting).
71. *New Jersey Bell Telephone Co. v. State Board of Texas and Assessment of New Jersey*, 280 U.S. 338 (1930) (Holmes, J., dissenting).
72. *Baldwin v. State of Missouri*, 281 U.S. 586 (1930) (Holmes, J., dissenting).
73. *Hoeper v. Tax Commission of Wis.*, 284 U.S. 206 (1931) (Holmes, J., dissenting).

ratio of dissenting votes to majority opinions authored is .083 to .098 to
.171, suggesting a rise, but one that is difficult to speculate about if one
compares only dissenting votes with majority authorships. What Table 1
shows clearly is that the percentage of cases in which Holmes dissented
increased during his last decade on the United States Supreme Court.

As prolific as he was, Holmes produced fewer dissents than Supreme
Court justices produce today (see Tables Two through Five), perhaps
because he did not have the same kind of assistance from law clerks that
United States Supreme Court justices have enjoyed since the 1960s, if not
earlier.[18] He did his own research and wrote his own opinions, and fewer
briefs and petitions reached the United States Supreme Court during
his tenure than they did during the latter half of the twentieth century
and into the new millennium. From 1940 to 1970 the number of petitions
before the United States Supreme Court "more than tripled."[19] Increased
caseloads, however, do not necessarily correlate with an increase in dissents because "the growth in caseload was not dramatic until the 1960s,
twenty years after the rise of dissent" as a popular medium.[20]

There are a few justices—Justice Brandeis, for instance—whose dissents
Holmes was likely to join and who were likely to join Holmes's dissents.
Of the dissenting opinions Holmes joined, 68% were authored by Justice
Brandeis and 12% were authored by Justice White. Holmes accordingly
appears to have been more aligned with the jurisprudence of certain justices. In 28% of the cases in which he joined the dissent of another justice,
Holmes wrote separately to register his reason for dissenting. Holmes
published 890 majority opinions during his tenure as a United States
Supreme Court justice. He dissented in only 8% of the cases in which
he authored an opinion, excluding concurrences. This percentage seems
unremarkable in light of the "rate of non-unanimous decisions [that]
mounted from under twenty percent in the early 1900s to over 70 percent
in the middle 1980s."[21] However, the percentage of cases in which Holmes
authored a dissent must be considered within historical context because
the "ratio of dissenting opinions to majority opinions was less than ten
percent in the early 1900s." By contrast, "in the middle 1980s, in number,
majority and dissenting opinions ran just about even."[22] Since the time
Holmes took his seat on the bench of the United States Supreme Court,
justices on that court have dissented with more frequency. The frequency
of dissenting opinions over time should not distract from the remarkable
frequency with which Holmes dissented during an era when dissents
were uncommon.

Perhaps the most interesting conclusion is that, although Holmes has
become known as "The Great Dissenter," entire terms passed in which
he never authored a dissent. He did not author a dissent in 1903, 1914, or
1916, although he joined one in 1903. By comparison, Justice Thurgood

Marshall, Chief Justice William Rehnquist, Justice John Paul Stevens, and Justice Sandra Day O'Connor never went a term without dissenting except during a year of retirement. As the tables below indicate,[23] Justice Marshall averaged 15 dissents per term; Chief Justice Rehnquist, 10 dissents per term; Justice Stevens, 21 dissents per term; and Justice O'Connor, seven dissents per term. Holmes sat on the United States Supreme Court for 10,627 days. Of the justices in the tables below, only Justice Stevens (12,611 days) and Chief Justice Rehnquist (12,293 days) served longer. The number of cases in which Holmes dissented during his entire career is roughly equivalent to the number of cases in which the justices in the tables below dissented within five to nine terms. Holmes's 73 dissents[24] seem insignificant in light of the 365 dissents of Justice Marshall (see Table 2), the 329 dissents of Chief Justice Rehnquist (see Table 3), the 710 dissents of Justice Stevens (see Table 4), and the 174 dissents of Justice O'Connor (see Table 5). In just three consecutive terms (1983-1985), Justice Stevens dissented 103 times, seven more times than Holmes dissented during his entire career. Such statistics appear to undermine Holmes's status as "The Great Dissenter," and I have selected only four justices to compare with him. A cursory review of the output of other United States Supreme Court justices since Holmes's retirement reveals that this exercise could be repeated with similar results for any number of them.

The dates listed in the tables below indicate the year *of the term* such that the corresponding figures amount to the number of votes *per term* rather than *per year*. The proper interpretation of Table 2 is that Justice Marshall dissented once during the 1967 term, three times during the 1968 term, twice during the 1969 term, ten times during the 1970 term, and so forth; these figures do not necessarily mean that Justice Marshall dissented that many times during that particular year. Moreover, these figures account for written dissents and not dissents by memorandum. Following the practice of the *Harvard Law Review*, which compiled the statistics for each term, I have considered a dissent as "written" even if it consists merely of a brief statement. I also have followed the *Harvard Law Review* by classifying a justice as dissenting if he or she voted to dispose of a case in a manner different from that of the majority and by categorizing as a "dissent" any opinions that concur in part and dissent in part.

Tables Two through Five suggest that Holmes, by comparison to Justice Marshall, Chief Justice Rehnquist, Justice Stevens, and Justice O'Connor, did not author many dissents. Yet none of these justices is known as "The Great Dissenter."

Holmes's admirers are partially responsible for his inflated standing as a prolific dissenter. One scholar accuses them of exaggerating Holmes's reputation by "emphasizing [his] occasional dissents and ignor[ing] the more numerous instances" in which he joined the opinions and dissents

Table 2.   Thurgood Marshall

1967	10 opinions; 1 concurrence; 1 dissent
1968	13 opinions; 0 concurrences; 3 dissents
1969	9 opinions; 1 concurrence; 2 dissents
1970	9 opinions; 4 concurrences; 10 dissents
1971	15 opinions; 3 concurrences; 20 dissents
1972	12 opinions; 8 concurrences; 21 dissents
1973	13 opinions; 4 concurrences; 19 dissents
1974	11 opinions; 4 concurrences; 8 dissents
1975	17 opinions; 8 concurrences; 19 dissents
1976	12 opinions; 6 concurrences; 21 dissents
1977	15 opinions; 4 concurrences; 20 dissents
1978	13 opinions; 4 concurrences; 15 dissents
1979	14 opinions; 7 concurrences; 21 dissents
1980	13 opinions; 1 concurrence; 12 dissents
1981	15 opinions; 5 concurrences; 4 dissents
1982	17 opinions; 3 concurrences; 27 dissents
1983	15 opinions; 2 concurrences; 16 dissents
1984	13 opinions; 6 concurrences; 13 dissents
1985	15 opinions; 6 concurrences; 31 dissents
1986	16 opinions; 1 concurrence; 20 dissents
1987	15 opinions; 1 concurrence; 13 dissents
1988	14 opinions; 0 concurrences; 18 dissents
1989	14 opinions; 4 concurrences; 15 dissents
1990	12 opinions; 2 concurrences; 17 dissents[1]

[1] Justice Marshall retired during the 1991 term, so I have omitted the statistics from 1991.

of other justices. Even this explanation is flawed. Table 1 indicates that Holmes joined just 25 dissents while authoring 73 dissents of his own.[25] There are other, more plausible reasons why Holmes acquired the moniker "The Great Dissenter" besides the number and length of his dissents. One is that he dissented more frequently than his predecessors on the United States Supreme Court.[26] Another is that he dissented frequently relative to the volume of cases filed in the United States Supreme Court during his career whereas later justices dissented even more frequently simply because of the increased volume of overall cases filed.

There is no single reason why Holmes became known as "The Great Dissenter." Evidence of his reputation as a literary judge, however, points to the probability that his rhetorical style earned him an audience and secured for his dissents a place in the legal canon. Holmes enjoyed an "uncanny ability to compact his thought into the confines of a powerful paragraph or a poignant sentence or a poetic phrase."[27] "One of the few points on which all commentators agree," notes Thomas Grey,

Table 3.   William Rehnquist

1971	11 opinions; 0 concurrences; 9 dissents
1972	16 opinions; 2 concurrences; 21 dissents
1973	17 opinions; 4 concurrences; 15 dissents
1974	15 opinions; 6 concurrences; 12 dissents
1975	16 opinions; 1 concurrence; 15 dissents
1976	15 opinions; 3 concurrences; 15 dissents
1977	14 opinions; 7 concurrences; 24 dissents
1978	16 opinions; 12 concurrences; 12 dissents
1979	15 opinions; 3 concurrences; 26 dissents
1980	15 opinions; 10 concurrences; 15 dissents
1981	17 opinions; 7 concurrences; 15 dissents
1982	20 opinions; 5 concurrences; 16 dissents
1983	19 opinions; 3 concurrences; 14 dissents
1984	17 opinions; 1 concurrence; 15 dissents
1985	19 opinions; 3 concurrences; 15 dissents
1986	17 opinions; 0 concurrences; 9 dissents
1987	15 opinions; 2 concurrences; 7 dissents
1988	15 opinions; 1 concurrences; 7 dissents
1989	15 opinions; 2 concurrences; 5 dissents
1990	14 opinions; 1 concurrence; 4 dissents
1991	11 opinions; 2 concurrences; 9 dissents
1992	14 opinions; 2 concurrences; 5 dissents
1993	10 opinions; 0 concurrences; 6 dissents
1994	11 opinions; 1 concurrence; 4 dissents
1995	10 opinions; 3 concurrences; 2 dissents
1996	11 opinions; 0 concurrences; 3 dissents
1997	12 opinions; 2 concurrences; 3 dissents
1998	9 opinions; 3 concurrences; 6 dissents
1999	9 opinions; 0 concurrences; 5 dissents
2000	9 opinions; 2 concurrences; 3 dissents
2001	10 opinions; 0 concurrences; 4 dissents
2002	8 opinions; 0 concurrences; 4 dissents
2003	9 opinions; 2 concurrences; 3 dissents
2004	7 opinions; 1 concurrence; 1 dissent[1]

[1]Chief Justice Rehnquist died in office on September 3, 2005; therefore, I have omitted the year 2005 from this table.

"is Holmes' greatness as a prose stylist."[28] Richard Posner has said that "Holmes was a great judge because he was a great literary artist."[29] Justice Frankfurter claimed that the greatness of most judges is determined by recounting "an analysis of specific decisions" but that Holmes was different because his "specialty was the great utterance," which he used to give "momentum" to "constitutional philosophy."[30] "[I]f we care for our literary treasures," Justice Frankfurter added, then "the expression of his

Table 4.   John Paul Stevens

1975	9 opinions; 9 concurrences; 17 dissents
1976	13 opinions; 17 concurrences; 27 dissents
1977	14 opinions; 10 concurrences; 21 dissents
1978	15 opinions; 7 concurrences; 13 dissents
1979	14 opinions; 12 concurrences; 21 dissents
1980	11 opinions; 17 concurrences; 25 dissents
1981	15 opinions; 15 concurrences; 26 dissents
1982	15 opinions; 12 concurrences; 27 dissents
1983	16 opinions; 18 concurrences; 34 dissents
1984	16 opinions; 9 concurrences; 33 dissents
1985	17 opinions; 15 concurrences; 36 dissents
1986	16 opinions; 14 concurrences; 32 dissents
1987	19 opinions; 6 concurrences; 17 dissents
1988	16 opinions; 14 concurrences; 22 dissents
1989	14 opinions; 17 concurrences; 29 dissents
1990	14 opinions; 5 concurrences; 25 dissents
1991	2 opinions; 11 concurrences; 22 dissents
1992	13 opinions; 10 concurrences; 21 dissents
1993	11 opinions; 9 concurrences; 13 dissents
1994	9 opinions; 6 concurrences; 19 dissents
1995	8 opinions; 6 concurrences; 21 dissents
1996	10 opinions; 5 concurrences; 17 dissents
1997	7 opinions; 8 concurrences; 15 dissents
1998	9 opinions; 6 concurrences; 19 dissents
1999	7 opinions; 7 concurrences; 18 dissents
2000	10 opinions; 7 concurrences; 17 dissents
2001	8 opinions; 3 concurrences; 14 dissents
2002	9 opinions; 10 concurrences; 9 dissents
2003	8 opinions; 9 concurrences; 12 dissents
2004	8 opinions; 9 concurrences; 13 dissents
2005	7 opinions; 6 concurrences; 15 dissents
2006	7 opinions; 8 concurrences; 16 dissents
2007	7 opinions; 8 concurrences; 13 dissents
2008	9 opinions; 3 concurrences; 17 dissents
2009	6 opinions; 13 concurrences; 14 dissents[1]

[1] Justice Stevens left office on June 29, 2010, so I have not included any statistics from the year 2010.

views must become part of our national culture."[31] Frederic R. Kellogg suggests that Holmes's "fame" was "made in several ringing dissents."[32] Posner would agree: "Holmes's innovations were dissenting opinions that, often after his death, became and have remained the majority opinion. [. . .] His majority and dissenting opinions alike are remarkable not only for the poet's gift of metaphor that is their principal stylistic distinction, but also for their brevity, freshness, and freedom from legal jargon; a directness bordering on the colloquial; a lightness of touch foreign to the

Table 5.   Sandra Day O'Connor

1981	13 opinions; 12 concurrences; 10 dissents
1982	16 opinions; 7 concurrences; 11 dissents
1983	17 opinions; 10 concurrences; 9 dissents
1984	16 opinions; 11 concurrences; 9 dissents
1985	17 opinions; 12 concurrences; 7 dissents
1986	18 opinions; 11 concurrences; 13 dissents
1987	16 opinions; 8 concurrences; 12 dissents
1988	13 opinions; 12 concurrences; 8 dissents
1989	17 opinions; 7 concurrences; 5 dissents
1990	16 opinions; 4 concurrences; 5 dissents
1991	15 opinions; 11 concurrences; 11 dissents
1992	13 opinions; 7 concurrences; 11 dissents
1993	12 opinions; 9 concurrences; 6 dissents
1994	10 opinions; 13 concurrences; 19 dissents
1995	9 opinions; 2 concurrences; 4 dissents
1996	9 opinions; 6 concurrences; 7 dissents
1997	10 opinions; 3 concurrences; 3 dissents
1998	10 opinions; 3 concurrences; 2 dissents
1999	8 opinions; 6 concurrences; 1 dissent
2000	9 opinions; 3 concurrences; 5 dissents
2001	8 opinions; 6 concurrences; 7 dissents
2002	9 opinions; 6 concurrences; 2 dissents
2003	8 opinions; 4 concurrences; 2 dissents
2004	8 opinions; 5 concurrences; 5 dissents
2005	3 opinions; 0 concurrences; 0 dissents[1]

[1] These numbers are low because Justice O'Connor retired before completing this term.

legal temperament; and insistence on being concrete rather than legalistic—on identifying values and policies rather than intoning formulas."[33] Posner concludes that most judges "lack Holmes's eloquence."[34] In light of the foregoing, I submit that Holmes's greatness as a dissenter and the reason he gained his reputation as "The Great Dissenter" has to do with the *content* rather than the frequency or quantity of his dissents. The literary and rhetorical excellence of his dissents enabled them to become canonized in leading textbooks and popularized in the American legal education system.

HOLMES'S STYLE

Holmes once wrote that the "tendencies of my family and myself have a strong natural bent to literature."[35] He is remembered as a writer like his father and like his hero, Emerson. "[H]ow like Emerson Holmes could sound," declares an early biographer of Holmes,[36] adding that "[t]here was a kinship of nobility between the two men."[37] Holmes himself wrote that the "only firebrand of my youth that burns to me as brightly as ever is Emerson, and I am bound to admit that for many years I have read but two or three pieces of his, coupled with *The Heart of Emerson's Journals* (I am not sure of the title) which impressed me a few years ago."[38] The present perfect tense of "have read" suggests that Holmes read these selections of Emerson repeatedly for many years, not that he read only a few pieces during a few years. In 1912 Holmes wrote to Patrick Sheehan, "You put it much too strongly when you say that I had no sympathy with Emerson. When he was breaking and I was still young, I saw him on the other side of the street and ran over and said to him: 'If I ever do anything, I shall owe a great deal of it to you,' which was true. He was one of those who set one on fire—to impart a [thought] was the gift of genius."[39] In 1919 Holmes wrote to Morris Cohen that "Emerson and [John] Ruskin were the men that set me on fire."[40]

Holmes was the Class Poet at Harvard, a position Emerson himself had held in 1821.[41] After the Civil War, when he was forced to embark upon a career, he "framed his choice as between Poetry and Philosophy, and then as between Philosophy and the Law. Philosophy was apparently the middle term, the psychological bridge between Poetry and the Law, and when he crossed that bridge it was 'law-law-law,' as he put it at the time in a letter to William James."[42] The celebrations of Holmes's talent as a writer seem to be endless and in many cases mawkish. Take, for instance, Francis Biddle's representatively sentimental acclaim:

> His words were feathered arrows, that carried to the heart of the target, from a mind that searched and saw. Words and thought were so closely knit that the thought could not have been said differently, the words re-arranged. They were warm with his own feeling, incisive with the precision of his mind, or tender, so that they became his words, and others had not used them before. He was a great stylist. Or, perhaps, as the word somehow conveys to our minds the suggestion of polish and surface without the depths below, I should suggest rather the inevitableness of his language.[43]

The following two dissents rendered in poetic form provide examples of the aesthetic properties to which Biddle refers. Regarding the first dissent, Justice Brandeis wrote to Justice Frankfurter in 1928 with the prediction that "Holmes's dissent in the Black & White Taxi Cab Case will stand among his notable opinions."[44] Justice Frankfurter himself wrote to Holmes about the dissent, saying, "I have just read your dissent in the *Black & White Taxicab* case and I'm all stirred with delight. You have written, if I may say so, a landmark opinion."[45] Later audiences concurred, calling the dissent "eloquent,"[46] "brilliant,"[47] "impassioned,"[48] "famous,"[49] and "famous and important."[50] These praises are not accompanied by explanations about what properties of the dissent make it extraordinary. Examining the dissent for such properties allows one to ascertain why the dissent gained its literary reputation that led to its vindication. Consider the following lines from the dissent, which I have reformatted as a poem:

> *Black & White Taxi:*[51] *A Poem*[52] (1928)
>
> It is very hard to resist the impression
> that there is one august corpus
> to understand which clearly is the only task
> of any Court concerned.
>
> If there were such a transcendental body of law
>
> outside of any particular State
> but obligatory within it unless and until changed by statute,
> the Courts of the United States might be right in using
> their independent judgment
> as to what it was.
>
> But there is no such body of law.
>
> The fallacy and illusion that I think exist
> consist in supposing that there is this outside thing to be found.
> Law is a word used with different meanings,
> but law in the sense in which courts speak of it today
> does not exist
> without some definite authority
> behind it.

One can almost sense Wallace Stevens in this "verse."[53] These lines appear abruptly in Holmes's dissent and in the context of a discussion about what the common law is. Holmes is refuting the majority's finding that the "cases cited show that the decisions of the Kentucky Court of Appeals holding such arrangements [i.e., railroad contracts granting certain companies exclusive privileges to do business on railroad property] invalid *are contrary to the common law as generally understood and applied.*"[54] Holmes is arguing that the common law is not one general body of abstract principles with definite applications that are binding in all times and places; he is suggesting that the common law may encompass different rules in different jurisdictions and that the law is ultimately whatever the government treats as the law at any given time and place. The implication is that the common law is not one thing but many, not the name for a fixed order of principles but for a process or methodology for handing down and following precedents. Because the common law in one place may differ from the common law in another place, Holmes reasons, the common law in Kentucky may consist of rules that are valid there but invalid elsewhere.

Holmes's background in poetry and literature warrants the inference that he deliberately chose his diction for its sound effects, including this succession of "c" sounds: "corpus-clearly-Court-concerned." He displays here alliteration, rhyme, and iambic feet, as this phonetic rendering demonstrates: "*clear*-LEE *is*-THEE *on*-LEE *task*-OF *an*-EE *court*-CON *serned*." This line might have rounded out an Emily Dickinson poem. Other alliterative, near-rhyming phrases include "It *iS*/*reS*-*iSt*/*impreSS*," "there *iS*/*auguSt*/*corpuS*," and "*exiSt*/*conSiSt*." Other iambic phrases include "*might*-BE *right*-IN *yoos*-ING" (note also the "might/right" rhyme), "*as*-TO *what*-IT *was*" (note also the "s" and "w" alliteration), "*that*-I *think*-EX *ist*" (note also the "th" alliteration), "*used*-WITH *diff*-RENT *mean*-INGS" (note also the "with-diff-rent" assonance), and "*speak*-OF *it*-TO *day*" (note also the "s" and "t" alliteration). These iambs would be unremarkable if they were not positioned alongside one another to create a rhythm and meter; the series of successive iambic phrases gives rise to feet, which gives rise to the presumption that the metrical patterns were not accidental but designed for rhetorical effect.

The manner in which Holmes employs metonymy by calling the majority's notion of the law "this outside thing" highlights his belief that the law consists of nothing more than the rules that are backed by government; there is, he seems to say, no law separate from and above that which the sovereign recognizes. He reinforces this point with the phrase "[l]aw is a word used with different meanings." Here as in the other lines in this dissent Holmes appears to have "elected to stick with already familiar and nonprofessional forms of language," turning plain idioms into resonant and memorable sounds through the careful organization of diction and syntax.[55] He eschews citations, logical reasoning, and case analogies and makes sweeping philosophical claims that raise ontological questions about what the law is and epistemological questions about how we know what the law is. Dissents ordinarily do not discuss the philosophical nature of the law, only how the case ought to have been decided and on what precedential basis. Holmes's sentiment could have been stated more simply: "It is understandable that people want there to be some higher form of law that governs how courts decide cases, but there is not a higher form of law—there are only the rules that the government establishes." Yet he went further than that, giving us lines that are memorable for their style and sound.

Compare Holmes's lines with the holding of the majority opinion:

The decree below should be affirmed unless federal courts are bound by Kentucky decisions which are directly opposed to this court's determination of the principles of common law properly to be applied in such cases. Petitioner argues that the Kentucky decisions are persuasive and establish the invalidity of such contracts, and that the Circuit Court of Appeals erred in refusing to follow them. But, as we understand the brief, it does not contend that, by reason of the rule of decision declared by section 34 of the Judiciary Act of 1789 (now R. S. 721, U. S. C. tit. 28, 725 (28 USCA 725)), this court is required to adopt the Kentucky decisions. But, granting that this point is before us, it cannot be sustained. The contract gives respondent, subject to termination on short notice, license or privilege to solicit patronage and park its vehicles on railroad property at train time. There is no question concerning title to land. No provision of state statute or Constitution and no ancient or fixed local usage is involved. For the discovery of common-law principles applicable in any case, investigation is not limited to the decisions of the courts of the state in which the controversy arises. State and federal courts go to the same sources for evidence of the existing applicable rule. The effort of both is to ascertain that rule. Kentucky has adopted the common law, and her courts recognize that its principles are not local but are included in the body of law constituting the general jurisprudence prevailing wherever the common law is recognized. Hunt v. Warnicke's Heirs Hardin (3 Ky.) 61; Lathrop v. Commercial Bank, 8 Dana, 114, 121, 33 Am. Dec. 481; Ray v. Sweeney, 14 Bush, 1, 9, et seq., 29 Am. Rep. 388; Aetna Insurance Co. v. Commonwealth, 106 Ky. 864, 876, 51 S. W. 624, 45 L. R. A. 355; Nider v. Commonwealth, 140 Ky. 684, 686, 131 S. W. 1024, Ann. Cas. 1913E, 1246. And see 1 Kent's Commentaries (14th Ed.) pp. 451, 602. As respects the rule of decision to be followed by federal courts, distinction has always been made between statutes of a state and the decisions of its courts on questions of general law. The applicable rule sustained by many decisions of this court is that, in determining questions of general law, the federal courts, while inclining to follow the decisions of the courts of the state in which the controversy arises, are free to exercise their own independent judgment. That this case depends on such a question is clearly shown by many decisions of this court.[56]

These lines lack the voice that is evident in Holmes's dissent. They explain the rationale without narrative asides such as "[i]t is hard to resist the impression" or "[t]he fallacy and illusion that I think exist." If there are alliterative phrases in the majority's holding, they appear to be incidental and not designed. Although there are iambs in the majority's holding, as there are iambs in all ordinary speech, they are not arranged in a series to create a rhythm or meter. There are no aphorisms, and the citations to authority tend to disrupt the flow of the passage. This comparison is not meant to suggest that Holmes's dissent was vindicated because it was more literary than the majority opinion—as if the literariness of an opinion were all that mattered, notwithstanding logical argument and legal reasoning—but the comparison does explain why *Black & White Taxi* has become famous not for the majority opinion but for Holmes's dissent. The fact that Holmes's dissent has been widely criticized for its reasoning and logical analysis only strengthens the proposition that its most lasting traits—the reasons it remains read, discussed, and quoted—are aesthetic and stylistic.[57] Its vindication could be attributed to his reaching the right result from logically specious or jurisprudentially questionable premises.

Holmes's dissent in this case was later vindicated in that it became the majority position.[58] Justice Breyer, writing for a unanimous court in *Hertz Corp. v. Friend*,[59] explained that the majority's holding in *Black & White Taxicab* had been superseded by statute. Statutes represent a form of majority opinion insofar as legislation reflects the dominant views of the populace as expressed through elected representatives. Even before the decision of the United States Supreme Court in *Hertz*, the majority holding in *Black & White* came under scrutiny in *Erie R. Co. v. Tompkins*[60] in which Justice Brandeis delivered the opinion of the United States Supreme Court. Allan C. Hutchinson claims that the *Erie* decision "vindicated" Holmes's dissent in *Black & White Taxicab* "in substance if not in rhetoric."[61] In 1988 a Fourth Circuit judge in *Capital Tool and Manufacturing Co., Inc. v. Maschinenfabrik Herkules*[62] recognized that the majority holding in *Black & White* had been abrogated. Two federal district courts declined to extend the precedent of *Black & White* in *Toste Farm Corp. v. Hadbury*[63] and *Lenco, Inc. v. New Age Industrial Corp., Inc.*[64] Although no judge or legislator overtly professed that the distinctive literary and aesthetic properties of Holmes's dissent in *Black & White* necessitated a formal reconsideration of that case, those properties lent Holmes's dissent a certain aura for which there can be no empirical measure but which stand out as unusual and memorable in the canons of American constitutional law. Subsequent chapters will demonstrate that other dissents by Holmes became known for their literary and aesthetic qualities and were likewise vindicated. *Black & White* therefore is not an aberration or an isolated example but merely one illustration within a pattern of vindication.

Holmes's dissent in *Gitlow v. New York*[65] provides another illustration, marked as it is by "extraordinary prose to find in [a] judicial opinion."[66] This dissent has been called "powerful,"[67] "prescient,"[68] "forcefully articulated,"[69] "stirring" for its "stylistic brilliance,"[70] and "classic" for its "memorable rhetoric."[71] One scholar has proposed that Holmes's dissent in *Gitlow* "is more an example of his distinctive literary style than an attempt to develop a new First Amendment jurisprudence."[72] Despite such acclaim, there is a glaring absence of commentary about what elements of the dissent make it literary or stylistic.

Consider the following lines, which I have reformatted as a poem:

Gitlow v. New York:[73] *A Poem*[74] (1925)

Every idea
is an incitement.
It offers itself for belief
and if believed
it is acted on
unless some other belief
outweighs it
or some failure of energy
stifles the movement
at its birth.

The only difference
between the expression
of an opinion and an incitement
in the narrower sense
is the speaker's enthusiasm
for the result.

Eloquence may set fire
to reason.

But whatever may be thought
of the redundant discourse
before us
it had no chance of starting
a present conflagration.

Aphorisms such as "[e]very idea is an incitement" and "[e]loquence may set fire to reason" are rare in judicial opinions. They "put the point memorably [. . .] with pragmatist resonance"[75] and have earned a reputation as "famous,"[76] "quotable,"[77] and "arresting and memorable."[78] They have become a "mantra" in First Amendment commentary.[79] Even more foreign to judicial opinions is personification of the kind expressed when Holmes treats an "idea" as an acting agent that can "offer itself." Holmes's alliterative use of the letter "n" emphasizes mobility, momentum, and ignition: "incitement," "energy," "movement," "incitement," "enthusiasm," "conflagration." These nouns suggest provocation, stimulus, and instigation; they are tied to ideas themselves, as in the line "every idea is an incitement," hence the correspondingly alliterative "n" sounds in the words "expression" and "reason." "For Holmes, expression remained combustible," and the metaphor of fire created in these lines evokes his pronouncement in *Schenck v. United States*[80] that the First Amendment does not protect someone who falsely shouts *"fire!"* in a crowded theater.[81]

The diction in these brief lines recalls Holmes's advice to Lewis Einstein: "A sentence gets its force from short words."[82] Even an economical use of ordinary nouns and adjectives can bring about the extravagance that characterizes Emersonian superfluity. Such superfluity signals an emphatic sound and style and not necessarily verbosity or prolixity. Richard Poirier explains that "[e]xtravagance in writing is more [. . .] than simply a matter of the local magnification of a word. It can involve a kind of rapid or wayward movement of voice, something often heard in the casual, idiomatic passages of speech, as it simultaneously focuses on particular things."[83] "Familiar, homey words," Poirier continues, "cannot, then, be dispensed with; they can, however, be reshaped, especially by alterations in any written syntax designed to catch those tones or sounds of speech that can substantially inflect or even reverse the meanings normally assigned to the words."[84] Holmes recognized in this vein that "the *normal* speaker of English" can be "a literary form."[85] Emersonian superfluity is not about verbosity or ornamentation of diction but occurs whenever writing and speech "create significances, especially by inflections of voice."[86] Emersonian superfluity can teach us "to hear sounds already deeply embedded in the caves of the human mouth and of the human ear."[87]

The sound of Holmes's prose in *Gitlow* exhibits superfluity. He follows a series of dactyls with spondaic feet just as he describes the possibility of combustion: "Eloquence [stress / slack / slack] may set fire [stress / stress / stress / slack] to reason [stress / stress / slack]." It is as though he wishes to create the sense of building pressure and then of sudden release or combustion. Two unstressed lines abruptly interrupt the heightened tension; the first appears with the transitional conjunction "But," which signals a change in the tone. Holmes appears to reverse the intensity as he assures us that the "redundant discourse," a phrase made cacophonous by the alliterative "d" and "s" sounds, has "no chance of starting a present conflagration." A sudden transition to iambic feet and a lightened tone round out these lines and suggest that Holmes has smothered or extinguished whatever energy had been building with the three-syllable feet. His ability to turn brief sentences and undemonstrative words into profound and demonstrative utterances heralds what Poirier calls the "American pragmatist heritage that goes back to Emerson, a philosophical heritage that is unique for the privileges it accords to casual, extemporized, ordinary idiom, to uses of language that translate into little more than sound."[88]

These lines from Holmes's *Gitlow* dissent develop an aesthetic characterized as much by the sound as by the meaning of Holmes's diction. "Style, I think, is sound—a matter of the ear," Holmes wrote to Lewis Einstein.[89] Poirier refers to the "*sound*" of certain American writers such as

Robert Frost, Gertrude Stein, and Wallace Stevens as the "central aspect of the Emersonian pragmatist contribution."[90] These pragmatic writers "made the value of sound explicitly a subject of their work."[91] At the time he authored the *Gitlow* dissent, Holmes had recently read and commented on the writings of Santayana,[92] T.S. Eliot,[93] Thomas Hardy,[94] James Joyce,[95] Rudyard Kipling,[96] and Sinclair Lewis,[97] among other modernists who were using ordinary idioms with extraordinary effect. Within the next few years he would read Ernest Hemingway,[98] D.H. Lawrence,[99] Robinson Jeffers,[100] Siegfried Sassoon,[101] and E.M. Forster.[102] He was, as he put it in a letter to Sir Frederick Pollock, "pleased" by Santayana's unique "style" and convicted that "*superfluity* of energy [. . .] makes it necessary for a man to act."[103] Holmes was attentive to the function of syllabics and meter in his prose, explaining in a letter to Albert J. Beveridge that "except in rare cases I try to end a paragraph with a monosyllable or word accented on the last syllable—so that the axe may fall—and the head drop. When you end on a polysyllable it gives a squashy feeling. Of course there are cases where although you make a new paragraph you only pause to take breath and then continue the previous line of thought."[104] Holmes's attention to the sound, style, meter, and syllabics of his prose suggests that his use of these features of language in *Gitlow* were intended for rhetorical effect.

The literary and rhetorical qualities of Holmes's *Gitlow* dissent contributed to its memorability, without which one probably could not have said that "the *Gitlow* dissent became law."[105] The aphoristic premises of this dissent—*every idea is an incitement; eloquence may set fire to reason*— "resonate with particular audiences" and "*continue* to resonate."[106] In a letter concerning *Gitlow*, Holmes complained to Lewis Einstein about "a criticism of my opinions that they might be literature but were not the proper form of judicial expression."[107] Such criticism makes the vindication of Holmes more remarkable because it suggests that his dissent is remembered more for *what* it says than *how* it says. If Holmes had not aestheticized his dissent, it might not have been canonized. Nor would it have shaped the trajectory of First Amendment jurisprudence. This dissent was considered nearly vindicated in 1951 by the United States Supreme Court in *Dennis v. United States*: "Although no case subsequent to *Whitney*[108] and *Gitlow* has expressly overruled the majority opinions in those cases, there is little doubt that subsequent opinions have inclined toward the Holmes-Brandeis rationale."[109] Writing for the majority of the United States Supreme Court in *Thomas v. Collins* (1945),[110] Justice Rutledge cited Holmes's *Gitlow* dissent to support this axiom: "The First Amendment is a charter for government, not for an institution of learning. 'Free trade in ideas' means free trade in the opportunity to persuade to action, not merely to describe facts."[111] In 1946 the United States Supreme

Court in *Pennekamp v. State of Florida*,[112] a case that relied on *Gitlow* to reach its conclusion, recalled this about Holmes's First Amendment jurisprudence: "No Justice thought more deeply about the nature of a free society or was more zealous to safeguard its conditions by the most abundant regard for civil liberty than Mr. Justice Holmes. He left no doubt that judicial protection of freedom of utterance is necessarily qualified by the requirements of the Constitution as an entirety for the maintenance of a free society."[113] Numerous federal and state court decisions have linked their freedom-of-speech rationale to Holmes's dissent in *Gitlow*. Chapter 3 will demonstrate that Holmes's complex notions of freedom of speech and expression are not reducible to his *Gitlow* dissent from which he eventually distanced himself. The point here is that the citational network of federal cases emanating from the *Gitlow* dissent would not have been possible if that dissent had been unremarkable, nor perhaps would Holmes's arguments about unrestrained speech have been revisited if they had been couched in boring or bland prose.

EMERSONIAN SUPERFLUITY

The hagiographic treatments of Holmes as a poetic genius signal a tendency in Holmes's own writing toward Emersonian superfluity. Holmes employed remarkable turns of phrase and insisted on rhythmic and memorable language where a mundane and mechanical style would have sufficed. Poirier's theory of superfluity, which refers to an extravagant literary style that Poirier attributes to Emerson, resonates in the context of Holmes's writings and in light of Holmes's devotion to Emerson. Poirier considered superfluity to be Emerson's recourse for overcoming the influence of his aesthetic predecessors while making his own mark on their tradition. He presented superfluity as a textual means for creative minds to struggle against the inherent limitations and vagaries of language and to experiment with diction and syntax to attract and affect future readers. Related to Harold Bloom's theory of the anxiety of influence, Poirier's notion of superfluity holds that Emerson and others in his revisionary tradition (William James, Robert Frost, Gertrude Stein, Wallace Stevens, and T.S. Eliot) drew creative inspiration from the angst that accompanied their desire to overcome their literary predecessors as well as the confines of language and representation. The agonism inherent in Emersonian superfluity goes lengths toward explaining how Holmes's dissents not only draw from Emerson's influence but also instantiate an aesthetic pragmatism that struggles to generate continuity and improvement in rules that are couched in binding utterances. The language of Holmes's dissents exemplifies the creative urge as against supine submission to other judges and justices and against the uncritical acceptance of established precedents. His memorable diction and syntax serve important rhetorical functions and shape judicial precedents to fit the present environment, as evidenced by the ability of his dissents to transition into law. Holmes's dissents counteracted the tendency among judges and justices to mechanically receive or repeat only partially relevant holdings that left current parties without an adequate remedy and future parties without guidance as to how old laws obtain in new contexts. The sonorous qualities of those dissents emphasized and popularized his normative utterances about what the law ought to be and thereby increased the probability that those utterances would impact if not become the law.

Emerson enacted the superfluity he described. He writes about superfluity in the form of "energies, processes, movements, transitions, and transformations" while making his "writing the literal embodiment of these vital forces."[114] He substantiates superfluity by couching his claim "that the world is a force" in language that "has a force" and that "draws on and extends the force."[115] The opening of "Circles," for example, announces that "[t]he eye is the first circle; the horizon which it forms is the second; and throughout nature this primary picture is repeated without end."[116] Here Emerson separates three short, emphatic independent clauses with two semi-colons, creating the sense that the sentence itself is flowing outward from the first "circle" and repeating a syntactical structure the way nature repeats her forms. The eye metaphor suggests that all experience is concentric in that it shares the same origin, which itself is not a point but a curved line having multiple points on it, to say nothing of the power to "see." All circles of knowledge and existence derive from the first. The metaphor applies not just spatially but temporally: the circles of the present develop out of past circles and enable future circles.

Emerson states that "[t]here are no fixtures in nature" because the "universe is fluid";[117] the constitution of each circle, he suggests, has to do with "laws" and "culture," the former being what regulates and explains the latter even as both change in synchronized stages.[118] The eye and circle metaphors exemplify superfluity by making figurative what could have been simple and literal but also less memorable; his punctuation and syntax exemplify superfluity by representing and resembling the circular processions that are Emerson's subjects. Emerson's use of auxesis also mimics the circularity that he depicts in the eye metaphor: "Our life is an apprenticeship to the truth, that around every circle another can be drawn; that there is no end in nature, but every end is a beginning; that there is always another dawn risen on mid-noon, and under every deep a lower deep opens."[119] This sequence of phrases beginning with the conjunctive "that" demarcates the stages in which each new circle is drawn and signals the endlessness and repetitiousness of natural phenomena.

This line, like the material world, resembles the "vast ebb of a vast flow."[120] In these opening sentences to "Circles" there is "no sleep" and "no pause" or "inertia" but instead "incessant movement and progression."[121] Emerson's prose performs the momentum it celebrates—it superfluously promotes superfluity.

Such moments are common in Emerson's essays. He might comment about the greatness of simplicity, for instance, in simple diction and syntax: "Nothing is more simple than greatness; indeed, to be simple is to be great."[122] This aphoristic sentence is indeed great; it is superfluous not because of prolixity or ornateness, which it lacks, but because it is rendered in a manner that reflects the philosophical point Emerson is making. Another example of such superfluity appears in "Spiritual Laws," where Emerson discusses a ship on a river surrounded by "obstructions on every side but one" in an independent clause stuck between two semicolons; he then submits that "on that side all obstruction is taken away" as he drops the repetition of semicolons and allows the sentence itself, like its subject, to flow forward.[123] In light of this creative and precise organization of punctuation, it is telling that Emerson immediately follows this sentence with the declaration that the "talent" and "call" to break through obstructions "depend on [. . .] organization."[124]

Poirier explains that "the democratic impulse shared by Emersonian pragmatists [. . .] involved a recognition that language, if it is to represent the flow of individual experience, ceases to be an instrument of clarification or of clarity and, instead, becomes the instrument of a saving uncertainty and vagueness."[125] Emersonian superfluity is in this sense an overcompensation or overreaction to skepticism about the ability of language—or what Holmes called the "uncertainty of speech"[126]—to summon forth absolute meaning. Holmes's dissents enacted Emersonian pragmatism by subverting the clarity of the law (the majority opinion) while displaying unforgettable language that diminished the persuasive force of the majority opinion. Holmes's dissents defamiliarized the majority rule by calling it into question with language that is provocatively aesthetic. Poirier employs the phrase "Emersonian individualist and dissenter" in a way that could have described Holmes.[127] Like judges and justices in a common-law system who are obligated to follow precedent, Poirier's Emerson is concerned with "the language we inherit."[128] "Every new compound / Is some product and repeater," intones Emerson in words that both substantiate Poirier's theory and evoke the mimetic rules within the common-law system.[129] He says elsewhere in thematically similar diction that "the experience of each new age requires a new confession"[130] and that "the inventor only knows how to borrow."[131] Like precedents in a common-law system, creativity for Emerson is mimetic and transmitted, not fashioned in a vacuum.

Poirier's pragmatist canon is subject to its own version of *stare decisis* whereby writers inevitably receive the precedents on which originality is predicated. Poirier coins the term "linguistic skepticism" to describe the struggle "to reveal, in the words and phrases we use, linguistic resources that point to something beyond skepticism, to possibilities of personal and cultural renewal."[132] Linguistic skepticism is tied to the idea that language can never represent reality; that vocabularies are social adjuncts standing in for concrete phenomena; and that words are signs for referents and cannot completely convey the sensations one feels while perceiving material objects. What characterizes Poirier's conception of superfluity is the attempt to overcome linguistic skepticism with poetic language and prominent style. Common-law judges and justices also avail themselves of superfluity: Although they are restrained by binding precedents, certain judges and justices may use such restraint as a source of creative originality for disrupting the majority positon or for swerving from the course of precedent.

"Although he was the most eloquent writer on the bench," observes one biographer, Holmes "could also be the most obscure."[133] Holmes himself admitted in a letter to Ellen A. Curtis that a surplus of meaning may have led his writing into the kind of obscurity or vagueness that characterizes the aesthetics of Poirier's pragmatists: "Obscurity has been my trouble, although I hardly should count that in estimating what I mean by style. Obscurity sometimes means, with me as with others, that one still is out on the fighting line of thought."[134] Holmes thus expressed an element of superfluity: the way in which "Emersonian pragmatism [. . .] never allows any one of its [key, repeated terms] to arrive at a precise or static definition."[135] The anxiety for the Emersonian pragmatist consists in breaking from the gridlock of influence and compensating for the obscurity inherent in language while always leaving room for future adaptation and influence. Poirier portrays Stevens's poem "Seventy Years Later" as articulated "in a vocabulary and syntax opaque even for Stevens, suggesting that a burden of obscurity is revealed to him in the very process of the poem's delivery to us."[136] This very burden "validate[s] the possibilities for new invention"[137] and motivates "an impatient rejection of defeat."[138] In Poirier's view, the inherent limitations of language are also conditions for its creative perpetuation; the struggle against the constraints of language enables originality to proliferate. The common-law judge or justice confronts not only language constraints but also the constraints of *stare decisis*. Superfluity can to some extent free the common-law judge or justice from these constraints. The anxiety of influence for the common-law judge or justice is creatively to achieve workable solutions in particular cases without allowing lines of reasoning to solidify into rigid rules that may not obtain in future contexts.

Holmes's dissents are on the order of superfluity insofar as they evoke the possibilities of language to make the past *"foreseen* in the present, a present always intent, as the past was, on transforming itself into a very different and better future."[139] Holmes's dissents consult the laws of the past while reaching future audiences to influence the law at later dates. Holmes's dissent in *Haddock v. Haddock*,[140] for example, consulted the legal history regarding matrimonial domicile to make possible the majority opinion in *Williams v. State of North Carolina*,[141] which expressly overruled the majority in *Haddock* and cited an aphorism from Holmes's dissent ("this is pure fiction, and fiction always is a poor ground for changing substantial rights") to establish a new majority position.[142]

As indicated in the opening of this chapter, Holmes dissented in *Dr. Miles*, stating, "There is no statute covering the case; there is no body of precedent that, by ineluctable logic, requires the conclusion to which the court has come. The conclusion is reached by extending a certain conception of public policy to a new sphere."[143] The United States Supreme Court eventually overruled the majority in *Dr. Miles* and vindicated Holmes's dissent. When it did so it borrowed from Holmes's Darwinian terminology, declaring that "[s]*tare decisis* does not compel continued adherence to the *per se* rule here" because the "rule of reason's case-by-case adjudication implements the common-law approach" whereby the statutory prohibition on the restraint of trade "evolves to meet the dynamics of present economic conditions."[144]

Another example of the ability of Holmes's dissents to shape the law long after his death appears in *Olsen v. State of Nebraska ex rel. Western Reference and Bond Association*,[145] which overruled part of the majority opinion in *Tyson* and credited Holmes's dissent for the reversal.[146] *Green v. United States*[147] explains that Holmes's dissent in *Kepner v. U.S.*[148] has been vindicated while *Green* itself vindicates the *Kepner* dissent. By concurring with the main opinion in *Fernandez v. Wiener*[149] on grounds presented in Holmes's dissent in *Hoeper v. Tax Commission of Wisconsin*,[150] Justice Douglas vindicated Holmes's dissent in *Hoeper*. Pushing back against the holding in *Farmer's Loan & Trust Co. v. State of Minnesota*,[151] the United States Supreme Court in *Curry v. McCanless*[152] nudged case precedent back in the direction of Holmes's dissent in *Farmer's Loan*, giving rise to a limited vindication of Holmes's views.

State Tax Commission of Utah v. Aldrich[153] vindicated Holmes's position on the Fourteenth Amendment as articulated in his dissent in *Baldwin v. State of Missouri*,[154] quoting Holmes's superfluous maxim that the Fourteenth Amendment was not "intended to give us carte blanche to embody our economic and moral beliefs in its prohibitions."[155] Writing for the majority in *Girouard v. United States* (1946),[156] Justice Douglas vindicated Holmes's dissent in *United States v. Schwimmer*,[157] proposing that Justice

Holmes's dissent exposed a fallacy underlying the general rule at issue in the case.[158] Vindication of Holmes's dissenting view was acknowledged in *Youngstown Sheet & Tube Co. v. Sawyer*:[159] "Although more restrictive views of executive power, advocated in dissenting opinions of Justice Holmes, McReynolds and Brandeis, were emphatically rejected by this Court in *Myers v. United States, supra*, members of today's majority treat those dissenting views as authoritative."[160] *North Dakota State Board of Pharmacy v. Snyder's Drug Stores, Inc.*[161] compared the majority opinion of Justice Sutherland in *Louis K. Liggett Co. v. Baldridge*[162] with Holmes's dissent in *Liggett* before adopting Holmes's position as the law: "The *Liggett* case, being a derelict in the stream of the law, is hereby overruled."[163] Finally, in *Harper v. Virginia Department of Taxation*,[164] Justice Thomas vindicated an aspect of Holmes's dissent in *Kuhn v. Fairmont Coal*.[165]

Holmes's dissents have influenced not just the United States Supreme Court and inferior federal courts but also state appellate courts. When a Florida appellate court declined to follow the majority in *Kuhn*, it did so partially on the ground of Holmes's dissent in *Kuhn*.[166] In *Monongahela River Consol. Coal & Coke Co. v. Jutte*,[167] the Pennsylvania Supreme Court, following the decision in *Northern Securities Company v. United States*, moved toward the position of Holmes's dissent in *Northern Securities*. Even the United States Supreme Court, without expressly vindicating Holmes, looked back to Holmes's writing in *Northern Securities* as a source of authority. In *Dennis v. United States*,[168] for example, Justice White adopted Holmes's opening dictum from *Northern Securities* about great cases making bad law and hence called attention to Holmes's oppositional reasoning. This dictum was so catchy that it was repeated in several United States Supreme Court cases, mostly in dissents: *Penn-Central Merger and N & W Inclusion Cases*;[169] *New York Times Co. v. United States*;[170] *United States v. Chavez*;[171] *Nixon v. General Service Administrator*;[172] *Larkin v. Grendel's Den, Inc.*;[173] *Pennzoil Co. v. Texaco, Inc.*;[174] and *Skinner v. Railway Labor Executives' Association*.[175]

These examples demonstrate that when a dissent registers legal positions that the present majority has rejected, later justices influenced by that dissent may register their own legal opinions until the dissenting position becomes vindicated. The constant process of working through differing viewpoints, of sifting through opposing arguments and antagonistic reasoning, results in what at any given moment is deemed "the law," a term that in the common-law system signifies the cumulative product of longstanding trial and error. Because it draws attention to itself, superfluity can ensure that judges and justices remain interested in the legal arguments lying beneath compelling language.

Poirier's notion of linguistic skepticism articulates a parallel between what a strong common-law judge like Holmes does and what a strong poet like Emerson does. Poirier does not mention judges or justices, but his take on what Emerson believed texts to be and to do is remarkably similar to what common-law judges and justices are trained to believe that textual precedent is and does. In a sense, Poirier portrays Emerson as a judge of and within the literary tradition who "wishes to point out [. . .] that no matter how appealing the historical nature of any text, especially as it gets expressed in uses of language, historicity is itself the germ of what could become the cultural obsolescence of that text."[176] By the standards of this hypothetical Emerson, a work of literature (or a legal opinion) that is too historically bound to remain relevant to future readers exhausts its importance. Authors (or judges and justices) who are too eager to break from precedent, whose "tiresome injunction" is "to make it new," are merely "weak Emersonians" who "fail to perceive that this is also to say that 'it' will become old and will not thereby be discredited."[177] Rather than altogether dispensing with precedents, the Emersonian modifies or adapts precedents for present conditions and purposes. He wrests control of the only natural constant: "life, transition, and the energizing spirit."[178] In the common-law system, the inheritance of acquired rules and principles embodied in case precedents supplies future judges and justices with a range of data on which to base their decisions. By dissenting, a judge or justice widens the range of data. Poirier's claim that even "words of resistance and dissent" are "products of 'previous human thinking'" therefore resounds in the context of the common-law system.[179]

Poirier's Emerson maintains that "every text is a reconstruction of some previous texts of work, work that itself is always, again, work-in-progress."[180] "[A]ccording to Emerson himself," Poirier submits, "nothing can be recognized as new unless it offers in itself some hint of its obligation to the past."[181] Or in Emerson's words, "There is not a piece of science but its flank may be turned tomorrow; there is not literary reputation, not the so-called eternal names of fame, that may not be revised and condemned."[182] "Every ultimate fact," Emerson says, "is only the first of a new series. Every general law only a particular fact of some more general law presently to disclose itself."[183] This evolutionary understanding of literary and intellectual history that Poirier attributes to Emerson nearly aligns with Holmes's view of the common-law system. Poirier even ascribes to Emerson a view of textual heritability that resembles the common-law processes by which majority opinions are advanced and opposed over time and in response to changing social and technological circumstances. He claims, for instance, that Emerson held the notion that the "same work gets repeated throughout history in different texts, each being a revision of past texts to meet present needs, needs which are perceived differently by each new generation."[184] This Emersonian idea of "creation consist[ing] of repetition with a difference, of repeating in a new text work already being carried on in the texts of the past," is in fact the basis of the common-law system that Holmes repeatedly called attention to in *The Common Law*.[185]

CONCLUSION

Holmes is "The Great Dissenter" not only because he dissented with literary sparkle but also because, as Poirier said of Emerson, he "ma[d]e oneself conscious of things before they [went] public, as it were, before they c[ould] be known publicly by virtue of having passed into language."[186] Holmes's dissents "lack the perspicuity of a logical demonstration" and have been resurrected "as fragments of American public culture that continue to circulate *beyond* the particularities of the decisions rendered in each case."[187] Poirier may as well have called Emerson a prophet. In a similar sense, Holmes's dissents not only provide normative utterances about what the law ought to be in theory but also prophesy about what the law will become in fact. It is indeed the Emersonian "virtue" of "superfluousness" and the "determination to show that excess is more important than necessity, energy more lasting than any meanings it may toss out to the intellectually sedentary," that marks Holmes's dissents with distinction and enables them to become prophetic.[188]

"[W]hat elevates the style of a great decision," explains one commentator on Holmes, "is its capacity to *gesture beyond the particularities* of a case without employing broad generalizations. This is why Holmes's dissents are so *stylistically memorable*—the metaphors they employ *gesture beyond the case at hand* to larger, more pressing paradoxes that *continue* to mark American political affairs."[189] Holmes appropriates Emersonian superfluity and vests certain legal arguments in resonant language to preserve those arguments in American legal discourse for future generations. His vindicated dissents suggest that the proliferating potential of any dissents to become majority positions is maximized by "mutations and superfluities of meaning";[190] by the "power of troping" or "turning or changing the apparently given";[191] and by inflecting language to "ever so slightly make some persons *feel* like changing the world."[192] If superfluity "points to a human desire to go beyond these usual stopping places in sentences, these nouns, abstractions, concepts that serve the function of homes or still points, making us their dependents," then dissents as rhetorical media are conducive to superfluity because they seek to push society forward by diversifying jurisprudential options for future judges and by placing ideas in constructive competition.[193] Dissents defamiliarize the law as expressed by the majority and enable the vagaries of meaning from which creativity is derived. Dissents are an oppositional genre, and opposition forces the struggle for creativity and originality that are the hallmarks of Emersonian pragmatism.

NOTES

1. Leegin Creative Leather Products, Inc. v. PSKS, Inc., 551 U.S. 877 (2007) at 899.

2. *Leegin* 551 U.S. 877 (2007).

3. Dr. Miles Medical Co. v. John D. Park & Sons Co., 220 U.S. 373 (1911).

4. *Dr. Miles* 220 U.S. at 413.

5. *Leegin* 551 U.S. 877 (2007) at 899.

6. Ibid.

7. See generally Daniel Gross, "An Empirical Study of the Vindicated Dissents of the New York Appellate Division, Fourth Department, From 2000 to 2010," *Albany Law Review* 74 (2010-11): 931-949, examining vindicated dissents in just the Fourth Department of the New York Appellate Division. Examples abound from the United States Supreme Court. Consider the majority opinion in Arizona v. Gant (556 U.S. 332 [2009]), which answered the call of the dissenters in New York v. Belton (453 U.S. 454 [1981]) to revise the latter case's interpretation of a vehicle search under the Fourth Amendment (Arizona v. Gant 556 U.S. at 338). See also Lawrence v. Texas (539 U.S. 558 [2003]) in which the majority quoted from Justice Stevens's dissent in Bowers v. Hardwick (478 U.S. 186 [1986]) and then declared, "Justice Stevens' analysis, in our view, should have been controlling [. . .] and should control here" (*Lawrence v. Texas* 539 U.S. at 578). Not all cases announce that they are vindicating a dissent by adopting its legal reasoning and rejecting the reasoning of the binding majority. An example is Katz v. United States (389 U.S. 347 [1967]), which rejects the majority reasoning in Olmstead v. United States (277 U.S. 438 [1928]) and thereby vindicates the dissents of Justice Holmes and Justice Brandeis, among others, without explicitly acknowledging the source of the vindication.

8. Chicago, M. & St. P. R. Co. v. State of Wisconsin, 238 U.S. 491 (1915).

9. Williams v. Standard Oil Co. of Louisiana, 278 U.S. 235 (1929).

10. E.g., Holmes's unpublished and undelivered dissent in Buchanan v. Warley (245 U.S. 60 [1917]). The dissent was withdrawn before publication.

11. Haddock v. Haddock, 201 U.S. 562 (1906).

12. American Column & Lumber Co. v. U.S., 257 U.S. 377 (1921).

13. U.S. ex rel. Milwaukee Social Democratic Pub. Co. v. Burleson, 255 U.S. 407 (1921).

14. Myers v. U.S., 272 U.S. 52 (1926).

15. Tyson & Bro.-United Theatre Ticket Offices v. Banton, 273 U.S. 418 (1927).

16. Olmstead v. U.S., 277 U.S. 438 (1928).

17. Baldwin v. State of Missouri, 281 U.S. 586 (1930).

18. See Todd C. Peppers, *Courtiers of the Marble Palace: The Rise and Influence of the Supreme Court Law Clerk* (Stanford, CA: Stanford University Press, 2006) at pages 30-35, 112-115, 130-132, 145-149, 156, 169, 186. Also see generally David J. Garrow, "'The Lowest Form of Animal Life?': Supreme Court Clerks and Supreme Court History," *Cornell Law Review* 84 (1999): 855-94. Regarding a distinct shift in the way Supreme Court clerks were hired in accordance with a model developed by Justice Brandeis, see William E. Nelson, Harvey Rishikof, I. Scott Messinger, and Michael Jo, "The Liberal Tradition of the Supreme Court Clerkship: Its Rise, Fall, and Reincarnation?" *Vanderbilt Law Review* 62: 1756-1766.

19. Joseph Jucewicz and Lawrence Baum, "Workload Influences on Supreme Court Acceptance Rates, 1975-1984," *Western Political Quarterly* 43 (1990): 125.

20. "The data suggest that the change in the number of cases is inversely related to the number of dissenting opinions. The fivefold increase in Supreme Court decisions in the 1860s was not accompanied by an increase in dissenting opinions. By contrast, the drop in the number of Supreme Court cases following the Judiciary Act of 1925 corresponds well with the increase in dissenting opinions. In addition, the Rehnquist Court heard fewer cases per year than any Court of the last 100 years [as of 2007], but nearly 50 percent of all opinions had a dissent; the Roberts Court appears to be following a similar pattern. This inverse relation suggests that it was more likely the change in the type of cases that resulted in more dissenting opinions rather than the change in the number of cases" (Henderson, "From Seriatim to Consensus," 326-27).

21. Ruth Bader Ginsburg, "Remarks on Writing Separately," *Washington Law Review* 65 (1990): 147.

22. Ibid.

23. These tables are drawn from the statistics provided by *Harvard Law Review* following each term of the United States Supreme Court.

24. As I have stated already, Holmes sometimes wrote a dissent and joined a dissent in the same case, and for such cases, I have categorized Holmes's writings as both "Dissenting Opinions Authored" and "Dissenting Opinions Joined."

25. G. Edward White, "The Canonization of Holmes and Brandeis: Epistemology and Judicial Reputations," *New York University Law Review* 70 (1995): 578.

26. M. Todd Henderson has examined trends in seriatim versus consensus among United States Supreme Court justices. He provides the following chart showing statistics for Chief Justices of the United States Supreme Court up until 2007 (Henderson, "From Seriatim to Consensus," 316):

Table 6.   Supreme Court Statistics

Chief Justice	Dates of Service	No. of Cases	No. of Chief Justice Dissenting Opinions	Dissent Proportion (%)
Marshall	1801–35	1,187	3	0
Taney	1836–63	1,708	38	2
Chase	1864–73	1,109	33	3
Waite	1874–87	2,642	45	2
Fuller	1888–1909	4,866	113	2
White	1910–20	2,541	39	2
Taft	1921–29	1,708	16	1
Hughes	1930–40	2,050	46	2
Stone	1941–45	704	95	13
Vinson	1946–52	723	90	12
Warren	1953–68	1,772	215	12
Burger	1969–85	2,755	184	7
Rehnquist	1986–2005	2,131	182	9
Roberts	2005–present	104	3	3

27. Ronald Collins, "Prologue," in *The Essential Holmes: A Free Speech Chronicle and Reader*, edited by Ronald Collins (New York: Cambridge University Press, 2010), xviii.

28. Thomas C. Grey, "Holmes and Legal Pragmatism," *Stanford Law Review* 41 (1989): 787.

29. Richard Posner, "Introduction," in *The Essential Holmes: Selections from the Letters, Speeches, Judicial Opinions, and Other Writings of Oliver Wendell Holmes, Jr.* (Chicago: University of Chicago Press, 1992), xvii.

30. Felix Frankfurter, *Mr. Justice Holmes and the Supreme Court* (Cambridge, MA: Harvard University Press, 1939), 28.

31. Frankfurter, *Mr. Justice Holmes*, 29.

32. Frederic R. Kellogg, *Oliver Wendell Holmes, Jr., Legal Theory, and Judicial Restraint* (Cambridge University Press, 2007), 8.

33. Posner, "Introduction," xiii.

34. Posner, "Introduction," xiv.

35. Holmes, *Autobiographical Sketch*, quoted in G. Edward White, *Justice Oliver Wendell Holmes: Law and the Inner Self* (New York: Oxford University Press, 1993), 8.

36. Francis Biddle, *Mr. Justice Holmes* (New York: Charles Scribner's Sons, 1943), 25.

37. Biddle, *Mr. Justice Holmes*, 24.

38. In 1930 letter to Pollock quoted in Posner, "Introduction," 16.

39. From 1912 letter to Sheehan quoted in Posner, "Introduction," 64.

40. From 1919 letter to Cohen, in Posner, "Introduction," 110.

41. Robert D. Richardson, *Emerson: The Mind on Fire* (Berkeley, CA: University of California Press, 1995), 6.

42. Saul Touster, "Holmes a Hundred Years Ago: *The Common Law* and Legal Theory," *Hofstra Law Review* 10 (1981-82): 682, citing Ralph Barton Perry, *The Thought and Character of William James* (New York: George Braziller, 1954), 90.

43. Biddle, *Mr. Justice Holmes*, 2.

44. Melvin I. Urofsky and David W. Levy, eds., *Letters of Louis D. Brandeis, Vol. 5: 1921-1942: Elder Statesman* (Albany, NY: State University of New York Press, 1978), 335.

45. Robert M. Mennel, and Christine L. Compston, eds., *Holmes and Frankfurter: Their Correspondence, 1912-1934* (Hanover, NH: University Press of New England, 1996), 225.

46. Lisa Litwiller, "A SLAPP in the Face: Why Principles of Federalism Suggest That Federal District Courts Should Stop Turning the Other Cheek," *Journal of Court Innovation* 67 (2008): 67-96, 76.

47. Robert Post, "Federalism in the Taft Court Era: Can It Be 'Revived'?" *Duke Law Journal* 51 (2001-2): 1595.

48. David W. Levy and Bruce Allen Murphy, "Preserving the Progressive Spirit in a Conservative Time: The Joint Reform Efforts of Justice Brandeis and Professor Frankfurter, 1916-1933," *Michigan Law Review* 78 (1980): 1291.

49. William F. Young, "The Federal Courts and the Federal System," *Texas Law Review* 32 (1954): 483-85; Young 1954, 486; David Goodnight, "Chaos on Appeal: The Tenth Circuit's Local Judge Rule," *Denver University Law Review* 67 (1990):

526; Henry Paul Monaghan, "Supremacy Clause Textualism," *Columbia Law Review* 110 (2010): 780; Earl C. Dudley, "Federalism and Federal Rule of Evidence 501: Privilege and Vertical Choice of Law," *Georgetown Law Journal* 82 (1994): 1790.

50. John Eastman, "Reflections on Justice Thomas's Twenty Years on the Bench," *University of Detroit Mercy Law Review* 88 (2011): 703.

51. Black & White Taxi & Transfer Co. v. Brown & Yellow Taxi & Transfer Co., 276 U.S. 518 (1928); Holmes, dissenting.

52. My addition.

53. For remarks about how Stevens's poetry seeks to overcome repose in the same way that Holmes's jurisprudence seeks to overcome repose, see Thomas C. Grey, *The Wallace Stevens Case: Law and the Practice of Poetry* (Cambridge, MA: Harvard University Press, 1991), and in particular pages 55, 85, 92, 94, 96, and 105.

54. Black and White Taxicab and Transfer Company v. Brown and Yellow Taxicab and Transfer Company, 276 U.S. 518 (1928) at 528; emphasis added.

55. Richard Poirier, *Poetry and Pragmatism* (London: Faber and Faber, 1992), 136.

56. *Black and White Taxi* 276 U.S.

57. "There is strong reason to doubt the claim by Justice Holmes in dissent," says Samuel Issacharoff ("Federalized America: Reflections on *Erie v. Tompkins* and State-Based Regulation," *Journal of Law, Economics & Policy* 10 [2013]: 207), not least of which is that there were "grave deficiencies in his argument, as it related to the intended meaning of section 34" of the Judiciary Act (William W. Crosskey, *Politics and the Constitution in the History of the United States* [Chicago: University of Chicago Press, 1953], 910). Another reason is that Holmes appears to formulate a "dogmatic rejection of general common law" (Jeremy Waldron, *"Partly Laws Common to All Mankind": Foreign Law in American Courts* [New Haven, CT: Yale University Press, 2012], 54). Yet another reason is that "the positivism represented by Justice Holmes's insights in the *Black & White Taxicab* case, the positivism that was apparently endorsed in *Erie Railroad*, is now regarded by most legal philosophers as crude and obsolete" (ibid.). William W. Crosskey claims that Holmes's dissent contained "irrelevant" wording and accuses Holmes of reasoning anachronistically about the common law in the dissent (*Politics*, 910).

58. "Justice Holmes dissented with observations that would be vindicated a few years later" (George T. Anagnost, "Trial by Jury and 'Common Law' Antecedents," *Arizona Attorney* 43 [2006]: 38-42).

59. Hertz Corp. v. Friend, 559 U.S. 77 (2010) at 85-89.

60. Erie R. Co. v. Tompkins, 304 U.S. 64 (1938) at 819-20.

61. Allan C. Hutchinson, *Laughing at the Gods: Great Judges and How They Made the Common Law* (New York: Cambridge University Press, 2012), 100.

62. Capital Tool and Manufacturing Co., Inc. v. Maschinenfabrik Herkules, 837 F. Supp. 171 (4th Circuit 1988) at 172.

63. Toste Farm Corp. v. Hadbury, Inc., 882 F. Supp. 240 (1995).

64. Lenco, Inc. v. New Age Industrial Corp., Inc. No. 99-2584-JWL, 2001 WL 492386 (April 23, 2001).

65. Gitlow v. N.Y., 268 U.S. 652 (1925).

66. Harry Kalven, *A Worthy Tradition: Freedom of Speech in America*, edited by Jamie Kalven (New York: Harper & Row, 1989), 156.

67. Gerald Gunther, *Learned Hand: The Man and the Judge*, 2nd Ed (New York: Oxford University Press, 2011), 239; Irving Louis Horowitz, *Persuasions & Prejudices: An Informal Compendium of Modern Social Science, 1953-1988* (New Brunswick, NJ: Transaction Publishers, 1989), 278.

68. Paula Abrams, *Cross Purposes: Peirce v. Society of Good Sisters and the Struggle Over Compulsory Public Education* (Ann Arbor: University of Michigan Press, 2009), 196.

69. Jeffrey M. Gamso, "Sex Discrimination and the First Amendment," *Texas Tech Law Review* 17 (1986): 1596.

70. Yosal Rogat and James M. O'Fallon, "Mr. Justice Holmes: A Dissenting Opinion—The Speech Cases," *Stanford Law Review* 36 (1984): 1401.

71. Gerald Gunther, "Learned Hand and the Origins of Modern First Amendment Doctrine: Some Fragments of History," *Stanford Law Review* 27 (1975): 751.

72. White, *Justice Oliver Wendell Holmes*, 445.

73. Gitlow v. N.Y., 268 U.S. 652 (1925).

74. My addition.

75. Vincent Blasi, "Holmes and the Marketplace of Ideas," *Supreme Court Review* (2004): 37.

76. Bernard Schwartz, "Holmes versus Hand: Clear and Present Danger or Advocacy of Unlawful Action?" *Supreme Court Review* (1994): 239.

77. Robert W. Gordon, "Holmes's *Common Law* as Legal and Social Science," *Hofstra Law Review* 10 (1981-82): 719-46.

78. White, *Justice Oliver Wendell Holmes*, 445.

79. Robert L. Tsai, "Fire, Metaphor, and Constitutional Myth Making," *Georgetown Law Journal* 93 (2004): 204.

80. Schenck v. United States, 249 U.S. 47 (1919).

81. Tsai, "Fire," 203.

82. James Bishop Peabody, ed., *The Holmes-Einstein Letters: Correspondence of Mr. Justice Holmes and Lewis Einstein, 1903-1935* (London: St. Martin's Press, 1964), 5.

83. Poirier, *Poetry*, 45-46.

84. Poirier, *Poetry*, 136.

85. Holmes, "Theory of Legal Interpretation," 418; emphasis added.

86. Poirier, *Poetry*, 46.

87. Poirier, *Poetry*, 136.

88. Poirier, *Poetry*, 166.

89. Peabody, *Holmes-Einstein Letters*, 322.

90. Peabody, *Holmes-Einstein Letters*, 155; emphasis in original.

91. Peabody, *Holmes-Einstein Letters*, 154.

92. On November 23, 1905, Holmes wrote to Sir Frederick Pollock, "I am just turning to Santayana's last two volumes of *The Life of Reason* which I like better than any philosophy I have read—or nearly so" (Mark DeWolfe Howe, ed., *Holmes-Pollock Letters: The Correspondence of Mr. Justice Holmes and Sir Frederick Pollock 1874-1932, Volume I* [Cambridge, MA: Harvard University Press, 1941], 122). In a letter dated June 23, 1906, Holmes again wrote to Pollock about Santayana, this time noting some of the elements of superfluity at work in Santayana's prose: "I write to Little Brown & Co. to send you Santayana—4 vols—but not big ones.

My wife says that the critics are not so warm as I in praise of it. I liked it because the premises are so much like my own. I always start my cosmic salad by saying that all I mean by truth is what I *can't help* thinking and that I have no means of deciding whether my can't helps have any cosmic worth. They clearly don't in many cases. I think the philosophers usually are too arrogant in their attitude. I accept the existence of the universe, in some unpredictable sense, just as I accept yours—by an act of faith—or by another can't help, perhaps. But I think the chances are much against man's being at the centre of things or knowing anything more than how to arrange *his* universe—according to his own necessary order. I dare say you will think Santayana something of an *improvisatore*, and say that he talks too much. But to my mind he talks like a civilized man, and with a good deal of charm of speech, though that also may weary, after you have caught his rhythm and trick. At all events his book was one which seemed to me to express the world as I should express it, more nearly than often befalls" (Howe, *Holmes-Pollock Letters*, 1:126-27).

In a letter dated December 5, 1913, he wrote to Lewis Einstein: "Last week while we were adjourned and my work being done I read with a great deal of admiration Santayana's *'Winds of Doctrine'*. Wonderful knowledge and easy criticisms of systems with many *aperçus* that I have shared without owing them to him. I said (considering his possible retention of his membership in the Catholic Church) that he stood on the flat road to heaven and buttered slides to hell for all the rest, so well does he state the fundamental scepticisms without committing himself" (Peabody, *Holmes-Einstein Letters*, 84). On June 13, 1918, he wrote this in a letter to Einstein: "I did reread Santayana's *Egotism in German Philosophy*, which a fellow sent to me the other day, with much more appreciation than the first time. I don't think it the best of his books, but he always hits me where I live with his prose. On his poetry I can't recite" (Peabody, *Holmes-Einstein Letters*, 167).

In a letter to Laski dated November 17, 1920, Holmes concluded by saying, simply, "Do you like Santayana's books? I do, though I believe Bill James didn't" (Mark DeWolfe Howe, ed., *Holmes-Laski Letters: The Correspondence of Mr. Justice Holmes and Harold J. Laski, 1916-1935, Volumes I and II* [Cambridge, MA: Harvard University Press, 1953], 292). On December 17, 1920, Holmes wrote to Laski, "When I get a chance I want to read Santayana's new volume on *Character and Opinion in the U.S.* He generally hits me pretty near to where I live—even though one does not wholly like either him or his way of thinking. He is a philosopher very much after my own heart" (Howe, *Holmes-Laski Letters*, 297). In a letter dated December 19, 1920, addressed to Justice Frankfurter, Holmes discussed reading Santayana along with William James: "I keep pretty close to books bearing on my general drift. I *have* read and with the usual pleasure Santayana's volume, *Character etc. in the U.S.* (a wonderfully keen appreciation of W. James in it). [. . .] I have received W. James's *Letters* which stir many old emotions in me, though I haven't read them—only opened here and there. Kimball (my secretary) wants me to reread W.J.'s *Pragmatism* that we may jaw. He has extracted more subtile [sic] significances than I remembered" (Mennel and Compston, *Holmes and Frankfurter*, 98). On August 19, 1922, he wrote the following lines to Laski: "Have you read Santayana's *Soliloquies* ('Soliquities' my nurse called them)? His scepticism seems most akin to my own—his dogmas or preferences the results of a temperament and Catholic bringing up that we have a perfect right not to share and I don't. When he speaks of life as hideous I venture to see the Church rather than a free aesthetic judgment" (Howe, *Holmes-Laski Letters*, 440).

On February 16, 1924, Holmes wrote a letter to Justice Frankfurter, stating, "I believe you sent me Santayana's *Unknowable*, which needs a second reading. His general way of thinking and mine have much in common—but he has a damned patronizing way of presenting himself—reserving the right to a strictly private smile as if he also is an illusion" (Mennel and Compston, *Holmes and Frankfurter*, 168). The next day Holmes wrote to Laski: "Frankfurter sent me a discourse of Santayana's on the Unknowable. It needs reading twice. In a general way his thinking more than that of other philosophers coincides with mine. But he has a patronizing tone—as of one who saw through himself but didn't expect others to" (Howe, *Holmes-Laski Letters*, 594). One day in 1924, Holmes met with Bertrand Russell and discussed Santayana. As Holmes explained to Laski in a letter dated April 18, 1924: "I had just read Santayana's *Scepticism and Animal Faith*. (By the way I think our starting point put in plain words would be about similar or the same, but there is such a mass of literary arabesques and variations that though the book may gain as literature, I think it is diminished in philosophical significance.) I spoke of the tone of patronizing irony—and thought it an echo of Catholicism. [Russell] said: more of the Latin—Santayana thinks the English good for football, but thinks that speculation should be left to the Latin races" (Howe, *Holmes-Laski Letters*, 608). On May 22, 1924, Holmes wrote again to Laski: "Cohen and his wife lunched here on Sunday—and his remarks led me to take down Santayana's *Life of Reason*, volume IV, *Reason in Art* and I am rereading it and also (on the same stimulus) *Huckleberry Finn*. There is such a dilution of literature in Santayana—so much pork for a shilling when he philosophises, that it makes me think by way of reaction how many mathematically compacted sentences would it take to give us all that is important. Yet I believe I am more in accord with the *motif* of his arabesque than perhaps with any other philosopher—who has expressed his system" (Howe, *Holmes-Laski Letters*, 618).

On January 27, 1931, he signed off on a letter to Justice Frankfurter by saying that "The Burroughs and Santayana are waiting" (Mennel and Compston, *Holmes and Frankfurter*, 261). He reacted strangely to reading Santayana in 1931, writing again to Justice Frankfurter in a letter dated February 7, 1931: "Santayana comes nearer to hitting me than most philosophers but I dislike him. He patronizes, as being rich with the past experience of a Catholic although no longer believing in the Church. He has the openness to all thought that is anti-dogmatic and yet he sneers like a dogmatist. I take back or qualify the 'dislike' above. He is a good sauce to have on hand, but not a food. He writes like a gentleman but I doubt if he quite is one. Good reading anyhow" (Mennel and Compston, *Holmes and Frankfurter*, 262).

Elsewhere Holmes had much more to say about Santayana. These excerpts suffice to prove his longstanding interest in Santayana.

93. On September 27, 1921, Holmes wrote to Harold Laski, "Thinking that I remembered the *New Republic* speaking of Eliot, presently unknown to me, as the greatest going poet I, or rather my wife, after my refusal bought a little volume. It reminded me of Bill Hunt (the artist) to a pupil—'Oh, I see you want to do some-

thing damned smart right off.' I am not prepared yet to say it is not pay dirt—but I suspect a good deal of watering will be needed to get any gold" (Howe, *Holmes-Laski Letters*, 373). On November 22, 1929, Holmes wrote to Laski that "I was pleased by a side slash at T.S. Eliot (poet and critic—did you ever hear of him—I am told regarded by youth as its prophet) in a periodical *Life and Letters* which has good reading in it" (Howe, *Holmes-Laski Letters*, 1196).

94. In a letter dated December 15, 1923, Holmes wrote to Harold Laski, "Hardy is a deity whom I have not worshipped. I have not read his later books, and the earlier ones read long, long ago with pleasure but without so far as I remember adoration" (Howe, *Holmes-Laski Letters*, 568). On September 8, 1925, having just read Homer's *Odyssey*, Holmes wrote a letter to Sir Frederick Pollock, stating that the book had left him "blank," adding, "I think of a novel by Hardy—a gent. whom I have left alone since I was young" (Howe, *Holmes-Pollock Letters*, 2:168).

95. Holmes refers to Joyce's *A Portrait of the Artist* in a letter to Harold Laski dated April 12, 1917 (Howe, *Holmes-Laski Letters*, 78). He mentions that book again in a letter to Laski dated April 20, 1917 (Howe, *Holmes-Laski Letters*, 80). On November 5, 1923, he wrote to Laski, "Then as to James Joyce I read his first book—I suppose—autobiographical of his own youth, and was struck by his use of dirty words as well as by his telling things that I hardly regarded as a gift to mankind, though I suppose he felt like Rousseau. I have seen that and *Ulysses* taken solemnly—but thus far have felt free to wait for *Ulysses*" (Howe, *Holmes-Laski Letters*, 556). On May 16, 1925, he wrote a letter to Lewis Einstein alluding to Joyce's *Portrait of the Artist* (Peabody, *Holmes-Einstein Letters*, 240). In a letter to Laski dated March 27, 1930, Holmes noted that he "read of few pages" of Joyce's *Ulysses* (Howe, *Holmes-Laski Letters*, 1236). Holmes then wrote the following lines in a letter to Lewis Einstein dated March 29, 1930: "I will ask you in your turn if you have read Joyce's *Ulysses*? I haven't and don't intend to, but I have looked into it. A reputable critic in the New Republic calls him a great poet. He may be, but he has what seems to me an abnormal propensity for dirty words and disgusting images of the lesser sort. I should think he must be queer in the nob, and so, though I think it possible that I am laying a genius on one side, I shall not read on" (Peabody, *Holmes-Einstein Letters*, 307).

96. In a letter to Harold Laski dated August 31, 1924, Holmes claimed that he had taken up "one of Kipling's short stories" (Howe, *Holmes-Laski Letters*, 653). On August 27, 1925, he wrote to Laski, stating, "Even Kipling will tear the word from the guts of the dictionary or from speech and make it his own" (Howe, *Holmes-Laski Letters*, 781). On March 7, 1928, he wrote to Laski, stating, "I am not impressed at what you say about Kipling. Many years ago I made up my mind that he did not interest me—that his view of the universe was too simple—and since then I thought that he had a breakdown. But as a story teller, and in spite of you, as a verse writer, I think he makes a direct appeal to the simpler emotions which we never are too sophisticated to feel when a man has the gift—as he has. Also, where Stevenson laboriously selects a word and lets you feel his labor, Kipling puts his fist into the guts of the dictionary, pulls out the utterly unavailable and makes it a jewel in his forehead or flesh of his flesh with no effort or outlay except of the pepsin that makes it part of him. But I thought he was finished years back" (Howe, *Holmes-Laski Letters*, 1034).

97. In a letter dated March 14, 1925, Holmes wrote to Harold Laski that he had read "Sinclair Lewis's new novel [*Arrowsmith*], which I thought brilliant in parts, but suffering from a tendency to sacrifice art to the thesis" (Howe, *Holmes-Laski Letters*, 721). In a letter dated May 6, 1925, Holmes wrote to Lewis Einstein, "Have you read *Martin Arrowsmith*? I enjoyed it thoroughly with its exposure of university and uplift bunk. The writer, Sinclair Lewis of *Main Street* fame, passed through here only the other day, gay and mellowed by success and no longer thinking that people wished to patronize him" (Peabody, *Holmes-Einstein Letters*, 237). Holmes again mentioned Lewis and *Arrowsmith* in a letter to Laski dated December 5, 1925 (Howe, *Holmes-Laski Letters*, 803). Weeks later, on December 17, 1925, Holmes wrote another letter to Laski referring to Lewis as "a pretty big chap" (Howe, *Holmes-Laski Letters*, 807). Holmes noted in a letter to Laski dated October 28, 1927, that he had read Lewis (Howe, *Holmes-Laski Letters*, 987).

98. Holmes wrote the following lines to Lewis Einstein in a letter dated July 28, 1928: "Also a book by a young American living in Paris (Hemingway), *The Sun Still* [sic] *Rises*, which excites some interest in others and in me. No events greater than going to a bull fight, much conversation without an idea in it, characterizing phrases replaced by damn and hell, no marked character, the chief interest of the parties food and drink with a discreet hint of fornication, and most of them drunk nearly every evening. I think of rereading the book to try to find out why it interests and why I suspect it to be a work of art" (Peabody, *Holmes-Einstein Letters*, 287). On January 30, 1929, he wrote to Einstein, "Did you ever read anything of Hemingway: *Men without Women, The Sun also Rises*? They would lend themselves to some remarks" (Peabody, *Holmes-Einstein Letters*, 293). Holmes read Hemingway at the recommendation of the author Owen Wister. A few weeks before his July 28, 1928, letter to Einstein, Holmes wrote the following lines to Sir Frederick Pollock in a letter dated July 12, 1928: "Owen Wister has sent me *The Sun Also Rises* by Ernest Hemingway, which he seemed to think of great promise when the writer got away from garbage. I haven't read it yet, but it sounds brisker than [Hugh] Walpole" (Howe, *Holmes-Pollock Letters*, 2:226).

Just over a month later, Holmes wrote again to Pollock in a letter dated August 30, 1928: "Thinking of [Chekhov] and of an American living in Paris, Hemingway, author of *Men Without Women* & *The Sun also Rises*, I wonder at the illusion that one is more real if one evokes sordid situations and bad smells, than if one invites one's readers to fresh air and agreeable and even noble people" (Howe, *Holmes-Pollock Letters*, 2:227). On the same day, Holmes wrote the following lines in a letter to Harold Laski: "I have read some stories by Chekov (qu.sp.?) well told but squalid—not the swinish instinct you attribute to Hemingway, but none the less displeasing to me" (Howe, *Holmes-Laski Letters*, 1091). He sent a similar note to Nina L. Gray: "I read a queer book by Hemingway (living in Paris) *The Sun also Rises*—The doings of some people in whom I felt no interest, whose talk was devoid of ideas and for want of discriminating words used damned and Hell, who continually got drunk and who had no events except to go to some bull fight in Spain, and yet I was interested—I think probably because the narrative had a masterly simplicity and fact followed fact of course" (Letter to Nina L. Gray).

On November 30, 1929, Holmes wrote to Laski, "Hemingway must be a clever writer for he interests me when I can't see any reason for it (in *The Sun Also Rises*).

Hemingway, I believe, is something of an athlete and Wister writes to me has been hurt lately in a bull fight—which seems good. I am told that he is one of the heroes of the young—as T.S. Eliot has been. I don't yet see the need to get very excited about him—but it is well to keep one's mind open to the fashions of the day. Every fashion is beautiful while it is a fashion" (Howe, *Holmes-Laski Letters*, 1205).

On December 18, 1929, Holmes wrote again to Laski: "You mentioned some-time back, *Farewell to Arms*—by Hemingway. I couldn't quite use the superlatives that you and some others have used about it—but it has some thrilling power. The author interested me by the wonder that he raised in my mind, especially by another book, *The Sun Also Rises*—as to why and how he interests me—extremely ordinary people and extremely ordinary talk (noted with intensity, I admit) and yet I read on. He certainly is something of a writer—whether a very great one I still doubt—as I, with due and sincere modesty, doubt about the great lights among the modernist painters—hastening to add that I have seen but little of Cézanne—their goddest God" (Howe, *Holmes-Laski Letters*, 1209).

Mentions of Hemingway appear in several more of Holmes's letters, but this sampling suffices to show Holmes's ambivalent interest in the man.

99. Holmes admitted in a letter to Justice Frankfurter dated October 23, 1931, that he "stopped Lawrence, *Lady Chatterley's Lover*, in transition" (Mennel and Compston, *Holmes and Frankfurter*, 266).

100. In a letter to Harold Laski dated November 7, 1932, Holmes wrote that "Owen Wister sent me a poem by Robinson Jeffers—*Thursto's Landing*—some marks of power in it, but I don't care for it—though the advertisements tell me that Jeffers is the greatest living American poet" (Howe, *Holmes-Laski Letters*, 1416).

101. Holmes read Sassoon at the recommendation of Lewis Einstein. He wrote the following lines in a letter to Einstein dated February 8, 1931: "Style, I think, is sound, a matter of ear. I liked Siegfried Sassoon's book. No special comment to make" (Peabody, *Holmes-Einstein Letters*, 322).

102. On July 6, 1924, Holmes wrote a letter to Laski promising "to try to get *A Passage to India*," adding that "Fred Pollock mentioned it also, the other day" (Howe, *Holmes-Laski Letters*, 631). Two months later, in a letter dated September 6, 1924, he wrote to Lewis Einstein, "Your recommendation of a *Passage to India* comes on top of so many from England and here that though I have resisted thus far I think I must yield and send for it to the Old Corner Book Store, Boston's principal dispensing agent" (Peabody, *Holmes-Einstein Letters*, 229-30). The only evidence that Holmes actually read Forster comes from a letter to Laski dated August 22, 1930, in which Holmes mentions that he was "beginning to wallow in easy literature," including "short stories by E.M. Forster" (Howe, *Holmes-Laski Letters*, 1277).

103. Howe, *Holmes-Pollock Letters*, 260-61; emphasis added.

104. Oliver Wendell Holmes, Jr. to Albert J. Beveridge, July 11, 1926, Harvard University Holmes Digital Suite, Mark DeWolfe Howe's research materials on Holmes, 1858-1968: Finding Aid, Beveridge, Albert J., 1915-1917, online.

105. Frederic R. Kellogg, *Oliver Wendell Holmes, Jr., Legal Theory, and Judicial Restraint* (Cambridge University Press, 2007), 155.

106. Robert Danisch, "Aphorism, Enthymemes, and Oliver Wendell Holmes, Jr. on the First Amendment," *Rhetoric Review* 27 (2008): 232; emphasis added.

107. Oliver Wendell Holmes, Jr. to Lewis Einstein, July 11, 1925, Harvard University Holmes Digital Suite, Mark DeWolfe Howe's research materials on Holmes, 1858-1968: Finding Aid, Einstein, Lewis, correspondent, June 4, 1924-September 21, 1925, online.

108. Whitney v. California, 274 U.S. 357 (1927).

109. Dennis v. United States, 341 U.S. 494 (1951) at 507.

110. Thomas v. Collins, 323 U.S. 516 (1945).

111. *Gitlow* 268 U.S. 652 (1925) at 537.

112. Pennekamp v. State of Florida, 328 U.S. 331 (1946).

113. *Pennekamp* 328 U.S. at 351-52.

114. Jonathan Levin, *The Poetics of Transition: Emerson, Pragmatism, & American Literary Modernism* (Durham, NC: Duke University Press, 1999), 2.

115. Ibid.

116. Emerson, "Circles," 403.

117. Ibid.

118. Ibid.

119. Ibid.

120. Emerson, "Circles," 406.

121. Emerson, "Circles," 412.

122. Ralph Waldo Emerson, "Spiritual Laws," in *Emerson: Essays and Lectures*, edited by Joel Porte. New York: The Library of America, 1983e.

123. Emerson, "Spiritual Laws," 310.

124. Ibid.

125. Poirier, *Poetry*, 3-4.

126. Holmes, "Theory of Legal Interpretation," 418.

127. Poirier, *Poetry*, 6.

128. Poirier, *Poetry*, 11.

129. Ralph Waldo Emerson, "The Visit," in *Emerson: Collected Poems and Translations*, edited by Harold Bloom and Paul Kane (New York: Library of America, 1994), 14.

130. Ralph Waldo Emerson, "The Poet," in *Emerson: Essays & Poems* (New York: Library of America, 1996), 450.

131. Ralph Waldo Emerson, "Plato, or the Philosopher," in *Emerson: Essays & Poems* (New York: Library of America, 1996), 634.

132. Poirier, *Poetry*, 11.

133. Thomas Healy, *The Great Dissent: How Oliver Wendell Holmes Changed His Mind—and Changed the History of Free Speech in America* (New York: Metropolitan Books, 2013), 103.

134. Oliver Wendell Holmes, Jr. to Ellen A. Curtis, April 26, 1908, Harvard University Holmes Digital Suite, Mark DeWolfe Howe's research materials on Holmes, 1858-1968: Finding Aid, Curtis, Ellen A., 1900-1933, online.

135. Poirier, *Poetry*, 129.

136. Poirier, *Poetry*, 162.

137. Poirier, *Poetry*, 163.

138. Poirier, *Poetry*, 164.

139. Poirier, *Poetry*, 13.

140. Haddock v. Haddock, 201 U.S. 562 (1906).

141. Williams v. State of North Carolina, 317 U.S. 287 (1942).

142. *Williams* 317 U.S. at 300.

143. *Dr. Miles* 220 U.S. at 411.

144. *Leegin* 551 U.S. at 879.

145. Olsen v. State of Nebraska ex rel. Western Reference and Bond Association, 313 U.S. 236 (1941).

146. *Olsen* 313 U.S. at 245.

147. Green v. United States, 355 U.S. 184 (1957).

148. Kepner v. United States, 195 U.S. 100 (1904).

149. Fernandez v. Wiener, 326 U.S. 340 (1945).

150. Hoeper v. Tax Commission of Wis., 284 U.S. 206 (1931).

151. Farmer's Loan & Trust Co. v. State of Minnesota, 280 U.S. 204 (1930).

152. Curry v. McCanless, 307 U.S. 357 (1939).

153. State Tax Commission of Utah v. Aldrich, 316 U.S. 174 (1942).

154. Baldwin v. State of Missouri, 281 U.S. 586 (1930).

155. *Baldwin* 281 U.S. 586 at 595.

156. Girouard v. United States, 328 U.S. 61 (1946).

157. United States v. Schwimmer, 279 U.S. 644 (1929).

158. *Girouard* 328 U.S. at 63.

159. Youngstown Sheet & Tube Co. v. Sawyer, 343 U.S. 579 (1952).

160. *Youngstown Sheet* 343 U.S. at 702.

161. North Dakota State Board of Pharmacy v. Synder's Drug Stores, Inc., 414 U.S. 156 (1973).

162. Louis K. Liggett Co. v. Baldridge, 278 U.S. 105 (1928).

163. *North Dakota State Board* 414 U.S. at 167.

164. Harper v. Virginia Department of Taxation, 509 U.S. 86 (1993).

165. Kuhn v. Fairmont Coal Co., 215 U.S. 349 (1910).

166. Robbat v. Robbat, 643 So. 2d 1153 (Fla. Dist. Ct. App. 1994) at 1156.

167. Monongahela River Consol. Coal & Coke Co. v. Jutte, 210 Pa. 288, 59 A. 1088, 105 Am. St. Rep. 812, 2. Am. Ann. Cas. 951 (1904).

168. Dennis v. United States, 341 U.S. 494 (1951).

169. Penn-Central Merger and N & W Inclusion Cases, 389 U.S. 486 (1968).

170. New York Times Co. v. United States, 403 U.S. 703 (1971).

171. United States v. Chavez, 416 U.S. 562 (1974).

172. Nixon v. General Service Administrator, 433 U.S. 425 (1977).

173. Larkin v. Grendel's Den, Inc., 459 U.S. 116 (1982).

174. Pennzoil Co. v. Texaco, Inc., 481 U.S. 1 (1987).

175. Skinner v. Railway Labor Executives' Association, 489 U.S. 602 (1989).

176. Poirier, *Poetry*, 16.

177. Ibid.

178. Emerson, "Circles," 413.

179. Poirier, *Poetry*, 27.

180. Poirier, *Poetry*, 17.

181. Poirier, *Poetry*, 16.

182. Emerson, "Circles," 407.

183. Emerson, "Circles," 405.

184. Poirier, *Poetry*, 17-18.

185. Poirier, *Poetry*, 18.
186. Poirier, *Poetry*, 25.
187. Danisch, "Aphorism," 227; emphasis added.
188. Poirier, *Poetry*, 37.
189. Danisch, "Aphorism," 227; emphasis added.
190. Poirier, *Poetry*, 38.
191. Poirier, *Poetry*, 39.
192. Ibid.
193. Poirier, *Poetry*, 40.

2

The Poetics of Transition
and Vindicated Dissents

This chapter explores Holmes's aesthetics with more attention and analyzes three of Holmes's most famous dissents to demonstrate that aesthetics impact the reception and legacy of his judicial writing. I begin by describing the "poetics of transition" that frames my discussion of Holmes's aesthetics. I then analyze these three dissents for specific examples of Holmes's superfluity, reveal how superfluity contributed to the vindication of the dissents, and integrate Jonathan Levin's theory of the poetics of transition into Poirier's formulation of superfluity and linguistic skepticism. Holmes's Darwinian "ethic of struggle" finds aesthetic expression in his use of sound in the dissents discussed in this chapter.[1] The legacy of these dissents suggests that Holmes's style enacted the poetics of transition that contributed to the vindication of his arguments.

Recent empirical scholarship has measured the importance of dissents by totaling the number of times federal appellate cases cited them.[2] Although this chapter accounts for citations to Holmes's dissents by federal appellate courts, it does not adopt the premise that federal appellate citations represent the only or best measure of a dissent's influence or vindication. Counting appellate court citations to Holmes's dissents proves that the dissents influenced future judges and justices, but citation numbers are not a proxy for vindication. Consider Colin Starger's observation about the limitation of the citation-based approach to evaluating influence or vindication:

An exclusively citation-based approach would apparently conclude that Holmes's dissent played no role in *Lochner*'s famous and definitive

overruling by *West Coast Hotel v. Parrish* in 1937. This is because Holmes'
Lochner dissent was cited exactly zero times in the *West Coast Hotel* majority
opinion and zero times in the authorities relied upon by the majority. [. . .]
I regard this absence of citation more as evidence of a methodological limitation in this empirical approach than as proof that Holmes' dissent failed
to contribute to the demise of *Lochnerism*. Despite the absence of citation, a
direct line unquestionably connects the *West Coast Hotel* majority opinion to
Holmes' *Lochner* dissent twenty-two years later.[3]

Starger uses graphs and tables to illustrate a "hermeneutic connection"
between dissents and subsequent opinions "notwithstanding the absence
of formal citation" from one case to the next.[4] This chapter follows Starger
by treating the citation of Holmes's dissents by future courts as evidence
of influence while acknowledging that other measures of influence exist.
Even when this chapter points out where appellate courts have explicitly
relied on Holmes, it does not consider these moments of agreement determinative of vindication. A number of dissents have been vindicated apart
from the ruling of a future court. For example, the Fourteenth Amendment may be interpreted as vindicating the dissents of Justice Benjamin
Curtis and Justice John McLean in the notorious *Dred Scott* case. Likewise,
Holmes's dissents were vindicated not merely because some future justice quoted them or borrowed from their reasoning but because the logic
and rules he recommended were adopted at some later date, if not by a
court then by a legislature or some other lawmaking body.

Poetics of Transition

Dissents prevent case precedents in a common-law system from reaching
a state of repose or stasis; they yield variety in rules and principles and
generate competition among different legal theories, thereby facilitating the forward mobility of judicial decision-making. In this respect, the
theory of the poetics of transition derived from Richard Poirier and made
comprehensive by Jonathan Levin pertains as much to poetry and works
of imaginative literature as to judicial opinions, especially in light of dissents that are inherently agonistic. Poirier's subjects thrive on opposition:
each author struggles against the ideas and practices of his or her greatest
influences while striking out against the stasis of unoriginality and the
restrictions of language. Poirier's trace accounts of literary influence and
his suggestion that forms and methods are passed from author to author
warrant a comparison with the common-law system in which judges and
justices struggle against their peers and established case precedents.

Poirier has argued that Emersonian superfluity counteracts repose in
writing and ideas and involves "a kind of rapid or wayward movement
of voice" that "is associated [. . .] with speed" and a "momentum or

volatility of style."[5] Poirier does not construe superfluity because obscurity and vagueness are aspects of superfluity. The nebulous meaning of superfluity must be inferred from the context in which Poirier uses the concept. Superfluity is about "generative interaction,"[6] "a struggle with language,"[7] the "continuous struggle with language,"[8] "creative energy,"[9] a "commitment" to "more than is necessary [for the] survival" of ideas and influences,[10] "accelerations of a process,"[11] the "power of invention,"[12] an "overwhelming excess of productivity,"[13] "words in excess of the minimum daily requirements of human beings,"[14] the "plenitude and power of language" that propels one's "voice into the future,"[15] "the power for new creation,"[16] "generative" and "creative power,"[17] "engendering,"[18] and "speaking to a posterity in no way bound by th[e] discourse" in which people in their specific time and place are immersed. These notions are emphatically against "a loss of creative powers,"[19] "immobility,"[20] "stand still,"[21] "the stasis achieved by former movements that have become textualized or intellectualized,"[22] and "bareness."[23]

Poirier surveys pragmatists who follow Emerson by resorting to superfluity to overcome the precedents of their influential predecessors as well as the inability of language to fully represent its referents. Judges and justices are subject to the same inquiry because they may also seek to overcome the precedents of their influential predecessors and to struggle against the vagaries of the language of the law that would seem to require clarity and interpretability for all members of society. Justices like Holmes who are known for their literary style provide a basis for examining judicial opinions and dissents for Emersonian superfluity. Holmes's dissents in particular make Poirier's and Levin's theories of influence both useful and legible beyond the typical pragmatist associations with William and Henry James, George Santayana, Wallace Stevens, Gertrude Stein, and Robert Frost.

Like Poirier, to whom Levin expresses his "luckiest debt," Levin attributes his theory of the poetics of transition to Emerson.[24] Defining superfluity and the poetics of transition is a betrayal of the terms: they have fluid, luminous, fluctuating meanings that pertain to language and its capacity to register meaning and feeling. They transport such registers into the future, achieving temporary influx in the works of writers who are sensitive to the past and concerned about the future. Poirier glosses the word and concept of "transition" throughout *Poetry and Pragmatism;*[25] Levin builds on and rounds out Poirier's glosses. Levin's theory of the poetics of transition is rooted in the belief that, "[o]nce we settle into a condition of repose, we compromise the vital energies that should constitute our power or [. . .] compromise the energies that should constitute power in our always elusive relationship to it."[26] Levin's theory of the poetics of transition both supplements and clarifies Poirier, whose writing is famously complex and ambiguous.

Poirier and Levin reject neopragmatism and the postmodernist spin on pragmatism popularized by Richard Rorty; they focus on the "demanding, uncertain struggle for renewal" in ideas and aesthetic forms.[27] Whereas Poirier decried mainstream scholarship and technical prose and adopted the expository, meandering style of his subject Emerson, Levin writes conventional scholarship that supplements, refines, and elucidates Poirier. Levin draws out the transitional implications of Poirier's theory of superfluity and frequently echoes Poirier, claiming, for instance, "Writing does not reflect or correspond to a world of things, but rather contributes to and extends the active processes and energies that flow through and thereby constitute the world."[28] Levin's and Poirier's theories are complementary if not intertwined discourses on the same themes: progress and momentum, creativity and vitality, rhetorical excess and its constructive and practical effects. Levin says at length and in detail what Poirier merely hints at and implies.

Although Levin's theory of the poetics of transition describes literary history and figures, the common-law system renders it more comprehensible insofar as the power of the law to facilitate cooperation and adjudicate disputes may be compromised when rules have settled into a condition of repose in the form of case precedent that is no longer relevant or workable in the present environment. The poetics of transition involves the use of aesthetic language to provoke and sustain the evolution of imaginative forms and ideas in both the literary and legal context because it signals a "process that extends knowledge further into the mysterious margin of things even as it defamiliarizes the very categories through which that movement is conducted."[29] In the legal context, for example, superfluous dissents may call into question the authority and clarity of majority opinions by defamiliarizing and unsettling the utterances in those opinions that constitute the law. Pragmatism in the common law and the literary context "is in many ways an extension of this transitional dynamic"[30] in that it recognizes and facilitates the "task of human intelligence," which is "to evolve, and to keep evolving, ideas of the world that meet constantly changing human needs."[31]

The prepositional phrase "of transition" signifies that poetry (or poetic prose) is the predicate concept and that transition is an adjectival construction separating one type of poetry from others: some poetry does not generate a practical influence whereas other poetry mobilizes future audiences to action and inspiration. The word "transition" refers to the tendency of poetic language to stimulate future poetic language in the form of troping, mimesis, and rhetorical superfluity derived from and breaking from precursor writers. Transition brings "the familiar into contact with the unknown"[32] such as when Robert Frost or Wallace Stevens creates "an abyss" or "a gap" in their writing by using "indistinct and loose phrasings, the kind people habitually use without expecting that the phrase will do more than keep them in touch with themselves and others."[33] Frost carves out gaps in lines about gaps in "Mending Wall." Five full lines after his previous mention of gaps, he says, in his characteristically colloquial way, "But they would have the rabbit out of hiding, / To please the yelping dogs. The gaps I mean, / No one has seen them made or heard them made, / But at spring mending-time we find them there."[34] For a genre that prizes concision and precision, the repetition of the conjunction "But" is unusual; then there is the ambiguity of the referent of "they," which is not clarified until Frost states, "The gaps I mean," as though the speaker, as all ordinary speakers might, remembers too late that his subject is unclear, especially as it consists of inanimate objects— gaps in a stone wall—that have no agency that could *intend* to have a rabbit out of hiding. Here we see the superfluity possible in common speech and the sort of personification that people use in everyday parlance. This carefully crafted sequence of words is supposed to seem natural and incidental, as if the rhetorical productions were only a mistake, merely chance phrases. Frost defamiliarizes familiar, basic language by making it figurative and difficult.

Frost and Stevens enact transition with sounds that "invite us to live with others in a space of expectation rather than deferral."[35] Notice how such expectation inheres in the third section of Stevens's poem "Credences of Summer":

> It is the natural tower of all the world,
> The point of survey, green's green apogee,
> But a tower more precious than the view beyond,
> A point of survey squatting like a throne,
> Axis of everything, green's apogee
>
> And happiest folk-land, mostly marriage-hymns.
> It is the mountain on which the tower stands,
> It is the final mountain. Here the sun,
> Sleepless, inhales his proper air, and rests.
> This is the refuge that the end creates.[36]

Like Frost, Stevens yields a vague pronoun reference. The "It" of these lines could refer back to the sun, the subject of the previous section of the poem, but that seems unlikely given the mention of the sun in the eighth line above. Each line in isolation is perfectly comprehensible. Taken together, however, this extract is exasperatingly obscure yet arrestingly beautiful. The meaning of the passage gets lost in the operation of its sound: the alveolar approximates and near trills resulting from the "r" in *natural, tower, world, survey, green, tower, precious, everything, marriage,*

Here, proper, air, rests, refuge, and *creates;* the voiceless alveolar stops and ejectives resulting from the "t" in *It, natural, tower, point, happiest, mostly, mountain, stands, rests, creates;* and the hissing sibilants resulting from the "s" in *is, survey, green's, precious, Axis, happiest, mostly, hymns, stands, sun, Sleepless, inhales, his, rests, This,* and *creates.* The hypnotic, trancelike sweep of these singing intonations—seemingly effortless—is complemented by the mechanical repetition of the words *It, green, apogee, tower,* and *mountain.* Without grandstanding, parading, or imposing himself, Stevens's speaker eases readers into the poem, driving his message forward with an unassuming lyrical eloquence that requires a heightened level of engagement. There appears to be no fussing with words, no tinkering with structure—just natural flow. The words seem spontaneous, inevitable. In fact they are a meticulous exercise in estrangement, distancing readers from any plain or ready understanding. The "It" is ultimately unknowable and unnamable even as it comes across as familiar, having assignable characteristics and a describable relationship to the surrounding words but defying exact identification: what is the subject of this passage? These lines evince the kind of emotional and imaginative obscurity Stevens believed to be intrinsic to poetry, which he described in terms germane to Poirier's characterization of superfluity:

> Things that have their origin in the imagination or in the emotions (poems) very often have meanings that differ in nature from the meanings of things that have their origin in reason. They have imaginative and emotional meanings, not rational meanings, and they communicate these meanings to people who are susceptible to imaginative or emotional meanings. They may communicate nothing at all to people who are open only to rational meanings. In short, things that have their origin in the imagination or in the emotions very often take on a form that is ambiguous or uncertain.[37]

Stevens, a lawyer himself, recognizes an open-ended and emotive aspect of communication that resists the logic and coherence that typify the law. Holmes's superfluity activates this moving, stirring potential in language.

Holmes creates transitions of a piece with Frost's and Stevens's not only by locating the "functional processes of intelligence and belief within the ongoing realm of experience" that he characterized as the "life of the law,"[38] but also by emphasizing explicitly in his jurisprudential writings and implicitly in his dissents "the constant need to adjust and readjust knowledge and belief about the world."[39] Holmes invoked the poetics of transition in his maxim that "repose is not the destiny of man."[40] Just as he left "absolute truth" and "absolute ideals of conduct" for "those who are better equipped,"[41] and opined that the "aim of the law is not to punish sins" (*Commonwealth v. Kennedy*[42]), so Levin's Emersonian pragmatists were "unwilling to accept any kind of transcendental, transexperiential force that guides or grounds moral and intellectual processes from with-out."[43] As Stevens said, "The notion of absolutes is relative,"[44] and "when the gods have come to an end, when we think of them as aesthetic projec-tions of a time that has passed, men turn to a fundamental glory of their own and from that create a style of bearing themselves in reality. They create a new style of a new bearing in a new reality."[45]

In law as in literature, the intellectual powers of the Emersonian prag-matists "are imperfect and everywhere subject to the vagaries of time and place, mood and belief, confusion and error," which happen also to be the "source of any impulse to rise above the worst effects of these limitations."[46] Poirier supplies examples in the "virtue and necessity of vagueness" as expressed in Robert Frost's attention to "voice," "sentence sounds," and the "sounds of sense," an attention that Poirier attributes to William James's "The Stream of Thought"[47] and to Emerson's "Self-Reliance," in which "a self in continuous transition is preferred to any self in repose."[48] Poirier is short on precise illustrations from Frost's work probably because there are so many to choose from. One illustration might have been the incantatory lullaby sound that rounds out "After Ap-ple-Picking." Readers of this poem become vicarious participants in the speaker's narcotic sleepiness and melancholy resignation by dint of the rhyme, enjambment, alliteration, slow rhythm, and mostly iambic meter:

> I feel the ladder sway as the boughs bend.
> And I keep hearing from the cellar bin
> The rumbling sound
> Of load on load of apples coming in.
> For I have had too much
> Of apple-picking: I am overtired
> Of the great harvest I desired.
> There were ten thousand thousand fruit to touch,
> Cherish in hand, lift down, and not let fall.
> For all,
> That struck the earth,
> No matter if not bruised or spiked with stubble,
> Went surely to the cider-apple heap
> As of no worth.
> One can see what will trouble
> This sleep of mine, whatever sleep it is.
> Were he not gone,
> The woodchuck could say whether it's like his
> Long sleep, as I describe its coming on,
> Or just some human sleep.[49]

More could be said about these lines—about their alternating length; their repetition of *sleep*; and their use of neologism (*overtired*), hyperbole (*ten thousand thousand fruit to touch*), and anthropomorphism (of the wood-chuck), all to the effect of drowsiness—but just as Levin appropriates the captivating ambiguity that is the strategy of his subjects, I leave Frost's words to speak for themselves.

Emersonian pragmatists, in Levin's view, embrace the notion that "there is no definitive ideal or belief that puts us in closer contact with the inherent nature of things or the absolute moral grounds or ethical impera-tives of being."[50] Levin locates this notion in Emerson's concept of God or Soul and Spirit,[51] in William James's formulations of thought and truth,[52] in Santayana's and Dewey's skepticism "toward any and all fantasies of the absolute,"[53] in Henry James's skepticism regarding metaphysical abstractions,[54] in the patterns of language employed by Gertrude Stein,[55] and in the "distinctive metaphorics of transition" in Wallace Steven's poetry.[56] Holmes himself postulates this Emersonian pragmatism in the common-law context by discarding the moral vocabularies that find their way into legal discourse[57] and by refusing to glorify the law as a collec-tion of absolute syllogisms. He complained about the "evil effects of the confusion between legal and moral ideas"[58] and went so far as to dismiss what he dubbed the "Hegelian" notion that one "can make a syllogism wag its tail—or less metaphorically, that he can get from logic into time and create the universe out of nothing."[59] Holmes maintained that the law "cannot be dealt with as if it contained only the axiom and corollaries of a book of mathematics."[60] "A page of history," he argued, "is worth a volume of logic."[61] Rather than logic or syllogisms, the law according to Holmes consisted of "systematized prediction" and the "scattered proph-esies of the past."[62]

The Emersonian pragmatists in Levin's canon profess that "noth-ing protects against our inevitable failures of imagination";[63] still these limitations can provoke a creative desire to transcend and move beyond, to anticipate and prophesy, and to "emphasize that only the ongoing process of continuous imaginative activity can provide adequate pro-tection against intellectual error and moral disaster."[64] Wallace Stevens nurtured his creative powers out of his acute sensitivity "to the way in which imaginative forms become inadequate to the experience of things that initially give rise to them."[65] Gertrude Stein abandoned any effort to "clarify a point or drive home a specific idea" and sought instead "to keep the movement—of words, of ideas, of self-awareness—on the go."[66] Her prose style and palpable modernism were responses to the inability of language to mirror the external world.[67] She saw to it that the contingency and plasticity of language inured to her benefit; she wittily exploited polysemy and rhetorical ambiguity to disrupt staid prose conventions. These lines from the introductory chapter of *The Autobiography of Alice B.*

Toklas reveal her superfluity as she contrives an inordinate vivacity with ordinary words and phrases:

> Before I decided to write this book my twenty-five years with Gertrude Stein, I had often said that I would write, The wives of geniuses I have sat with. I have sat with so many. I have sat with wives who were not wives, of geniuses who were real geniuses. I have sat with real wives of geniuses who were not real geniuses. I have sat with wives of geniuses, of near geniuses, of would be geniuses, in short I have sat very often and very long with many wives and wives of many geniuses.[68]

Playful repetition and word inversion invest these rhythmic sentences with velocity and opacity, forcing the reader to question and interpret Stein's message and intent. Although styled an autobiography in which Stein plays center stage while the narrator defers to her, Stein is in fact the author of the book. Her presiding focus is art itself and how modernism is supposed to look and act on the page. The previous extract might remind one of her portrait of Cezanne:

> The Irish lady can say, that to-day is every day. Caesar can say that every day is to-day and they say that every day is as they say.
> In this way we have a place to stay and he was not met because he was settled to stay. When I said I settled I meant settled to stay. When I said set-tled to stay I meant settled to stay Saturday. In this way a mouth is a mouth. In this way if in as a mouth if in as a mouth where, if in as a mouth where and there. Believe they have water too. Believe they have that water too and blue when you see blue, is all blue precious too, is all that that is precious too is all that and they meant to absolve you. In this way Cezanne nearly did nearly in this way. Cezanne nearly did nearly did and nearly did. And was I surprised. Was I very surprised. Was I surprised. I was surprised and in that patient, are you patient when you find bees. Bees in a garden make a specialty of honey and so does honey. Honey and prayer. Honey and there. There where the grass can grow nearly four times yearly.[69]

Thus concludes Stein's tribute to the French painter that exhibits just how deep and wide is her bag of rhetorical tricks. She is concerned in this passage with representation: how can her writing *do* what Cezanne's paintings *do*? To this end, her repetition of diction mimics the repetition characteristic of Cezanne's brushstrokes, as though this passage were a canvass in miniature in which she labors against the inevitable failing of the written word to completely and convincingly match its visual subject, a modernist painting.

Holmes's transitional dynamic, like that of Stevens and Stein, appeared in his striking prose. His beliefs about the transitional possibilities of the common law find expression in the Emersonian pragmatist notion that "[m]istakes contribute to the unfolding process by stimulating fresh adjustments and modifications in practice and belief" and that "creative intelligence posits no definitive ideal or standard of truth, beauty, or goodness, but cultivates a transitional dynamic that at once assimilates and recasts available ideals and standards."[70] This transitional dynamic occurs in the common-law system whenever future courts find a mistake in a previous ruling and therefore adjust or modify the law as it is uttered in the previous ruling; the process of receiving, adjusting to, and modifying precedent likewise undermines the notion that law is the articulation of a definitive ideal or the absolute standard of truth. By dissenting creatively and memorably, Holmes called attention to mistakes in the law and laid the groundwork for modifications and adjustments. His dissent in *Adair v. U.S.*,[71] for example, enabled the United States Supreme Court to recognize that the "course of decisions in this Court since *Adair v. United States* [. . .] have completely sapped those cases of their authority."[72] Still later courts would then refer to the majority position in *Adair* as a "regime" that had been "effectively overruled."[73] Like Poirier, Levin does not focus on the law *per se* but on language generally and the ideas language represents. The law, however, consists in language: each legislative or judicial imperative stands in the place of and reacts to ideas that are embedded in the practices and habits of the community. The law is a field of language in which Poirier's and Levin's theories reveal and enact themselves in practice.

The poetics of transition is a process "designed to include mistakes—false beliefs and moral failures—from which both individuals and larger social communities learn."[74] Like judges and justices in a common-law system whose holdings are essential to the evolutionary process of social development, the authors of poetry and imaginative literature to whom Levin attends contribute "to the unfolding process" of social development "by stimulating fresh adjustments and modifications in practice and belief."[75] If poetic language in the pragmatic tradition appeared in layers from Emerson to William and Henry James, from Santayana to Stevens, from Stein to Frost, and so forth, then the poetics of transition would demarcate the blurry line of sedimentation between each author. The poetics of transition involves the pragmatic, aesthetic features of writing that are common to each author in the Emersonian tradition but that also strive toward originality. The aesthetic Emersonian canon of pragmatism advanced by Poirier and Levin consists of traces of the poetics of transition between each creative author who extends while modifying the inspired tradition. In the context of American constitutional law, the poetics of transition marks the noticeable shifts from Holmes to jurists such as Brandeis, Cardozo, Stevens, and Scalia, who make up their own canon of creative dissenters. What makes the poetics of transition resonate in the context of judicial dissents is its concentration on transition and "the tendencies-in-realization latent in any given condition."[76] The nature and function of a judicial dissent is to be transitional and to make latent in case precedent the possibility of change, progress, and mobility—or, in Levin's words, "to make the transition from repose to a state of unsettled possibility."[77]

The doctrine of *stare decisis* preserves common-law precedents in a state of relative repose. The implementation of this doctrine in cases maintains the stability and uniformity that together organize judicial imperatives. Inevitable changes of the political environment and unpredictable revolutions in culture and technology may unsettle the social order and necessitate the adaptation of the law as it is expressed in cases. Sudden or extreme shifts in values may cause the minority opinion—or the dissent—to become the majority opinion, or the majority opinion to become the minority opinion, the dissent. The common-law system offers latitude within which rules may move and flexibility with which rules may adjust to unexpected change. In the context of language, such latitude and flexibility *are* the poetics of transition inasmuch as this concept reflects "a core dissatisfaction with all definite, definitive formulations, be they concepts, metaphors, or larger formal structures."[78]

To the extent that Levin treats the poetics of transition as an element of pragmatism it is also an element of the common-law system, albeit one that is underappreciated and overlooked by scholars of constitutional law. "Pragmatism is in many ways an extension of [a] transitional dynamic," Levin explains, because the pragmatists "typically locate the functional processes of intelligence and belief within the realm of ongoing experience."[79] Using similar language, Holmes opined in *The Common Law* that the "life of the law has not been logic" but "experience,"[80] and that the law is made up of "seemingly self-sufficient propositions" that are "but a phase in a continuous growth."[81] The following three dissents by Holmes employ superfluities of language to bring about the poetics of transition and the eventual vindication of ideas that the majority rejected. The aesthetic properties of these dissents enabled them to compete with and eventually to overcome the majority opinion. These dissents suggest that Holmes is to the American constitutional canon what Emerson is to the American pragmatic literary canon. Holmes inaugurated an aesthetic tradition among jurists such as Brandeis, Cardozo, Stevens, and Scalia, who are known for their impressive language and memorable dissents.

Holmes's dissents stood out for their sound and in particular for their cadence, rhythm, rhyme, feet, alliteration, and assonance. Considered alongside his letters that discuss sound and style, which demonstrate that he was acutely aware of the possibilities of language and the modes of reception effectuated by certain syntax, the following dissents display the measured words and carefully executed phrases of a justice seeking to persuade his audience to his point of view. Holmes was raised in a nineteenth-century culture that valued public speaking both in the political realm and among Christian audiences at church and revival meetings. He also bridges the twentieth century and would have been able to listen to music and speeches on the gramophone. He might have even listened to the radio, which was in full broadcast mode by the 1920s. The technologies of recording and radio and their marketing of sound in the early twentieth century would surely have influenced Holmes's attention to the sonorous qualities of his writing.

Lochner v. New York (1905)

Lochner is among the most famous if not the most formative cases in American legal history.[82] It is what "blissfully unversed" lawyers associate with "unbridled judicial activism" as well as "a shorthand description of a court overreaching its constitutional authority and thwarting a majority will as represented in the legislature."[83] Richard Posner has called Holmes's dissent in *Lochner* "the most famous opinion by our most famous judge."[84] Posner refers to the dissent as a "rhetorical masterpiece"[85] and mines it for evidence that Holmes was a "fine legal stylist."[86] Writing for the majority in *Roe v. Wade*, Justice Blackmun referred to Holmes's dissent in *Lochner* as "now-vindicated."[87] Charles Fairman affirmed the vindication of this dissent even earlier, stating, "An entire philosophy compressed into three paragraphs. Many men know those sentences by heart. A number of Holmes' best remembered opinions in later years were but the application of the Lochner dissent to the circumstances of the particular case. His point of view has now become a part of the accepted doctrine of the [United States Supreme] Court."[88]

Holmes positioned himself—his dissent—against this so-called judicial activism and alongside the New York legislature. The legal community has always tried to cabin Holmes within some label to make sense of his dissent in *Lochner*.[89] "Progressives" laud his dissent for challenging the interests of big-business and industry and for sticking up for the "little guy" or the "worker,"[90] whereas "conservatives" celebrate his dissent for its rejection of judicial activism and its deference to the state legislature.[91] Regardless of their accuracy, these attempts to label Holmes and his *Lochner* dissent have contributed to the canonization of the dissent, the first in the United States to become canonized when it became widely accepted as the correct view.[92]

Lochner reached the United States Supreme Court as an appeal from the Court of Appeals of New York, which held that an employer had violated a New York labor statute prohibiting employers from allowing employee bakers to work more than 60 hours per week or 10 hours per day. The employer owned a biscuit, bread, and cake bakery, and he allowed—indeed required—a certain baker to work more than 60 hours in one week. The employer was convicted of violating the labor statute. He sued in the County Court of Oneida County, lost; appealed to the New York Supreme Court, lost; appealed to the New York Court of Appeals, lost; and then appealed to the United States Supreme Court. Justice Peckham, writing for the majority and reversing the New York decisions, held in favor of the employer, reasoning that the right to contract free from government interference was a protected liberty under the Fourteenth Amendment,[93] that the labor statute was not necessary to ensure the health and welfare of bakers,[94] that bakers' tasks were not so dangerous or unhealthy as to justify the legislature's interference with them,[95] and that restricting bakers' working hours bore little relation to the statute's alleged purpose of enhancing the quality of bread.[96] Therefore, Justice Peckham concluded, the labor statute interfered with the liberty to contract and impeded business activities in violation of the United States Constitution.

Holmes disagreed. "This case is decided upon an economic theory which a large part of the country does not entertain," he wrote.[97] He also explained that he would not decide whether he agreed with the statute but that, if forced to do so, he would "desire to study it further and long before making up my mind."[98] Holmes believed that "my agreement or disagreement has nothing to do with the right of a majority to embody their opinions in law."[99] He then portrayed the United States Constitution as organic and pointed out the flaws of treating the Constitution as representative of any particular ideology:

> [A] Constitution is not intended to embody a particular economic theory, whether of paternalism and the organic relation of the citizen to the state or of *laissez faire*. It is made for people of fundamentally differing views, and the accident of our finding certain opinions natural and familiar, or novel, and even shocking, ought not to conclude our judgment upon the question whether statutes embodying them conflict with the Constitution of the United States.[100]

The Constitution, so interpreted, is accommodating and does not service the political ideas of particular groups but addresses and applies to all groups irrespective of ideology. Holmes explains that "[g]eneral propositions do not decide concrete cases" because judicial decisions depend upon "a judgment or intuition more subtle than any articulate major premise."[101] According to Holmes, judges and justices should not "prevent the natural outcome of a dominant opinion, unless it can be said that a rational and fair man necessarily would admit that the statute proposed would infringe fundamental principles as they have been understood by the traditions of our people and our law."[102]

Holmes directs readers' attention to the fact that the New York statute is simply the latest in a long line of statutes dealing with ancient Sunday and usury laws and more recently with lotteries.[103] He states that the "liberty of the citizen to do as he likes so long as he does not interfere with the liberty of others to do the same, which has been a shibboleth for some well-known writers, is interfered with by law schools, by the Post-office, by every state or municipal institution which takes his money for purposes thought desirable, whether he likes it or not."[104] Holmes seems to be suggesting that the principle of liberty propagated by the majority is undermined by the very existence of laws and institutions that deprive citizens of the allegedly fundamental principle of liberty at issue in the case.

In what is perhaps the most recognizable and quoted line of the *Lochner* dissent,[105] Holmes announces that the "14th Amendment does not enact Mr. Herbert Spencer's Social Statistics."[106] This line represents the "most terse and eloquent statement" in the dissent and is "an example of synecdoche" inasmuch as it professes "a belief in the 'natural' authority of an economic theory in terms of one particular book."[107] This line has also been called "the most famous line from the most famous dissent of all."[108] Having contextualized the labor statute within an historical framework, Holmes launches into this remark about Spencer as if to trumpet the fact that this case arose in a particular moment defined by a particular ethos. By doing so he signals to future judges and justices who will be writing in a different moment defined by a different ethos. He anticipates later courts' citations to his dissent "not as a justification for overturning the Old Court's established line of precedent, but in recognition of its ultimate vindication and as an admonition against repeating the egregious mistakes of the *Lochner* era."[109] His dissent is "politically convenient for later generations of lawyers and judges" who will use it to attack both progressive and conservative policies.[110]

Holmes wrote that "[i]t is settled by various decisions of this court that state constitutions and state laws may regulate life in many ways which we as legislators might think as injudicious, or if you like as tyrannical, as this, and which, equally with this, interfere with the liberty to contract."[111] With impeccable timing, he then offers this short, clipped statement: "A more modern one is the prohibition of lotteries."[112] This abrupt move generates a rhythm carried on by a succession of "s" and "th" sounds: "settled," "various," "decisions," "*this*," "*that*," "constiutions," "state," "laws," "ways," "as," "legislators," "*think*," "as," "injudicious," "as," "as *this*," "wi*th this*," "wi*th*," "*the*." Add to these the other alliterative combinations—"l" as in "laws," "life," "legislators," "like," and "liberty"; "t" as in "It," "court," "state," "constitutions," "state," "regulate," "might," and "contract"; "r" as in "various," "court," "regulate," and "contract"; "w" as in "ways," "which," "we," "which," "with," and "with"—and this sentence begins to attest to Holmes's fascination with sound. Alliteration may be a basic feature of ordinary speech, but the extent to which Holmes employs it suggests something more: a deliberate effort to produce memorable tonality. In this respect, Holmes taps into the "extraordinary dimension of the ordinary" that Stevens's poetry "sets out to reveal."[113]

"[G]reat works survive by sound," Holmes wrote in a letter to Harold Laski.[114] "Style," he added, "seems to me fundamentally sound,"[115] a line he would later repeat to Lewis Einstein after having read Siegfried Sassoon, Helen Waddell's *Medieval Latin Lyrics* (1929), Samuel Hoffenstein's *Poems in Praise of Practically Nothing* (1928), and *The Stuffed Owl: An Anthology of Bad Verse* (1930), a book edited by D. B. Wyndham Lews and Charles Lee.[116] Holmes expressed appreciation for the profundities of even commonplace sounds such as "those Sunday morning church bells—and hymn tunes—and the sound of the citizen's feet on the pavement,"[117] "the sound of many bobolinks singing in the meadow below the house,"[118] "the sound of a waterfall and birds,"[119] and finally "some shells put to the ear [that] give a sound like the faint echo of waves."[120] He once worried that he had breached decorum by writing in a light tone about certain judges, but he at last decided that "it makes a letter sound like a guide book unless one should turn to the other end of the wire."[121] Holmes's ear for tone guided his awareness of genre: he could tell how the sounds of particular sentences were more appropriate for a guide book, for example, than for a friendly letter. The tones he employed in his judicial writings set him apart from other justices and were not likely accidental but rather creative registers that pushed the bounds of genre.

After rereading Francis Bacon's essays in 1926, Holmes dashed off a missive to Ellen A. Curtis, averring that "a large part of the success of the past depends upon its sound."[122] "Shakespeare does enormously," he continued, "and Bacon is good to the ear even when as is not infrequent or unnatural he talks drool."[123] Holmes referred to Dante as a "troubadour and a poet" and deemed him to have possessed "the divinest singing gift that ever was among man."[124] Dante's sound, Holmes concluded this letter, "has sung in my ears for a week."[125]

Holmes likewise professed to Morris Cohen that "the first survival of a great work is its sound" and that "without the song of his words Shakespeare would not be read as he is."[126] Bacon's essays would go unread, Holmes added, "if they didn't sound so well."[127] Ten years earlier Holmes remarked to Margaret Bevan that Shakespeare "is kept going largely by his song, the enchanting sound of his words."[128] He wrote to Curtis, "Sounds vanish but sound is the secret to immortality—witness the Bard

[Shakespeare]. He is up, today."[129] Holmes's theory about Shakespeare's longevity is related to Poirier's assertion that Shakespeare's plays survive as "examples of superfluity."[130] Holmes like Poirier finds in sound the potential superfluity that endures because of its lasting effect on readers and listeners. For Holmes as for Poirier the aural properties of language protect the ideas it represents from the constant pressures and onslaught of sweeping change.

That Holmes connects sound with literary survival in each of these letters is telling in light of his treatment of legal principles in the common-law system as products of natural selection. If sound is a condition or enabler of survival, then arguments rendered in certain tones may be more likely to withstand the selective elimination of the unfit. Sound alone does not mark the survival of the fittest legal doctrines. But arguments about legal doctrines are more likely to be remembered—and hence reexamined and kept alive—if they are couched in language that is notable for its sound. The notion that legal doctrines rendered in memorable sounds might persist in the legal canon dovetails with the Emersonian pragmatic premise that language is an "organism" responding to its "accidental environment" and shaping "the profligacy of forms necessary to ensure the possibility of adaptation or fit to constantly changing conditions."[131] Holmes, like Emerson and Darwin, "understood language as a fundamental power."[132] He doubted "if any writer of English except Darwin [had] done so much to affect our whole way of thinking about the universe."[133] Holmes's association of sound with survival or endurance anticipates Poirier's portrayal of Emerson and Emerson's pragmatic successors as preoccupied with the aural properties of language that give it lasting value.

Holmes's letters prior to *Lochner*, some of which have been quoted above, suggest that he had been interested in the properties and effects of sound long before he penned his *Lochner* dissent. In 1893, when he was the Chief Justice of the Massachusetts Supreme Judicial Court, he wrote to Sir Frederick Pollock about the "sound of the polyphloisboian, the mosquito and the crow."[134] In 1898, he wrote to Pollock, "I hear the sound of music as I write these words—probably some fellows going off—or it may be only down to some of our seacoast defences—but such sounds are frequent and recall old days. It gives a certain ache."[135] These excerpts attest to his attentiveness to the *effects* of sound, although not necessarily to the properties of sound that brought about the sensations he describes. On April 19, 1868, however, he rounded out a letter to William James with the following lines:

> O! passionate breezes! O! rejoicing hills! How swells the soft full chorus—for this earth which slept hath awakened, and the air is tremulous with multiplied joyous sound.

Sing, sparrow—kissing with thy feet the topmost tassels of the pines.

Cease not thy too much sound, O! robin. Squirrels grind thy scissors in the woods. Creek, blackbirds. Croak, frogs. Caw, high-flying crows, who have seen the breaking of the ice in northern rivers and the seaward moving booms.

A keen, slender, stridulous vibration—almost too fine for the hearing, weaving in and out, and in the pauses of the music dividing the silence like a knife—pierces my heart with an ectasy [sic] I cannot utter. Ah! what is it? Did I ever hear It? Is it a voice within, answering to the others, but different from them—and like a singing flame not ceasing with that which made it vocal?[136]

Holmes was 27 at the time of this letter, which is different tonally from his later correspondence but similar in its use of alliteration, rhythm, and assonance. It raises the possibility that sound technology changed the way he used sound over the course of his life. These lines appeared when the primary medium for sound was public oration, whereas his later writing, which was less lyrical, appeared in the age of the gramophone and radio. These lines also reveal Holmes's awareness of the properties of sound and not just of their sensory effects. They seem influenced by Walt Whitman's *Leaves of Grass* and especially "Song of Myself," several editions of which had appeared by 1861.

This passage to James performs the subjects it describes; it is characterized by sigmatism: the repetition of "s" sounds for dramatic and musical effect ("passionate," "breezes," "rejoicing," "hills," "swells," "soft," "chorus," "this," "slept," "is," "tremulous," "joyous," "sound," "Sing," "sparrow," "kissing," "topmost," "tassels," "pines," and so forth). Holmes resorts to a device characteristic of Emerson and the transcendentalists when he employs apostrophe, addressing directly the breezes, the hills, the sparrow, the robin, the squirrel, the blackbirds, the frogs, and the crows. There can be little doubt that he meant for these sonorous lines to ring of their subjects: the "full chorus" of the hills and the singing sparrow and the squirrels' grinding teeth. With the creaking and the croaking and the cawing, Holmes reanimates the "stridulous vibration" and "music" that have apparently moved him to ecstasy. The diction and tempo are too distinctive and lyrical to be accidental; they affirm that Holmes was careful about the effect of his language and suggest that his meticulousness with words emerged when he was still a young man, long before Leland B. Duer, who was Holmes's secretary (or law clerk) from 1909 to 1910, wrote to Justice Frankfuter, "You know how carefully he [Holmes] chose his words, and how he delighted in a well termed phrase. I never knew him in doubt as to how he believed a case should be decided, but I have seen him re-cast more than once an opinion for the sake of a phrase, or even a word."[137]

Holmes's correspondence reveals that he was fascinated by other writers' use of sound and diction. On July 2, 1908, he wrote to the Brazilian statesman Joaquim Nabuco about the French translation of a book that is not identified by title in the letter. "Th[r]ough it all there is the sound of steel and the music of singing words," Holmes stated, admitting that he "could have cried over the sad, highhearted song of a fighting man."[138] In a letter to Laski dated May 12, 1922, Holmes mentioned a "breath stopping theory," a designation with a double meaning insofar "breath stopping" is not just an adjectival hyperbole but also a description of what happens phonetically when certain phrases are pronounced.[139] In context Holmes's remark seems sarcastic, the implication being that the book he is reading— George Willis's *The Philosophy of Speech*[140]—is not exciting. That Holmes would consult such a book at all indicates his interest in the subtleties and nuances of language and speech. The "breath stopping" theory maintains that all "substantives," or adjectives that are used as a noun or that take the place of a noun rather than modifying a noun, derive "from a preposition postponed—e.g., serve = servo-de = servod = servô with the o lengthened on the dropping of the consonant and as I becomes Ai when we drop the k from IK."[141] "Here is a sample sentence," Holmes continues, "'the' 'bi' in 'tibi' = to thee, the 'bus' in 'omnibus' = for all, and the by in 'thereby' would seem to be the same word.'"[142] This is a rough quotation of Willis.[143] Holmes's scrutiny was not limited to the written word; in another letter he lamented the "degeneration" of pronunciation in the "middle west" owing to the "obliteration of consonants."[144] He playfully claimed in one letter that he had "spent every spare minute in browsing over the dictionary of Modern English Usage for forty eight hours," marveling at "the pronunciation of girl" that made him "whinny with delight."[145] He also observed that Southerners tend to say "you all" for the second-person plural[146] and wondered whether "the accent of the e [in *Karénina*] merely indicates the pronunciation of the vowel" or "the accent of the syllable."[147]

In light of these letters, the alliteration, rhymes, and pararhymes in Holmes's *Lochner* dissent seem premeditated and carefully constructed: "ways" and "laws," "with" and "this" and "injudicious," "state" and "regulate," "tyrannical" and "liberty." The phrase "do not decide concrete cases" can be read as iambic; the repetition of "d" and "c" is alliterative. "Propositions" nearly rhymes with "cases." Depending on how one pronounces "Every" (i.e., whether one enunciates three syllables or elides the final two syllables to say "Ev'ry"), the hyperbolic aphorism—"Every opinion tends to become a law"—can be read as dactylic; at any rate the line consists of a falling rhythm that lends itself to recall. Rather than simply stating that "reasonable men would uphold the law," Holmes goes for intonation and emphasis by accentuating an understatement for rhetorical effect: "Men whom I certainly could not pronounce unreasonable would uphold [the law] as a first installment of a general regulation of the hours of work." The deliberate negation of an affirmative ("certainly could not pronounce unreasonable would uphold") marks this line as litotes. Holmes might be accused of prolixity here if it were not for the superfluity at work that makes the line striking and memorable and likely to be revisited and repeated by its readers. In a line already quoted above he supplies one of the most memorable and repeated aphorisms in American legal history: "General propositions do not decide concrete cases." The inference is that the facts and experiences embodied in individual cases shape what the rules and principles will be: because each case is unique, the facts and experiences of the case do not fit neatly within some operative paradigm of law. Instead the rules and principles are derived from facts and experience, which themselves determine which rules and principles obtain in the case.

Court references to Holmes's *Lochner* dissent number in the thousands. There is no empirical way to measure whether the literary devices and memorable language that Holmes used in *Lochner* caused his dissent to become known as "the canonical rejection of the anti-canonical decision."[148] However, the continued praise bestowed upon Holmes's style in his *Lochner* dissent, coupled with the vindication of that dissent, suggests that this case is memorable not because of its holding but because of its dissent.[149] Holmes's style instantiated the poetics of transition by representing his legal argument with aesthetic coding and signaling; the memorability of his words stimulated future attention to his point of view. The *Lochner* dissent earned him the reputation as "the greatest—or only—literary figure of the Lochner Court."[150] Anita S. Krishnakumar calls his *Lochner* dissent "thoroughly vindicated."[151] Citations to the dissent by later judges and justices suggest that the aesthetic qualities of his dissent gave his argument lasting power. Examples of such citations appear in *Winters v. New York*,[152] *Griswold v. Connecticut* (1965),[153] *Roe v. Wade* (1973),[154] and *Planned Parenthood v. Casey* (1992),[155] the latter three of which reference Holmes favorably while applying Fourteenth Amendment jurisprudence that Holmes would have rejected. The absence of agreement with Holmes on the Fourteenth Amendment, which determined how the United States Supreme Court ruled in these four cases, makes these references to Holmes's *Lochner* dissent even more revealing. It suggests that the later justices were drawn to Holmes's dissent less for its logic than for its style and sound as well as the totemic reputation it had earned.

Abrams v. United States (1919)[156]

Holmes's dissent in *Abrams* was also vindicated[157] and is known for its "language [that] approached poetry in its rhetorical power."[158] It was vindicated because it expressed views that became widely and generally accepted as correct. It has been dubbed "canonical,"[159] "a classic,"[160] "the supreme achievement of an otherwise largely uninspiring period" for the United States Supreme Court,[161] and "brilliant."[162] Justice Felix Frankfurter claimed that "[i]t is not reckless prophesy to assume that [Holmes's] famous dissenting opinion in the *Abrams* case will live as long as English prose retains its power to move."[163] The dissent is said to have marked "the beginning of modern First Amendment theory"[164] and to have "sow[ed] the seeds of a new tradition that would bear fruit in later times."[165]

The facts of *Abrams* are as follows. In the trial court, the defendants—five Russian-born individuals, three of whom considered themselves rebels, revolutionists, or anarchists—were charged with conspiring to violate the Espionage Act of Congress when they published statements deemed disloyal to the United States, which at the time of publication was at war with Germany. The defendants argued that the prosecution lacked the evidence needed to convict them of inciting resistance to the war and of curtailing the production of ammunition. They claimed that the Espionage Act was unconstitutional because it conflicted with the First Amendment. Writing for the majority of the United States Supreme Court, Justice John Hessin Clarke used the "bad tendency" test rather than the "clear and present danger" test to hold that substantial evidence supported the finding that the defendants incited violence and curtailed ammunition, that the Court did not have to evaluate the sufficiency of the evidence as to each count, and that the defendants had not convinced the Court that their pamphlets intended to thwart setbacks to the Russian cause. The Court therefore upheld the defendants' conviction.

Holmes dissented in what was later called "as strong a self-revision as American legal culture has known."[166] This dissent is a self-revision because in two previous decisions—*Schenck v. United States*[167] and *Debs v. United States*[168]—Holmes affirmed convictions under the Espionage Act. "By dissenting in *Abrams*," explains Robert Cover, "Holmes not only *argued* that the Constitution tolerated dissent, he also exemplified the dissent."[169] Adapting his earlier views to the new political climate, perhaps to placate critics of his earlier decisions,[170] Holmes began by describing each count against the defendants. He then undertook a close reading of the leaflets that had brought about the defendants' conviction. This led him to conclude that the defendants had not violated the Espionage Act because they had posed no clear and present danger. "Holmes might have ended his opinion there," since he had "explained why the defendants had not violated the Sedition Act and why their speech did not pose a clear and present danger."[171] He was "under no obligation to say anything further."[172] If he had "stopped there," however, "his dissent might have faded into the fog of history, another well-intentioned yet ultimately futile attempt to curb the excesses of popular government."[173] Rather than stopping, Holmes turned to superfluity. As an Emersonian pragmatist who wished his posterity to discover the "traces of productive energy that pass through a text or a composition or an author, pointing always beyond any one of them,"[174] Holmes produced in *Lochner* "that plenitude and power of language" that propelled "his voice into the future."[175]

In the most aphoristic and arguably the most famous line in the dissent, Holmes went on to declare, "But when men have realized that time has upset many fighting faiths, they may come to believe even more than they believe the very foundations of their own conduct that the ultimate good desired is better reached by free trade in ideas—that the best test of truth is the power of the thought to get itself accepted in the competition of the market, and that truth is the only ground upon which their wishes safely can be carried out."[176] The metaphor of the unregulated marketplace recalls both John Stuart Mill and Adam Smith, whom Holmes had read that year.[177] Emerson too had adopted the metaphor of capitalism as an "aboriginal power" and a "human invention designed to satisfy the rage for the superfluous."[178] As a metaphor, "capitalism is preeminently the economy of superfluity."[179] Such a metaphor asks to be noticed and hence enables Holmes's sentence to be recognized as "rich," "profound," and "unforgettable,"[180] as well as "one of the [. . .] most-quoted justifications for freedom of expression in the English-speaking world."[181]

Holmes intoned that "[e]very year if not every day we have to wager our salvation upon some prophecy based upon imperfect knowledge."[182] The words "every year if not every day" are in a strict sense unnecessary: without them the sentence bears the same meaning. Nevertheless, they lend flair with their tempo and rhythm and stand out for their parallel structure: the nouns "year" and "day" share an adjective ("every") and are divided by the words "if not":

[every year → *if not* ← every day]

The words "if not" separate nearly mirrored dactylic expressions; in this respect the phrase represents palistrophe, a symmetrical structure related to chiasmus. The nouns "year" and "day" are notable for their strong, nasal "y" sounds that form dipthongs. These nouns designate units of time and approximately establish an alphabetic and grammatical inversion inasmuch as "year" begins with a "y" whereas "day" terminates with a "y" and inasmuch as "*year*" forms a rising dipthong (a phoneme beginning with a less prominent semivowel and ending with a more prominent semivowel) whereas "*day*" forms a falling dipthong (a phoneme beginning with a more prominent semivowel and ending with a less prominent semivowel). The pronunciation of the gliding vowel sounds in these units of time generates a euphonic and syllabic pattern. As a sonorous predicate phrase, "every year if not every day" underscores the subject that follows: "prophesy based on imperfect knowledge"—words that signal key elements of Holmes's pragmatic jurisprudence, namely, the predictive nature of the law and the fallibility of human intelligence.

Like the aphoristic lines in *Lochner*, these aphoristic lines attest to Holmes's literary discernment and his ability to employ resonant language to highlight important jurisprudential points. The phrases "best test of truth," "to get itself accepted," and "which their wishes" are alliterative and describe the function of speech according to one hermeneutic under the First Amendment. "Best test of truth" not only rhymes "best" and "test" but also forms a dispondee in that it consists of back-to-back spondees (or four consecutive stressed syllables); the effect is emphatic, accenting the nature of truth as consensus-based. Other near rhymes include "safely," "be," and "carried." Holmes's stark combinations of sound produce staccato deliveries that are memorable and that make his *Abrams* dissent more quotable and recitable than textbook commentaries on the First Amendment.

Between colloquial phrases with no discernable measure, Holmes alternates iambic and trochaic patterns as if to emphasize certain statements and to validate Poirier's claim that we learn "from the sounds we hear in the movements of sentences, or fragments of sentences."[183] The iambic phrasing—"I am aware," "the word intent as vaguely used," "means no more than knowledge at the time," "said to be intended will ensue," "Even less than that," "A man may have to pay," "may be sent to prison," "if at the time"—generates a rhythm (da-DUM-da-DUM-da-DUM-da-DUM) that calls attention to the philosophical positions Holmes takes in relation to free expression. Discussions of acts, knowledge, and consequences, common to all criminal treatises, usually do not display the aphoristic flair displayed in these lines. The alliteration, rhymes, and pararhymes—"man *may* have to *pay*," "at the time of his *act* he knew *facts*," "when words," "deed is not done," "does not do the act," "produce . . . proximate"—make Holmes's phrases memorable, and memorability is essential to "the continuity of successful forms of expression in the evolution of thinking" and to the "context of language as an organic form."[184] One may be tempted to recall a stanza by Emily Dickinson that uses iambic meter to make a point about dissent:

> Great streets of silence led away
> To neighborhoods of pause—
> Here was no notice—no dissent—
> No universe—no laws.[185]

This risks overstating the point, but is it not remarkable that Holmes's choice of feet reflects Dickinson's lines about dissent and laws and that in Dickinson's poem stasis corresponds with a lack of dissent and laws, whereas in Holmes's jurisprudence dissents enable activity and competition, the opposite of stasis? It is almost as if Dickinson associates dissent with activity and the law and the lack of dissent with repose. If so, then her construction dovetails with the thesis of this work that dissents enable the gradual spread of workable rules through constant competition.

The *Abrams* dissent "not only breaks from and misreads the authority of precedent," proclaims David Cole, "it ultimately becomes the authoritative precedent itself," and not just any authoritative precedent but one that "gains more precedential power than the three unanimous opinions that preceded it."[186] Referencing the "stirring" final paragraph of this dissent has become a "time-honored ritual."[187] The *Abrams* dissent is "illustrative of [. . .] Holmes's aphoristic style."[188] His aphorism regarding free speech and the marketplace of ideas not only represents superfluity but also enacts the poetics of transition by marking "a beginning in free speech decisions" that gestures *"beyond itself* to the living, mysterious, unfinished debates that *will come* regarding the limits of free speech."[189]

Two days after *Abrams* was decided, Felix Frankfurter, not yet a justice on the United States Supreme Court, wrote to Holmes about "the pride I have in your dissent" because it contains "the voice of the noble human spirit."[190] Frankfurter could not have known how many commentators would issue similar tributes. The United States Supreme Court has referenced the dissent several times.[191] Numerous state and federal courts have likewise quoted Holmes's catchiest phrases from the dissent. It is not just the free-speech concept but the words in which the free-speech concept is couched that make the arguments in Holmes's *Abrams* dissent worthy of reconsideration. Holmes was aware that "a word even in the dictionary has shades of meaning" and that "the meaning of words according to the usage of speech" can alter the "external character of the law."[192] Words themselves, he maintained, are meaningful only within a context: "In like manner, still by the usages of speech the rest of the document may qualify the sentence."[193] Holmes's use of sound and metaphor in *Abrams* appears to have been designed to shape the external character of the law and to have succeeded in attaining lasting power. One biographer of Holmes beams that the "splendid language" of this "great dissent [. . .] added to our national heritage a concept of freedom to speak that Americans will cherish as long as they cherish freedom."[194] Another commentator suggests that "[f]rom Holmes we learn that the practice of rhetoric is vital for democratic life and that the theory of our Constitution allows for the 'free trade in ideas' in which only what proves persuasive will succeed."[195]

Over the course of his career, "Holmes took great pride in his writing and worked hard to make every sentence shine," believing as he did that "judicial opinions should be agreeable to the ear when read aloud."[196] By the time he authored his *Abrams* dissent, "he had grown into his style and was now the most assured writer on the Court."[197] By crafting the *Abrams* dissent with style, he "produced a document that far exceeded his own estimation" that would "survive long after he was gone."[198] The *Abrams* dissent was "direct and provocative" and possessed "the qualities that made his voice as a judge distinctive," including "an almost aggressively colloquial style."[199] The *Abrams* dissent "continues to make its presence felt [. . .] in a vast range of expressive activity, from commercial advertisements and campaign spending to defamation of public figures and the burning of the American flag."[200] The "centrality of free speech in our legal culture today" is largely attributable to this dissent.[201] Moreover, the "metaphor of the marketplace of ideas and [the] concept of 'clear and present danger' have worked their way into our collective consciousness" and have become "part of our language," "view of the world," and "identity as a nation."[202] Generations of readers have "internalized" Holmes's words in *Abrams* and have "come to regard" such words as their own.[203] By "re-animating" his audience's "emotional commitment" to both rhetoric and the "underlying, metaphoric value embedded in law," Holmes hoped "to *move beyond* the original emotional directive behind the laws banning speech against U.S. involvement in the First World War."[204] His ability to employ stylistic rhetoric "to *move* the audience someplace" enacts the poetics of transition by guaranteeing the perseverance of his legal arguments amid the constant struggle for survival among cases.[205]

Tyson & Brother v. Banton (1927)[206]

Tyson & Brother v. Banton involved an appeal from the United States District Court for the Southern District of New York, which had denied a request for a temporary injunction brought by a licensed ticket-broker to restrain certain New York officials from revoking the ticket-broker's license and from prosecuting the ticket-broker because of the ticket-broker's refusal to comply with a statute fixing the price at which theater tickets could be resold. The practical effect of the statute was to prohibit the scalping of theater tickets. The ticket-broker challenged the severity of the statute, the violation of which was punishable by one-year imprisonment or a $250 fine or both. The ticket-broker alleged that execution of the statute would deprive the ticket-broker of its property and liberty rights under the Equal Protection Clause of the Fourteenth Amendment. The United States Supreme Court framed the operative issue on appeal as "whether every public exhibition, game, contest, or performance to which an admission charge is made is clothed with a public interest, so as to authorize a lawmaking body to fix the maximum amount of the charge which its patrons may be required to pay."[207]

Justice Sutherland issued the opinion for the majority, striking down the New York statute on the grounds that the New York legislature possessed the authority to police businesses or properties with a "public interest" but that places of entertainment such as theaters were private enterprises not similar in kind to gas or electric providers that were clothed with a public interest; therefore, the majority held, the statutory price-fixing violated the Fourteenth Amendment.

Holmes began his dissent with an aphorism: "We fear to grant power, and are unwilling to recognize it when it exists."[208] Holmes adored aphorisms, labored over them, and took pride when he at last stated them to his satisfaction. As one example, on January 16, 1910, he informed the Baroness Marie Moncheur that he had been reading Oscar Wilde for Wilde's "Civilized Speech" and "was rather pleased with an aphorism I touched off at dinner the other night to Mrs. Harry White—'Things that are just as good as things, aint.'"[209] Robert Danisch has argued that Holmes's "use of aphorisms demonstrates a philosophical commitment to understanding law as a competition between different rhetorics."[210] Danisch claims that Holmes's "job as a judge was to keep the public competition between rhetorics as open as possible. To do so, he used a style of argument that was suggestive, allusive, and terse, not final or complete."[211]

Holmes's use of aphorism often reflected the underlying philosophical point he was making. His use of aphorisms in *Abrams*, for example, accented the belief that "the world is made up of competing aphorisms" and that we "defend the right to free speech because we are open to the possibilities of multiple interpretations."[212] The powerful opening aphorism in the *Tyson* dissent highlights not only those powers vested in the New York legislature by the citizens of the State of New York but also those powers vested in the federal courts by way of the Fourteenth Amendment. "Holmes's style carries his worldview and mimics his philosophy," Danisch says to this end,[213] observing, too, that Holmes's "literary skill is not used merely to convey the truth he is after, but as an argumentative device itself designed to foreground values and emotions that are always already part of the legal process."[214] The aphorism about fearing power so much that we turn a blind eye to its existence indicates Holmes's apparent indifference to the good or bad content of the statute. "I am far from saying that I think this particular law a wise and rational provision," he concludes, adding, "That is not my affair."[215] Suggesting that we casually accept the things we most fear once they become part of our experience or that anticipated fears are never as obvious or devastating once their cause materializes or moves from a mere concept to a tangible reality, Holmes's aphorism in *Tyson* calls out for interpretation and context. It is a mechanism for Holmes to bring about the poetics of transition by evoking "the quality of alertness to possibilities of meaning as they lurk in the always dynamic margins of experience."[216]

Holmes's dissent in *Tyson* can be summed up in one phrase: the State of New York did not violate the Fourteenth Amendment by legislating a price-cap on theater-ticket resales. Not content with such a trite statement that would do little to inspire the imaginations of future judges and justices, Holmes launched into a critique of the signifier "police power," which he called "apologetic" and "convenient [. . .] to conciliate the mind to something that needs explanation."[217] "[P]olice power," he announced, "often is used in a wide sense to cover and, as I said, to apologize for the general power of the Legislature to make a part of the community uncomfortable by a change."[218] Holmes then used the word "machine" as a metaphor for the state legislature and "joints" as a metaphor for the law, stating, "some play must be allowed to the joints if the machine is to work."[219] His use of metaphor transfers the mechanical characteristics of a piece of equipment or a powered device to statutory regulations and thus highlights the difference between planned or designed legislative codification and the unplanned and spontaneous ordering of the common-law system. This subtle recourse to figurative language establishes a rhetorical framework within which Holmes may exposit his Fourteenth Amendment jurisprudence that favors deference to local political branches. When he commissions the resonant metonym "some moral storm of the future" to minimize the gravity of the present legislation, which he contextualizes alongside changing attitudes about the regulation of wine and lotteries, he evinces his pragmatic view of the common-law system as responsive to rather than determinative of cultural consensus.[220] Holmes's resort to superfluity in the form of metonymy underscores his refusal to arrogate to himself the authority to divine the best interests of communities not his own.

Aphorism and metonymy are just two elements of superfluity working in Holmes's *Tyson* dissent. Other examples of superfluity in the *Tyson* dissent include auxesis, a form of incremental overstatement that, in this instance, stresses the power of the state government to interfere with private property: "*the fact that* the constitutional requirement of compensation when property is taken cannot be pressed to its grammatical extreme; *that* property rights may be taken for public purpose without pay if you do not take too much; *that* some play must be allowed in the joints if the machine is to work."[221] This sentence repeats the conjunctive "that" to enlarge the importance of the culminating metonym; it is also an example of asyndeton in that it drops the conjunction "and" for rhetorical and aural effect. The hyperbole that "respect for art" is "one of the glories of France" anticipates the claim that "to many people the superfluous is necessary."[222] There is playfulness in this superfluous hyperbole that precedes a remark about superfluity that prefigures Poirier's celebration of "the human need for superfluousness."[223] One is reminded of Levin's observation that Emerson used forceful language when writing about the "vital forces" that constitute our universe.[224]

Each of the literary and rhetorical strategies used by Holmes in the *Tyson* dissent amplifies his language and contributes to the momentousness of his argument that would in time become vindicated. The majority in *Tyson* was overruled in part by *Olsen v. State of Nebraska*[225] and criticized in *Nebbia v. People of New York*[226] and *Gold v. DiCarlo*.[227] An implied overruling of the *Tyson* majority was recognized by *State v. Cardwell*[228] and *People v. Rosenblatt*.[229] An abrogation of the majority in *Tyson* was recognized by *New Jersey Association of Ticket Brokers v. Ticketron*,[230] *People v. Concert Connection, Ltd.*,[231] and *Arlotta v. Bradley Center*.[232] The majority in *Tyson* was called into doubt by *Blue v. McBride*.[233] Numerous courts have distinguished the majority in *Tyson* from the fact patterns in the case before them to arrive at a different legal result. Holmes's ability to influence future judges and justices with his *Tyson* dissent evidences the fact that he, like the Emersonian pragmatists in Poirier's canon, was "writing for the future and into the future."[234]

Holmes validated with *Tyson* the pragmatist notion that "language [. . .] and thinking [. . .] can be changed by an individual's acts of imagination and by an individual's manipulation of words."[235] Holmes capitalized on the "value" of his words that, "as pragmatism recommends," points "toward future realization, toward the existence of things" such as potential rules and principles that "it cannot verbally re-present."[236] As if tracking the Emersonian pragmatists, Holmes fashioned in his dissents in *Lochner*, *Abrams*, and *Tyson* "sounds [that] invite us to live with others in a space of expectation," always forcing us to wonder how his dissents will be received and whether they will be vindicated by future courts or legislatures.[237]

CONCLUSION

Techniques of prosody reveal much about the meaning and reception of Holmes's dissents. He experimented with language and tried to endow aesthetics with a legal function and the law with aesthetics. Liberated from the periphrasis that characterizes legal discourse, his prose exemplifies superfluity as that term is deployed by Poirier and enables the poetics of transition as that term is deployed by Levin. It has been observed that "Holmes consistently argued that legal reasoning requires more than logic, and the 'more' that he pointed to included passions, values, timing, and style."[238] He spoke of "the fallacy of the logical form"[239] and worried that "logic does not carry us far" in our understanding of the law.[240] His style is "deeply indicative" of "enthymematic reasoning."[241] Rather than couching his reasoning in complete syllogisms, he advanced his arguments and facilitated the poetics of transition by cultivating superfluity and moving the law toward a vague state from which his dissenting rationale might be redeemed.

Holmes began *The Common Law* by acknowledging that syllogisms alone do not advance the common-law system: "The felt necessities of the time, the prevalent moral and political theories, intuitions of public policy, avowed or unconscious, even the prejudices which judges share with their fellow-men, have had a good deal more to do than the syllogism in determining the rules by which men should be governed."[242] Enthymematic reasoning in the form of rhetorical superfluity enabled him to tap into these other sources for the rules of governance. "If style matters to enthymematic reasoning," then Holmes's use of literary devices "presents a unique opportunity for analyzing how the style of a particular genre of writing can advance a reasoned argument."[243] Holmes's superfluity substantiates Posner's submission that "rhetoric counts for a lot in law because many legal questions cannot be resolved by logical or empirical demonstration."[244] Holmes developed the medium of dissent as a literary genre that Brandeis, Cardozo, Stevens, and Scalia would build upon with their own distinctive sounds and style. The combination of Holmes's aphoristic charm with his enthymematic reasoning not only allowed him "to perform and articulate his version of pragmatism" but also "to conceptualize law as a kind of perpetually unfinished task that requires special attention to language."[245] This was his way of implicating "the democratic impulse shared by Emersonian pragmatists."[246] He accelerated the flux and flow of the law and made possible the realization of his arguments in future cases.

Poirier and Levin insinuate that superfluity serves a rhetorical function, assuages the anxiety of influence, and earns the writer (or for my purposes a judge or justice) a wider audience and possibly even a place in the canon. To the extent that superfluity represents the urge to progress, overcome, transcend, improve, increase, advance, extend, and outdo, it is conducive to judicial dissents, the most memorable of which are stylistic and predictive appeals for change to unnamed future lawyers, judges, justices, and legal academicians. As the canon of case precedents grows and expands, dissents can serve as corrective mechanisms: they can provide alternative theories from which to adopt lines of reasoning and with which to shape the normative orders that reflect and define the ethos of the time and place while retaining what is indispensable from past times and places.

Dissents ensure that the struggle for the right rules and principles continues. Aesthetic dissents are, because of their appealing properties, likely to succeed in redirecting the common-law system towards workable solutions and practical applications once some majority position becomes untenable or disagreeable. Rules and principles in a common-law system do not merely reflect the selection of outcomes attained in appellate cases. They also evidence the accumulated experience and prevailing reasoning of acting agents within a given territory. By contrast, dissents are signals of what might be accomplished through the concerted efforts of future litigants to secure for themselves what is just and reasonable in their own particular context and in light of their own particular arguments. Vindicated dissents such as Holmes's prove that a state of deliberate unrest in the law can facilitate juridical adaptation to the social environment and overcome dominant trends toward bad judicial decisions. Vindicated dissents also suggest that triumphant legal norms and judicially established value systems make up but a fraction of the potential options for arranging and responding to the complexities of human behavior.

The three aestheticized dissents discussed in this chapter reveal why Holmes was called the Great Dissenter. Chapter 3 extends this focus on Holmes's literary talent and places it in conversation with pragmatic theories about agon and canonicity that characterize the work of Harold Bloom. As in this chapter, the following chapter analyzes the dissent as a rhetorical medium that prevents case precedent from fossilizing into a state of immobility when the exigencies of the social order demand revision, modification, and adjustment.

NOTES

1. James W. Springer, "Natural Selection or Natural Law: A Reconsideration of the Jurisprudence of Oliver Wendell Holmes," *Georgetown Journal of Law & Public Policy* 3 (2005): 57, citing Holmes, "Law in Science," 443, 460; Vegelahn v. Guntner, 167 Mass. 92, 106 (1896) (Holmes, J., dissenting); and Holmes, "Path of the Law," 457, 466.

2. See, e.g., Lee Epstein, William M. Landes, and Richard Posner, "Why (and When) Judges Dissent: A Theoretical and Empirical Analysis," *Journal of Legal Analysis* 3 (2011): 101-37.

3. Colin Starger, "Exile on Main Street: Competing Traditions and Due Process Dissent," *Marquette Law Review* 95 (2010): 1256.

4. Starger, "Exile," 1257.

5. Poirier, *Poetry*, 45.

6. Poirier, *Poetry*, 47.

7. Poirier, *Poetry*, 52.

8. Poirier, *Poetry*, 67.

9. Poirier, *Poetry*, 50.

10. Poirier, *Poetry*, 55.

11. Ibid.

12. Poirier, *Poetry*, 57.

13. Poirier, *Poetry*, 58.

14. Ibid.

15. Poirier, *Poetry*, 60.

16. Poirier, *Poetry*, 71.

17. Poirier, *Poetry*, 73.

18. Poirier, *Poetry*, 74.

19. Poirier, *Poetry*, 47.

20. Poirier, *Poetry*, 59.

21. Poirier, *Poetry*, 58.

22. Poirier, *Poetry*, 65.

23. Poirier, *Poetry*, 70-71.

24. Levin, *Poetics*, xv.

25. Poirier, *Poetry*, 25, 28-29, 45-46, 67, 122, 150.

26. Levin, *Poetics*, ix.

27. Levin, *Poetics*, 22.

28. Levin, *Poetics*, 2.

29. Levin, *Poetics*, 3.

30. Ibid.

31. Levin, *Poetics*, 4.

32. Levin, *Poetics*, 3.

33. Poirier, *Poetry*, 149-50.

34. Robert Frost, *The Poetry of Robert Frost*, edited by Edward Connery Lathem (New York: Henry Holt and Company, 1975), 33.

35. Poirier, *Poetry*, 150.

36. Wallace Stevens, "Credences of Summer," *Stevens: Collected Poetry & Prose*, Frank Kermode and Joan Richardson, eds. (New York: The Library of America, 1997), 323.

37. "A Comment on Meaning in Poetry," in Kermode and Richardson, *Stevens*, 825.

38. Levin, *Poetics*, 3; Holmes, *Common Law*, 1.

39. Levin, *Poetics*, 4.

40. Holmes, "Path of the Law," 465.

41. Oliver Wendell Holmes Jr., "Ideals and Doubts," *Law Student's Helper* 23 (1915): 4.

42. Commonwealth v. Kennedy, 170 Mass. 18 (1897).

43. Levin, *Poetics*, 14.

44. "From the Notebooks," in Kermode and Richardson, *Stevens*, 901.

45. "Two or Three Ideas," in Kermode and Richardson, *Stevens*, 844.

46. Levin, *Poetics*, 14.

47. William James, *The Principles of Psychology, Vol. 1* (New York: Henry Hold and Company, 1890).

48. Poirier, *Poetry*, 137-39.

49. Frost, *Poetry*, 68-69.

50. Levin, *Poetics*, 197.

51. Levin, *Poetics*, 33-35.

52. Levin, *Poetics*, 50-52.

53. Levin, *Poetics*, 92.

54. Levin, *Poetics*, 117-18.

55. Levin, *Poetics*, 152-58.

56. Levin, *Poetics*, 169.

57. "For my own part, I often doubt whether it would not be a gain if every word of moral significance could be banished from the law altogether, and other words adopted which should convey legal ideas uncolored by anything outside the law" (Holmes, "Path of the Law," 464).

58. Holmes, "Path of the Law," 458.

59. Oliver Wendell Holmes, Jr. to Lewis Einstein, August 9, 1921, Harvard University Holmes Digital Suite, Mark DeWolfe Howe's research materials on Holmes, 1858-1968: Finding Aid, Major Correspondence: Einstein, Lewis, correspondent, October 10, 1920-March 31, 1922, online.

60. Holmes, *Common Law*, 1.

61. New York Trust Co. v. Eisner, 256 U.S. 345 (1921), at 349.

62. Holmes, "Path of the Law," 458, 457.

63. Levin, *Poetics*, 43.

64. Levin, *Poetics*, 44.

65. Levin, *Poetics*, 89.

66. Levin, *Poetics*, 150.

67. Levin, *Poetics*, 149-51.

68. Gertrude Stein, *The Autobiography of Alice B. Toklas* (New York: Vintage Books, [1933] 1990) 14.

69. Gertrude Stein, "Three Portraits of Painters," in *Selected Writings of Gertrude Stein* (New York: Vintage Books, [1945] 1990), 329.

70. Levin, *Poetics*, 44.

71. Adair v. U.S., 208 U.S. 161 (1908).

72. Phelps Dodge Corp. v. N.L.R.B., 313 U.S. 177 (1941) at 187.

73. Hotel and Restaurant Employees and Bartenders International Union Local 54 v. Danziger, 709 F. 2d 815 (3rd Circuit 1983) at 823.

74. Levin, *Poetics*, 44.

75. Ibid.

76. Levin, *Poetics*, ix.

77. Ibid.

78. Levin, *Poetics*, x.

79. Levin, *Poetics*, 3.

80. Holmes, *Common Law*, 1.

81. Holmes, *Common Law*, 25.

82. "[I]t is perhaps true that no case illustrates the metonymic nature of the constitutional canon better than Lochner. It has lent its name to an entire chapter of constitutional history: the so-called Lochner Era. But what exactly are the associated meanings to which the metonym points us? What do we mean when we

accuse someone of 'Lochnering'? Some modern commentators have suggested that the case's metonymic meaning remains unclear; that it is difficult to say with any certainty what is wrong with Lochner. But this confusion is, I think, rhetorical, as scholars struggle to draw a principled distinction between the Court's efforts to protect the liberty of contract in the early twentieth century, and its determination to enforce civil and reproductive rights under Earl Warren and Warren Burger. I suggest that, in truth, all of these uncertainties—the revilement, the revision, the distinctions, and the clarifications—are simply part of an ongoing battle to distill Lochner's metonymic meanings within constitutional practice. They are a manifestation of the continuing struggle to reclaim or refine the 'hard' spot the case occupies in the constitutional riverbank; the perpetual effort to define what Lochner stands for, or, more importantly, what it stands against" (Ian Bartrum, "Constitutional Canon as Argumentative Metonymy," *William and Mary Bill of Rights Journal* 18 [2009]: 347).

83. Bartrum, "Constitutional Canon," 348.

84. Richard Posner, "Law and Literature: A Relation Reargued," in *Law and Literature: Text and Theory*, edited by Lenora Ledwon (New York: Garland Publishing, 1996), 77.

85. Posner, "Law and Literature," 271.

86. Posner, "Law and Literature," 266.

87. Roe v. Wade, 410 U.S. 113 (1973) at 117.

88. Charles Fairman, *American Constitutional Decisions* (New York: Holt, 1950), 335.

89. "First, there is the problem of assessing Holmes's popularity and the meaning to be attributed to his famous dissent in *Lochner v. New York*. Is the orthodox wisdom about Holmes's dissent correct in portraying Holmes as an enemy of substantive due process? Was Holmes a modernist hero who helped to push us into the twentieth century, or was Holmes a troubled modernist thinker who was still caught up in the nineteenth century jurisprudence of his day? What explains the popularity of Holmes's Lochner dissent in the progressive era, and why did it take so long for Holmes to be lionized?" (Gary Minda, "Commentary: The Dragon in the Cave," *Brooklyn Law Review* 63 [1997]: 129-30).

90. "Professor Felix Frankfurter was the first to praise Holmes, with a eulogistic essay in the *Harvard Law Review* entitled *The Constitutional Opinions of Justice Holmes*. It took some time for others to follow suit, but during the late 1920s and early 1930s, a series of articles appeared in the *New Republic* and other progressive New Deal magazines hailing Holmes as the 'idol' of the progressive movement and casting him as 'the great dissenter.' The authors of these articles were members of the liberal elite who sought to promote the New Deal and embraced Holmes's methodology as a means of reversing the Old Court's jurisprudence and ushering in President Roosevelt's reforms. It was this conscious desire to elevate Holmes that led Frankfurter to compare Holmes's reasoning to John Marshall's in one of his eulogistic *Harvard Law Review* essays about the Justice—for such comparison lent legitimacy to the progressives' project to convince the nation and the Court of the New Deal's consonance with the Constitution. Similarly, others praised Holmes's 'faith that . . . our social system is one of experimentation subject to the ordeal of experienced consequences,' and commented that 'no judge who

has sat upon the bench has ever been more progressive in his attitude'" (Anita S. Krishnakumar, "On the Evolution of the Canonical Dissent," *Rutgers Law Review* 52 [2000]: 792-93).

91. See Robert H. Bork, *The Tempting of America: The Political Seduction of Law* (New York: Free Press, 1990), 45.

92. Krishnakumar, "Evolution," 788.

93. "The general right to make a contract in relation to his business is part of the liberty of the individual protected by the 14th Amendment of the Federal Constitution" (*Lochner* 198 U.S. at 53).

94. "There is, in our judgment, no reasonable foundation for holding this to be necessary or appropriate as a health law to safeguard the public health, or the health of the individuals who are following the trade of a baker" (*Lochner* 198 U.S. 45 [1905] at 58).

95. "We think that there can be no fair doubt that the trade of a baker, in and of itself, is not an unhealthy one to that degree which would authorize the legislature to interfere with the right to labor, and with the right of free contract on the part of the individual, either as employer or employee" (*Lochner* 198 U.S. 45 [1905] at 59).

96. "It is impossible for us to shut our eyes to the fact that many of the laws of this character, while passed under what is claimed to be the police power for the purpose of protecting the public health or welfare, are, in reality, passed from other motives. We are justified in saying so when, from the character of the law and the subject upon which it legislates, it is apparent that the public health or welfare bears but the most remote relation to the law. The purpose of a statute must be determined from the natural and legal effect of the language employed; and whether it is or is not repugnant to the Constitution of the United States must be determined from the natural effect of such statutes when put into operation, and not from their proclaimed purpose." (*Lochner* 198 U.S. 45 [1905] at 64)

97. *Lochner* 198 U.S. 45 (1905) at 75.

98. Ibid.

99. Ibid.

100. *Lochner* 198 U.S. 45 (1905) at 75-76.

101. *Lochner* 198 U.S. 45 (1905) at 76.

102. Ibid.

103. *Lochner* 198 U.S. 45 (1905) at 75.

104. Ibid.

105. Richard Posner calls this sentence "the most famous sentence in Holmes's dissent—one of the most famous in the history of law and as precious to those who think the statute bad policy as it is to advocates of regulating the employment relation" (Richard Posner, *Law and Literature*, Cambridge, MA: Harvard University Press, 1998).

106. *Lochner* 198 U.S. 45 (1905) at 75.

107. Danisch, "Aphorism," 230.

108. Paul S. Gillies, "Dissents and Deceptions," *Vermont Bar Journal and Law Digest* 25 (1999): 10.

109. Krishnakumar, "Aphorism," 789-90.

110. Gillmore, Howard. "De-Lochnerizing Lochner," *Boston University Law Review* 85 (2005): 861.

111. *Lochner* 198 U.S. 45 (1905) at 75.

112. Ibid.

113. Levin, *Poetics*, 169.

114. Oliver Wendell Holmes, Jr. to Harold Laski, November 23, 1926, Harvard University Holmes Digital Suite, Mark DeWolfe Howe's research materials on Holmes, 1858-1968: Finding Aid, Major Correspondence: Laski, Harold, correspondent, October 16-November 21, 1926, online.

115. Ibid.

116. Peabody, *Holmes-Einstein Letters*, 322.

117. Oliver Wendell Holmes, Jr. to Harold Laski, May 18, 1918, Harvard University Holmes Digital Suite, Mark DeWolfe Howe's research materials on Holmes, 1858-1968: Finding Aid, Major Correspondence: Laski, Harold, correspondent, March-May 1918, online.

118. Oliver Wendell Holmes, Jr. to Lady Pollock, July 20, 1897, Harvard University Holmes Digital Suite, Mark DeWolfe Howe's research materials on Holmes, 1858-1968: Finding Aid, Complete set of typescripts, interfiled, 1896-1902, online.

119. Oliver Wendell Holmes, Jr. to Margaret Bevan, May 18, 1915, Harvard University Holmes Digital Suite, Addenda, 1818-1978, Correspondence: Bevan, Margaret, correspondent, 1913-1915, online.

120. Oliver Wendell Holmes, Jr. to Nina L. Grey, August 30, 1904, Harvard University Holmes Digital Suite, Mark DeWolfe Howe's research materials on Holmes, 1858-1968: Finding Aid, Major Correspondence: Gray, Nina L., correspondent, July 23, 1904-September 26, 1904, online.

121. Oliver Wendell Holmes, Jr. to Ellen A. Curtis, January 12, 1913, Harvard University Holmes Digital Suite, Mark DeWolfe Howe's research materials on Holmes, 1858-1968: Finding Aid, Curtis, Ellen A. 1900-1933, online.

122. Oliver Wendell Holmes, Jr. to Ellen A. Curtis, November 16, 1926, Harvard University Holmes Digital Suite, Mark DeWolfe Howe's research materials on Holmes, 1858-1968: Finding Aid, Curtis, Ellen A. 1900-1933, online.

123. Ibid.

124. Oliver Wendell Holmes, Jr. to Ethel Scott, February 18, 1910, Harvard University Holmes Digital Suite, Mark DeWolfe Howe's research materials on Holmes, 1858-1968: Finding Aid, 1908-1912, online.

125. Ibid.

126. Oliver Wendell Holmes, Jr. to Morris Cohen, November 29, 1926, Harvard University Holmes Digital Suite, Mark DeWolfe Howe's research materials on Holmes, 1858-1968: Finding Aid, Cohen, Morris Raphael, 1909-1934, online.

127. Ibid.

128. Oliver Wendell Holmes, Jr. to Margaret Bevan, August 19, 1913, Harvard University Holmes Digital Suite, Addenda, 1818-1978, Correspondence: Bevan, Margaret, correspondent, 1913-1915, online.

129. Oliver Wendell Holmes, Jr. to Ellen A. Curtis, February 9, 1926, Harvard University Holmes Digital Suite, Mark DeWolfe Howe's research materials on Holmes, 1858-1968: Finding Aid, Curtis, Ellen A. 1900-1933, online.

130. Poirier, *Poetry*, 74.

131. Joan Richardson, *A Natural History of Pragmatism: The Fact of Feeling from Jonathan Edwards to Gertrude Stein* (Cambridge, UK: Cambridge University Press, 2007), 8.

132. Richardson, *Natural History*, 81.

133. Oliver Wendell Holmes, Jr. to Lady Pollock, July 2, 1895, Harvard University Holmes Digital Suite, Mark DeWolfe Howe's research materials on Holmes, 1858-1968: Finding Aid, Typescripts with footnotes, 1874-1895, online.

134. Oliver Wendell Holmes, Jr. to Sir Frederic Pollock, August 27, 1883, Harvard University Holmes Digital Suite, Mark DeWolfe Howe's research materials on Holmes, 1858-1968: Finding Aid, Typescripts with footnotes, 1874-1895, online.

135. Oliver Wendell Holmes, Jr. to Sir Frederick Pollock, May 13, 1898, Harvard University Holmes Digital Suite, Mark DeWolfe Howe's research materials on Holmes, 1858-1968: Finding Aid, Typescripts with footnotes, 1896-1909, online.

136. Oliver Wendell Holmes, Jr. to William James, April 19, 1868, Harvard University Holmes Digital Suite, Mark DeWolfe Howe's research materials on Holmes, 1858-1968: Finding Aid, James, William, 1867-1907, online.

137. Oliver Wendell Holmes, Jr., Letter from Leland B. Duer to Justice Frankfurter, February 16, 1938, Harvard University Holmes Digital Suite, John G. Palfrey (1875-1945), collection of Oliver Wendell Holmes, Jr. Papers, 1715-1938: Finding Aid, Secretaries (OHW's law clerks), 1912-1938, online.

138. Oliver Wendell Holmes, Jr. to Joaquim Nabuco, July 2, 1908, Harvard University Holmes Digital Suite, Mark DeWolfe Howe's research materials on Holmes, 1858-1968: Finding Aid, Nabuco, Joaquim, 1907-1910, online.

139. Oliver Wendell Holmes, Jr. to Harold Laski, May 12, 1922, Harvard University Holmes Digital Suite, Mark DeWolfe Howe's research materials on Holmes, 1858-1968: Finding Aid, Major Correspondence: Laski, Harold, correspondent, April-June 1922, online.

140. George Willis, *The Philosophy of Language* (New York: MacMillan Company, n.d.), original on file in the Cornell University Library, gifted to Cornell in 1891, Cornell University Library, Internet Archive, online.

141. Holmes to Laski, May 12, 1922.

142. Ibid.

143. Willis, *Philosophy*, 143-44.

144. Oliver Wendell Holmes, Jr. to Harold Laski, April 12, 1931, Harvard University Holmes Digital Suite, Mark DeWolfe Howe's research materials on Holmes, 1858-1968: Finding Aid, Major Correspondence: Laski, Harold, correspondent, January-April 1931, online.

145. Oliver Wendell Holmes, Jr. to Laurence Curtis, November 18, 1926, Harvard University Holmes Digital Suite, Holmes, Oliver Wendell, Jr., Addenda, 1818-1978, Correspondence: Curtis, Laurence, correspondent, 1921-1929, online.

146. Oliver Wendell Holmes, Jr. to Margaret Bevan, November 6, 1913, Harvard University Holmes Digital Suite, Addenda, 1818-1978, Correspondence: Bevan, Margaret, correspondent, 1913-1915, online.

147. Oliver Wendell Holmes, Jr. to Harold Laski, September 9, 1929, Harvard University Holmes Digital Suite, Mark DeWolfe Howe's research materials on Holmes, 1858-1968: Finding Aid: September 9-November 3, 1929, online.

148. Jack M. Balkin, "Wrong the Day It Was Decided: *Lochner* and Constitutional Historicism," *Boston University Law Review* 85 (2005): 677-725.

149. "Lochner is never cited for its legal authority. Although it has never been formally overruled, it is well understood among constitutional lawyers that relying on Lochner would be a pointless, if not a self-destructive, endeavor" (Richard

A. Primus, "Canon, Anti-Canon, and Judicial Dissent," *Duke Law Journal* 48 (1998): 244).

150. Gerald Leonard, "Holmes on the Lochner Court," *Boston University Law Review* 85 (2005): 1003.

151. Krishnakumar, "Evolution," 789.

152. Winters v. New York, 333 U.S. 507 (1948) at 527.

153. Griswold v. Connecticut, 381 U.S. 479 (1965) at 1703.

154. *Roe* 410 U.S. at 709.

155. Planned Parenthood of Southwestern Pennsylvania v. Casey, 505 U.S. 833 (1992) at 846-50.

156. Abrams v. U.S., 250 U.S. 616 (1919).

157. "Years later, a majority of justices vindicated Holmes's minority position, and free expression became a constitutional 'lodestar'" (Stephen M. Feldman, "Free Speech, World War I, and Republican Democracy: The Internal and External Holmes," *First Amendment Law Review* 6 [2008]: 192).

158. Anthony Lewis, *Make No Law: The Sullivan Case and the First Amendment* (New York: First Vintage Books Edition, [1991] 1992), 80.

159. Blasi, "Holmes," 2.

160. Schwartz, "Holmes," 88.

161. David P. Currie, *The Constitution in the Supreme Court* (Chicago: University of Chicago Press, 1990), 130.

162. Leonard Oppenheim, "Civil Liberties Doctrines of Mr. Justice Holmes and Mr. Justice Cardozo," *Tulane Law Review* 20 (1945): 194.

163. Felix Frankfurter, *Mr. Justice Holmes and the Supreme Court* (Cambridge, MA: Harvard University Press, 1938), 54-55..

164. Samuel Walker, *In Defense of American Liberty: A History of the ACLU, Second Edition* (Southern Illinois University Press, 1999), 27.

165. James F. Fagan, Jr., *"Abrams v. United States*: Remembering the Authors of Both Opinions," *Touro Law Review* 8 (1992): 454.

166. David Cole, "Agon at Agora: Creative Misreadings in the First Amendment Tradition," *Yale Law Journal* 95 (1986): 882.

167. 249 U.S. 47 (1919).

168. 249 U.S. 211 (1919).

169. Robert Cover, "The Left, the Right, and the First Amendment: 1918-1928," *Maryland Law Review* 95 (1981): 373.

170. See generally Fred D. Ragan. See also Feldman, "Free Speech," 229-34.

171. Healy, *Great Dissent*, 203.

172. Ibid.

173. Ibid.

174. Poirier, *Poetry*, 38.

175. Poirier, *Poetry*, 60.

176. *Abrams* 250 U.S. 616 (1919) at 630.

177. Healy, *Great Dissent*, 204-6.

178. Poirier, *Poetry*, 54.

179. Poirier, *Poetry*, 51.

180. Healy, *Great Dissent*, 206.

181. Baker, *Justice*, 539.

182. *Abrams* 250 U.S. 616 (1919) at 630.

183. Poirier, *Poetry*, 137.

184. Richardson, *Natural History*, 6.

185. Emily Dickinson, *The Selected Poems of Emily Dickenson* (Hertfordshire, United Kingdom: Worsdsworth Editions, Ltd., 1994), 171.

186. Cole, "Agon," 887.

187. Vincent Blasi, "Reading Holmes through the Lens of Schauer: The Abrams Dissent," *Notre Dame Law Review* 72 (1997): 1343.

188. Danisch, "Aphorism," 224.

189. Danisch, "Aphorism," 226; emphasis added.

190. Mennel and Compston, *Holmes and Frankfurter*, 75.

191. Some examples are *Dennis*, Brandenburg v. Ohio, 395 U.S. 444 (1969) at 451-52; New York Times Co. v. Sullivan 376 U.S. 254 (1964) at 276; *Winters* 333 U.S. at 540; Thornhill v. State of Alabama, 310 U.S. 88 (1940) at 105; Curtis Pub. Co. 388 U.S. 130 (1967) at 148-49; First Nat. Bank of Boston, 435 U.S. 765 (1978) at 790-91. These together represent a mere sampling; other United States Supreme Court cases reference *Abrams*, 250 U.S.

192. Oliver Wendell Holmes, Jr. to James Bradley Thayer, December 11, 1898, Harvard University Holmes Digital Suite, Mark DeWolfe Howe's research materials on Holmes, 1858-1968: Finding Aid, Thayer, James Bradley, 1890-1900, online.

193. Ibid.

194. Biddle, *Mr. Justice Holmes*, 163.

195. Danisch, "Aphorism," 234.

196. Healy, *Great Dissent*, 209.

197. Ibid.

198. Ibid.

199. Ibid.

200. Healy, *Great Dissent*, 249.

201. Healy, *Great Dissent*, 250.

202. Ibid.

203. Ibid.

204. Danisch, "Aphorism," 231; emphasis added.

205. Ibid.; emphasis added.

206. Tyson & Brother v. Banton, 273 U.S. 418 (1927).

207. *Tyson* 273 U.S. 418 (1927) at 429.

208. *Tyson* 273 U.S. 418 (1927) at 445.

209. Oliver Wendell Holmes, Jr. to Baroness Marie Moncheur, July 16, 1910, Harvard University Holmes Digital Suite, Mark DeWolfe Howe's research materials on Holmes, 1858-1968: Finding Aid, October 1909-1910, online.

210. Danisch, "Aphorism," 228.

211. Ibid.

212. Danisch, "Aphorism," 225.

213. Danisch, "Aphorism," 233.

214. Ibid.

215. *Tyson* 273 U.S. 418 (1927) at 447.

216. Levin, *Poetics*, xii.

217. *Tyson* 273 U.S. 418 (1927) at 445.

218. *Tyson* 273 U.S. 418 (1927) at 446.

219. Ibid.

220. *Tyson* 273 U.S. 418 (1927) at 446-47.

221. *Tyson* 273 U.S. 418 (1927) at 445-46; emphasis added.

222. *Tyson* 273 U.S. 418 (1927) at 447.

223. Poirier, *Poetry*, 54.

224. Levin, *Poetics*, 2.

225. Olsen v. State of Nebraska ex rel. Western Reference and Bond Association, 313 U.S. 236 (1941).

226. Nebbia v. People of New York, 291 U.S. 502 (1934).

227. Gold v. DiCarlo, 235 F. Supp. 817 (S.D.N.Y. 1964).

228. State v. Cardwell, 20 Conn. L. Rpt. 292 [not reported in A.2d] (1997).

229. People v. Rosenblatt, 667 N.Y.S. 2d 886 [slip op. 97674] (N.Y. 1997).

230. New Jersey Association of Ticket Brokers v. Ticketron, 226 N.J. Super 155, 543 A.2d 997 (1988).

231. People v. Concert Connection, Ltd., 211 A.D.2d 310, 629 N.Y.S.2d 254 (1995).

232. Arlotta v. Bradley Center, 349 F.3d 517 (7th Cir. 2003).

233. Blue v. McBride, 252 Kan. 894, 850 P.2d 852 (Kan. 1993).

234. Poirier, *Poetry*, 131.

235. Poirier, *Poetry*, 135.

236. Poirier, *Poetry*, 148.

237. Poirier, *Poetry*, 150.

238. Danisch, "Aphorism," 231.

239. Holmes, "Path of Law," 468.

240. Holmes, "Ideals," 5.

241. Danisch, "Aphorism," 228.

242. Holmes, *Common Law*, 1.

243. Danisch, "Aphorism," 221.

244. Posner, *Law and Literature*, 271.

245. Danisch, "Aphorism," 220.

246. Poirier, *Poetry*, 3–4.

3

Canon Formation and the Marketplace of Ideas

Clair L'Heureux-Dubé, a former justice on the Supreme Court of Canada, has argued that dissents have prophetic potential and reflect the complexity of judicial reasoning, a complexity that is, she suggests, more necessary than unanimity for the evolution of the law.[1] She adopts former United States Supreme Court Chief Justice Charles Evans Hughes's proverb that a "dissent in a court of last resort" is "an appeal to the brooding spirit of the law, to the intelligence of a future day, when a later decision may possibly correct the error into which the dissenting judge believes the court to have been betrayed."[2] She suggests, moreover, that dissents are unlike the monovocal Gregorian chants sung by Medieval European choirs, in that dissents sound "new melodies" in a "polyphonic world"[3] and enable courts to speak with "a plurality of voices."[4] L'Heureux-Dubé's proposition that dissents facilitate constructive deviations among case precedents comports with the arguments made in my earlier chapters that dissents ensure the continuity of the common-law system by making possible judicial malleability and reproductive variation among legal principles. The common law is as much about building room for new institutions consistent with changed values and traditions as it is about sustaining the residual form of the old institutions and their outmoded values and traditions. The aesthetic liberties that Holmes took in his dissents on the First Amendment underscore the liberty to speak that he sought to protect with those dissents. Holmes's dissents ensured that the system had some "play" in the "joints."[5]

L'Heureux-Dubé's commentary about dissents resonates with the idea proffered in earlier chapters that agon has the potential to generate societal progress and creative jurisprudence—or what L'Heureux-Dubé refers to as "a blossoming of legal concepts and solutions."[6] Maintaining what appear to be irresolvable tensions prevents one absolutism or essentialism from dominating another by force or by the threat of force; such tensions tend to correct each other or to cancel each other out.

The process of creating and sustaining a binding legal canon involves agonistic struggles similar to those that characterize the gradual formation of literary canons. Harold Bloom's declaration that there "can be no strong, canonical writing without the process of literary influence, a process vexing to undergo and difficult to understand," applies to legal canons as well as to literary canons.[7] Holmes more than any other United States Supreme Court justice substantiates this claim insofar as his influence on the development of the American legal tradition comes in equal measure from his philosophical rigor and his rhetorical force.[8]

Holmes also demonstrates, as earlier chapters have shown, that judicial dissents can be a literary genre. The canon formation resulting from Holmes's dissents reveals an interesting connection between the common-law system of sorting through judicial precedents and Bloom's observation that "[a]ny strong literary work creatively misreads and therefore misinterprets a precursor text or texts."[9] The connection has to do with the agonistic tensions between case precedents that reveal both the "burden of influence" and the "conflict between past genius and present aspiration" among judges and justices.[10] The same "literary survival" and "canon inclusion" that mark the literary tradition also mark the American constitutional canon.[11] In both canons the tensions between present and past creations enable originality to flourish. As Justice Frankfurter put it, the rhetorical expression of national habits in Holmes's judicial writings "is itself a creative force" for constantly renewing the law, first in the minds of the public and of jurists and then in the formation of new decisions and new precedents.[12]

Like the agonism essential to Bloom's postulations about literary influence, this judicial agonism is paradoxically and simultaneously disabling and enabling; the restrictions it imposes are sources for creative modeling and borrowing. I acknowledge that Bloom's treatment of the canon can be problematic and controversial because of the exclusionary tactics he recommends. His formulation of the Western Canon was a progenitor of the academic culture wars of the late twentieth century. And his allegedly apolitical framing of literary studies is susceptible to fair characterization as political. Nevertheless, those who study the common-law tradition will find his evolutionary approach to canon formation rewarding and possibly more insightful in the context of judge-made opinions. Applying Bloom's evolutionary theories of the canon to opinions of the United States Supreme Court narrows our interpretative focus to the processes rather than the results of canon formation, bypasses heated polemics about the importation of politics to literary study, and, because of the inherently political nature of the law, avoids any pretense that the text object can be isolated from political considerations.

It is the aim of this chapter to approach dissents as seeds planted for the growth of the legal system and to consider the agonistic nature of the legal canon, which drives abstract jurisprudence toward practical applications within changing social and political environments. This chapter also brings together the salient arguments of the preceding chapters by uniting the themes of agonism, creativity and aesthetics, precedent, evolutionary struggle, and constructive competition. Keeping pace with fluctuating social conditions and technological advances, the common-law system incorporates and has adjusted to new customs and activities with which dissenting viewpoints have corresponded and may eventually correspond. Because he recognized the meliorative potential of the common-law system, Holmes authored creative, aesthetic dissents to ensure a productive tension between permanence and stability on the one hand and adaptation and flexibility on the other.

This chapter begins by examining the Darwinian processes of canon formation to suggest that the so-called prophetic quality of Holmes's writing is attributable, in part, to its rhetorical style. The canon versus anti-canon paradigm for classifying decisions of the United States Supreme Court substantiates Holmes's theories about the evolutionary disposition of the common-law system within a constitutional framework. It also highlights parallels between theories of common-law formation and Bloom's theories of canon formation as they pertain to heroism, greatness, influence, staying power, and continuity. Having contextualized Holmes's common-law theories in terms of canon formation, this chapter then turns to Holmes's writing on freedom of speech and the First Amendment to demonstrate that, consistent with his evolutionary approach to the common law, Holmes saw the free interplay of varying ideas as requisite to the constructive advancement of society. In his view the agonism that inheres in a system of free expression neutralizes conflict by allowing a critical mass of opinion to moderate extreme ideologies and to enable more profitable claims to win out over their less advantageous competition. Holmes was a warrior who enlisted martial language and metaphor in his writings, yet his agonism is about peace, not violence; it restrains conflict at the level of rhetoric and discourse rather than instigating physical aggression.[13] The common-law paradigm is thus an antecedent theoretical cognate to Holmes's First-Amendment jurisprudence.

A renewed appreciation for the peacefulness at the core of Holmes's free-speech jurisprudence requires a teasing out of Holmes's complicated understanding of the most violent conflict of his life: the Civil War.

Accordingly, I round out the chapter with a discussion of Holmes's "bet-tabilitarianism," which supplies the best premise from which to approach Holmes's attitude toward the Civil War. Defined at length later in the chapter, "bettabilitarianism" is Holmes's notion that lived experiences combine to form valid inferences from which we rationally deliberate, or bet, about the place of our actions and beliefs in the complex order of the cosmos. A thrice-wounded veteran, Holmes identified with the average, unranked soldier, who was, he thought, a noble victim of the ideological certitude of his more powerful superiors. Insofar as the common-law system consisted of decentralized networks of jurists responding to residual customs and communal assent rather than legislative or parliamentary imperatives, it stood in marked contrast to the military system whereby the top-down commands of centralized powers (the president and his generals and officers) controlled and disposed of the lives of inferiors and disregarded the antagonistic sentiments within lower ranks. Judges in the common-law system were accountable to ordinary people in a way that military leaders were not. Therefore, Holmes believed that the common-law system, being responsive to the community, minimized violence, whereas the military system, in which a small elect commanded orders to the community, maximized violence.

HOLMES AS "PROPHET"

Holmes has often been described in reverential terms as a prophetic judge. L'Heureux-Dubé refers to Holmes as a "great dissenter" because he "embodied the role of the prophetic dissenting judge."[14] Justice Benjamin Cardozo memorialized Holmes as a "philosopher" and a "seer."[15] G. Edward White attached to Holmes the label of "inspiring judge,"[16] "prophet,"[17] and "visionary,"[18] and Holmes has been dubbed "an agnostic prophet to an agnostic age."[19] Holmes has emerged in the American constitutional canon as a "prophet" whose words are "quoted with almost Biblical reverence."[20] What did he produce that he should be likened to a prophet or a visionary or a seer? The answer involves a key element of American pragmatism, what Cornel West calls the "future-oriented instrumentalism that tries to deploy thought as a weapon to enable more effective action."[21]

The inherently pragmatic and instrumental common-law system is forward-looking and future-oriented inasmuch as it concerns itself with the reception and extension of judicial precedents by the legal community and especially by future judges and justices. Dissents add to the store of options and resources that judges and justices are obligated to consult before issuing an opinion that gives normative preference to one rule or assemblage of rules over another. The primary role of a dissent in the common-law system is to provide accessible alternatives so that when abrupt transitions of culture and business necessitate shifts in legal paradigms, there remains a substitute theory to meet new needs.

The free interplay between dissenting and majority opinions results in canon construction. The law is essentially a process of canon formation and continuation, because the whole practice involves calling on the authority of specific past rules or precedents to determine the outcome of any specific case.[22] As Hutchinson explains, "[g]reat cases" are "the heart and soul of the common law"[23] and become canonized when they demonstrate pragmatically the ability of the common law to keep up with and respond to changes in the moral attitudes and social order of the nation.[24] Judges and justices inherit rules and principles that are approved by their workability and that reflect the acquired characteristics of everyday social systems within a given jurisdiction. These rules and principles are embodied in common-law precedents that evolve even as they draw from tradition and modify historical standards and norms. Judges and justices must predict which heritable traits of different rules and principles are most advantageous for the legal system now and in the future. When they are faced with competing paradigms in the form of prior majority opinions and dissents, judges and justices must choose which paradigm is operative and profitable in light of the facts at hand and must locate their decision in both custom and reason while balancing demands for stability with demands for adaptation. This process entails predictions, or "prophecies": how will a rule or principle obtain in society if it alters slightly the normative guides that are authorized by the accretion of case precedents? What will it mean for the durability and credibility of the law if certain canonical opinions are challenged by judges and justices as unreasonable, impracticable, or obsolete?

Holmes recognized that, on account of the agonistic manner in which canons are constructed and sustained, there is a prophetic element to judicial writing. He maintained that the law consisted of the "*prophesies of what the courts will do in fact*"[25] as well as the "scattered prophecies of the past."[26] In this respect, and perhaps only in this respect, religious and legal canons operate according to similar modes of development and implicate what Bloom calls "the true Emersonian test for the American religion," which is that such religion cannot gain its status "*until it first is canonized as American literature.*"[27] Holmes's dissents have been canonized as legal masterpieces because of their literary and rhetorical distinction, and Bloom's point, which is relevant to Holmes's style as a vehicle to legal authority, seems to be that a particular, subsidiary canon tailored to literary merit is different from the larger, more general canon rooted in pragmatic utility and widespread acceptance. "Poetry and criticism," Bloom expounds on this score—and he might have added judicial opinions and dissents to these genres—"are useful not for what they really are, but for whatever poetic and critical use you can usurp them to."[28] Bloom styles this formulation "wholly pragmatic."[29] It suggests that texts comprising the literary canon are not inherently or intrinsically canonical but must be made canonical by future readers; those works that continue to compel, move, and attract future readers outlast their competition in the struggle for survival. Although there is nothing inherent in a case that can ensure that it will form a part of the canon, the history of Holmes's dissents suggests that a memorable style and sound can attract readers and generate discussion and thereby increase the likelihood that a dissent will become canonical.[30]

Bloom is sometimes unfairly maligned as the promoter of a fixed canon when in fact he treats the canon as open and fluctuating and always evolving. He does, however, argue for demonstrably fixed standards by which canonical texts should be measured and suggests that the canon is stable, although never unchanging. The distinction between his treatment of the canon and his standards for canonicity is important because it means that the canon is not set and static. But implicit in Bloom's theory of the canon is the warning that, if we discard the good and proper standards by which to measure the lasting value of literature, we risk the degeneration of the canon and the concomitant loss of knowledge about the survival probability of texts.

Richard Posner, who is known for his unique contributions to the legal canon, shares Bloom's belief that "the survival of works of literature is, broadly speaking, Darwinian."[31] He explains that if there is any one thing that causes a text to enter the canon, it is probably the text's flexibility or ambiguity and usefulness to people writing under the unforeseeable cultural circumstances of the future.[32] The workings of the literary canon as described by Posner mirror the workings of the legal canon, in which a case becomes canonical simply because people (especially lawyers and judges) in the future *use it* as canonical.[33] The ambiguity to which Posner refers with regard to the literary canon has its counterpart in the ambiguities or vagaries that dissents necessarily produce in the common-law system. Dissents cause ambiguity by undermining the authority of the majority position and by preserving viable alternatives to it. Logical soundness and syllogistic reasoning are only equally or possibly even less important to the survival of a literary or legal text than is its ability to interest and attract future readers.[34] And therefore, a memorable or literary style can help a case to gain canonicity by reaching future legal writers' ears and inkwells.[35]

The Darwinian pragmatics of Bloom's and Posner's theories are more evident in legal decisions than in works of imaginative literature such as novels or poems because legal decisions more obviously and practically demonstrate their influence in the workaday world. A law is meaningless unless and until it regulates social behavior; the value and effect of a legal canon is unclear until its role in the social sphere can be ascertained.

The canonical status of both literary and legal texts depends upon the customs and traditions of the people to whom the texts are directed. Like a literary text, a legal opinion or dissent becomes canonical when by general consensus it represents an accepted source of cultural authority on which most people rely when making decisions about how to act or what to believe. However, the failure or refusal to accept the legal canon as authoritative or to act in accordance with its mandates may trigger punitive consequences meted out by the government. By contrast, there are no punitive consequences meted out by the government for the failure or refusal of ordinary citizens to acknowledge or to follow the authority of the literary canon. Lacking any centralized enforcement mechanism or apparatus, the literary canon is looser and more permeable than the legal canon, even if it functions in a similar manner: shifting and improvising, revising and resituating, adapting and modifying, incorporating and discarding.

Holmes's prophetic voice and vision have elevated him to the status of a cultural hero figure, symbolic of the great traditions of American law and lawyers.[36] Holmes's canonization came not only from the appeal of his writing but also from his usefulness to the Progressives.[37] Both parties benefited from their mutual admiration. Progressive journalists, with whom Holmes disagreed about most things, canonized Holmes because, in the pursuit of their own political goals, they found ways to use him as a symbol of what they wanted the Supreme Court to be, and what they wanted the Constitution to mean.[38]

The canonization of Holmes was a singular event in that he marked a shift in the cultural currency of the United States Supreme Court.[39] No legal figure besides Holmes has become a prominent symbol of American culture.[40] And not since Chief Justice John Marshall had a justice on the United States Supreme Court been elevated as a symbol for a mode of jurisprudence.[41] The following lines from legal scholar Anita S. Krishnakumar represent a condensed version of a commonly retold narrative about the elevation of Holmes to the status of heroic prophet and his dissents to the status of judicial ideals:

> Holmes's canonization was part and parcel of the project to reconstitute the [Supreme] Court's interpretation of the Fourteenth Amendment. Once the switch in time had effected this reconstitution, and permitted the New Deal to become a pervasive element in American society, commentators began to hail Holmes, not just as their champion of right, but as a "prophet" and a cultural hero.[42]

The canonization of Holmes the man cannot be divorced from the canonization of his judicial writings; the two are reciprocal and mutually reinforcing. If Holmes has achieved the status of a cultural hero or icon, it is because admiring and emulating readers, especially judges, justices, and legal academics, have cultivated that status for him and have encouraged others to read and interpret his work. Holmes's writings gained value and appeal as his image and reputation began to stand for models of constitutional jurisprudence such as judicial restraint, deference to state legislatures, freedom of speech, and common-law processes and procedures. The fact that Holmes authored a dissent invested that dissent with authority notwithstanding the coherence, cogency, or validity of the argument itself.[43] The stature of Holmes's judicial opinions and dissents magnified and spread as more commentators began to recycle praises of his jurisprudence and to mythologize his influence on constitutional law. As Holmes became a symbol of justice and fairness, wisdom and excellence, restraint and moderation, his opinions and dissents gained force and influence. By decorating his opinions and dissents with unique and memorable language, he called attention to his style, enhanced his reputation, and slowly gained his spot in the American constitutional canon.

CANON AND ANTI-CANON

The concept of the common-law canon bifurcates into two categories: the canon itself, and the anti-canon. An understanding of canon is requisite to an understanding of the anti-canon. Holmes's position as a United States Supreme Court justice situated his judicial writings within the *constitutional canons* that have received more scholarly attention than the canons of particular areas of law—for instance, torts or contracts or criminal law, disciplinary categories that interest mainly practitioners and specialists. A constitutional canon is a "set of greatly authoritative texts that above all others shape the nature and development of constitutional law."[44] Those authoritative texts are excerpted and aggregated in casebooks and hornbooks to be used by law students and legal academics and in treatises to be used by the practicing bar, including the courts. The purpose of a legal canon in casebooks is chiefly pedagogical. The creators of casebooks determine which cases students need to absorb in order to be properly prepared as lawyers. The purpose of a legal canon in treatises is chiefly practical: lawyers, judges, and justices consult treatises for summaries of the prevailing rules and practices within certain jurisdictions.[45]

A constitutional anti-canon stands in contrast to a constitutional canon because it represents a set of important but regretted legal decisions that have been overturned.[46] In the history of the United States Supreme

Court, anti-canonical cases include *Dred Scott v. Sandford* (1857), *Plessy v. Ferguson* (1896), *Lochner v. New York* (1905), and *Korematsu v. United States* (1944).[47] The anti-canon reflects the "dual structure" of the constitutional canon[48] that distinguishes a legal canon from a literary or religious canon. A literary or a religious canon tends to preserve only what is considered best. A legal canon must also preserve decisions and legislations that are believed in hindsight to be reprehensible.[49] Jamal Greene explains that the anti-canon is the body of decisions in which the Supreme Court has done an "especially poor job" of drawing on the common-law traditions and adapting them to present circumstances.[50] To understand the basics of American constitutional law, it is necessary to master texts in both the canon and the anti-canon. Establishing the canon versus anti-canon paradigm yields an agonistic frame of reference for explaining how competing legal positions can orchestrate social coordination despite the variety of rules they recommend. The canonical and the anti-canonical by their very opposition create the potential for alternating authorities that guide the interactions of people and communities. Although some anti-canonical opinions may be possible to revive as law, most will fall into disuse to allow another form of opposition to take their place.

The undesirable qualities of cases in the anti-canon can be set off by dissenting opinions that are viewed more favorably by later audiences; these dissents provide choice and diversity for later judges and justices who must select the right rules and rationales for their opinions. When later courts vindicate or validate the legal arguments of a dissent about a matter with immediate importance or vast ramifications, the dissent becomes canonized.[51] Every time a jurist uses a dissent as if it were a canonical authority, he or she implicitly reasserts that the canon of the common law is mutable. This is because every dissent, by its nature and function, was at one time not authoritative.[52] The dissent becomes canonized by transitioning from being a memorable, non-binding legal argument to being a vindicated, binding legal argument. Such canonization arises as a result of the anti-canonical reasoning embedded in the majority opinion; the canonical and the anti-canonical are therefore mutually exclusive and yet dependent upon one another.

Any theory that attempts to determine which dissents have the potential for canonicity based on some property inherent in the dissent is limited.[53] The canonicity or redeemability of a dissent comes not from the dissent itself but from later decisions that, as Richard Primus puts it, "restructure the constitutional canon by reversing yoked pairs."[54] This yoked-pairs model is another name for what I have been calling agonism. It indicates that the very structure of the common-law constitutional canon and the dissents therein creates the ineradicable possibility that some past dissent will be redeemed and some past canonical decision will become anti-canonical.[55] Under this model, every canonical text is linked to an anti-canonical text; every prevailing argument has a corresponding non-prevailing argument: "The argument that the court adopted and the argument that it rejected are bound together [. . .], and the judicial canon is composed not just of a series of free-standing texts but of a series of members of yoked pairs, each canonical text dragging its partner along with it."[56] The purpose and function of dissents make them "presumptively members of yoked pairs" and "natural candidates for being made authoritative and even canonical." Primus echoes Bloom and Posner in stating that canonicity happens to a text and is not built into the text. In Primus's paradigm, the potential of a dissent is not in its supposedly self-contained, independent features cut off from the externalities of human activity but in its capacity to interact with some future community by contributing to ongoing legal conversations.

Primus writes that the "role of dissenter is conducive to heroism" inasmuch as "it is in the struggle with adversity that [. . .] heroism is established."[57] This theory of the hero in Primus's writing is comparable to Bloom's theory of the genius. The measure of genius, according to Bloom, is vitality.[58] In language similar to that which I have used to describe Holmes's evolutionary paradigm of the common law, Bloom argues that for a writer, drawing on the ideas and style of past authors increases the chances of one's own work surviving in the public imagination. Like Emersonian superfluity as described by Richard Poirier, Bloom's genius is characterized by the urge "to beget" and to "cause to be born," invoking great themes of the past in order to shape the minds of readers in the future.[59]

Bloom's and Posner's notion of canonicity harmonizes with Ross Posnock's pragmatic exposition of the "politics of nonidentity" apparent in the philosophical and literary principles that worked for both Henry and William James. Posnock alleges that social life is necessarily an agonistic experience not unlike the dialectic of dissenting and majority opinions.[60] The cosmopolitan James brothers resisted the homogenizing rush to assimilate and synthesize the assorted mores, practices, and attitudes of disparate and even alien communities into monistic units and preferred, at least in theory, to balance the competing varieties of human experience within divided jurisdictions, permitting social and economic interaction and coordination among anonymous actors to shape the overall polity. Henry James moves between psychic and subjective categories and habits of mind and cuts across totalizing labels and states of inquiry, disrupting his chosen identity as soon as he adopts it. His openness toward alien peoples and cultures is pragmatic because it reveals an "inordinate receptivity" that "replaces theory with practice, the a priori with contingency, clarity with shock, information with immersion."[61] Henry James thus wrote and lived "between cultures"[62] in a manner that was congruous with his brother William James's unwillingness to be subsumed to any political labels and his dogged insistence on open, conversational inquiry, "which conceives the aim of politics to be the circulation of differences rather than their imperial subjugation."[63]

Holmes's skeptical, hands-off jurisprudence is similar to this Jamesian politics of nonidentity, committed to no political program or partisan creed but deferential to the composite will of unlike, far-off communities. This will is reflected in the legislative enactments of elected representatives who derive their power from local majorities. An unaffiliated, uncommitted Holmes could, without passing judgment on the wisdom or goodness of local laws, stare into the laboratories of state legislatures and uphold any statutory scheme that did not clearly offend constitutional provisions. Holmes, like the James brothers, considered himself a residuum, or a cultural leftover, who worried about the capacity of American society and institutions to absorb the alien "into a homogenous social order."[64] Cognizant of the unpredictability of the future, Holmes and the James brothers offered an alternative to the absolutist dream of a central, final law for all places and times.[65] Holmes did this by eschewing the totalizing certitude of natural-law theories used to justify imperial expansion of the kind that the James brothers denounced in Theodore Roosevelt's international military policy.[66] While the James brothers found "incongruity and contradiction crucial to their identities," Holmes fashioned a jurisprudence of abjectness and submissiveness that simply accepted the hereditary variety of local laws as evidence of natural, unconscious selection, guided by different legislatures that responded to the disparate norms and behaviors within their jurisdiction, with the sifting and sieving electoral processes always ensuring that representatives remained just that: representative of the characteristic features of the community.

JUDICIAL AESTHETICS

Primus's model of heroism in which every dissenter needs an adversary,[67]and in which "the holding of a dissent is retrospectively created"[68] accords with my argument that agonism as represented by dissents energizes the common-law system by facilitating necessary changes in jurisprudence. Primus rejects the commonly held idea that dissents are necessarily more literary than majority opinions, but he acknowledges that some dissents are wonderfully literary and that dissents as a class tend to be thought of as a literary form.[69] Primus is right that by itself "literary merit is a slim reed on which to rest a theory of redeemed dissent"[70] and that some redeemed dissents, most notably Justice Harlan's in *Plessy v. Ferguson*, are hardly literary *tours de force*.[71] But literary merit alone does not bring about vindication; rather, the literary qualities of a dissent draw attention to the reasoning that is itself worthy of vindication but likely to be ignored absent some aesthetic dressing. A literary opinion that is irrational or unsound is not likely to be redeemed. The coupling of sound argument with aesthetics, however, increases the probability of a dissent's vindication and contributes to the heroic reputation of the author of the dissent. Holmes's literary aptitude, accordingly, is not the sole cause of the vindication of his dissents but merely a contributing factor. The anxiety of influence for a judge or justice "is assuaged insofar as legitimacy rests on following precedent, but it is exacerbated to the extent that greatness lies in breaking from precedent."[72] The tension between the organic and dynamic methods of adjudication in the common-law system and the need for order and stability among case precedents compels judges and justices to exercise a principled creativity. Those judges and justices who are inclined to institute changes in rules and principles while also attending to landmark antecedents are more likely to generate memorable and lasting opinions or dissents. There is little reason to doubt that what Bloom says of the anxiety of influence applies to jurists to the same degree as to strong poets: both jurists and poets are concerned "not that one's proper space has been usurped already, but that greatness may be unable to renew itself, that one's inspiration may be larger than one's own powers of realization."[73] Such anxiety of influence is no doubt heightened for those dissenting judges and justices who already have a sense that their arguments and interpretations have been rejected by the majority.

As Bloom suggests, value, whether of literature or of dissents, "has much to do with the idiosyncratic, with the excess by which meaning gets started."[74] Value proves itself over time, either running its course or advancing in gradual stages. In the common-law system, the value of an opinion or dissent is determined by the constant struggle of the canonical versus the anti-canonical, the precedential versus the novel, and the rule versus the exception. To guarantee that the legal system continues to grow in keeping with the values and priorities of society, prophetic judges like Holmes will dissent: the textual record thus will retain whatever advantageous traits preserve and generate practices that effectively govern human activity. Although dissents do not constitute *binding* precedents, they are nevertheless precedents. Judges and justices who believe their theory is superior to the majority's must register their position in a dissent to safeguard it for future consideration. The failure to preserve constructive legal theory in a dissent leaves future judges and justices without a textual basis for vindicating that theory.

VINDICATION AND THE MARKETPLACE OF IDEAS

The vindication of Holmes's dissents demonstrates the value of preserving legal theories that happen to be rejected by a majority at a particular moment. Such vindications are most apparent in Holmes's First Amendment jurisprudence regarding freedom of speech and expression in part because the presence of the First Amendment in our constitutional order indicates why dissents are so important in our legal tradition.[75] The jurisprudence of the First Amendment, after all, is based on the protection of the rights of the minority.[76] And the dissenter is almost by definition in the minority and in need of protection.[77] Holmes saw the need for such protection and for ensuring that the First Amendment "clears the field for antithetical battle and affirms the place of such struggles in the self-governance of the nation."[78] His First Amendment jurisprudence is a signpost for all who came after him; it warns of the disabling consequences of attempts to eliminate political opposition.

In a case involving college students who had distributed leaflets critical of the university administration, Justice Thurgood Marshall had this to say regarding the vindication of Holmes's writings on the First Amendment:

> It seems to me altogether too late in the constitutional history of this country to argue that individuals can properly be punished for pamphleteering[.] [. . .] These pamphlets are similar in some ways to the broadsides circulated by popular writers in England and the Colonies, official suppression of which helped lead to adoption of the First Amendment; to the writings of Republican polemicists, against which the Sedition Act prosecutions were aimed—prosecutions this Court has said violated the First Amendment [citation omitted]; and to leaflets distributed by protestors during the First World War and the 1920's, which evoked *the classic opinions* of Holmes and Brandeis, *since vindicated by history*, upon which so much of our law of free speech and the press is based.[79]

Justice Marshall verifies that Holmes's First Amendment dissents have become classic or canonical as well as vindicated. He adduces as evidence Holmes's dissents in *Abrams v. United States* and *Gitlow v. New York*.

Justice Marshall is not alone among United States Supreme Court justices in announcing Holmes's dissents to be thoroughly vindicated. Shortly after Holmes's death, in *Craig v. Harney*, Justice Frankfurter wrote in his own dissent that the "Court minimizes these findings by pointing to a likeness between them and those that were made in *Toledo Newspaper Co. v. United States* [citation omitted], and found inadequate by Mr. Justice Holmes' dissent, an inadequacy subsequently supported by our decision in *Nye v. United States*."[80]

Holmes's notion of free speech changed over time, most notably in a series of cases decided in 1918 and 1919.[81] In *Toledo Newspaper Company v. United States* (1918),[82] Holmes dissented from the majority's affirmance of a lower court's criminal conviction of a newspaper company for allegedly obstructing that court's ability to discharge its duties. The case involved a popular newspaper that had published articles about pending litigation regarding a railroad company and its creditors; according to the trial court, the articles attempted to incite readers, intimidate the judge, and turn the public against the creditors, who had sought an injunction against the railroad company. The trial court found the newspaper guilty of criminal contempt. Refusing to overturn the trial court, Chief Justice White, writing for the majority, rejected what he characterized as the notion that "the freedom of the press is the freedom to do wrong with impunity" that itself "implies the right to frustrate and defeat the discharge of those governmental duties upon the performance of which the freedom of all, including the press, depends."[83]

Holmes dissented, noting that the statute criminalizing the newspaper's activities had only recently gone into effect and that the newspaper, which was on the popular side of the conflict between the railroad and its creditors, was merely publishing the same type of material it had published before the enactment of the statute. "Misbehavior," Holmes declared, "means something more than adverse comment or disrespect."[84] He pointed out that the danger of violence had been abated and concluded that none of the published materials "would have affected a mind of reasonable fortitude."[85] Although not an ardent call for freedom of expression and far from asserting that freedom of speech and of the press are absolute privileges, Holmes's *Toledo* dissent, which was later vindicated,[86] does undercut a criminal scheme designed to suppress forms of protest. In four subsequent cases, however, Holmes stood on a different side of the free-speech issue.

The first was *Sugarman v. United States* (1919),[87] in which Justice Brandeis, writing for a unanimous court, dismissed for want of jurisdiction an appeal brought by a socialist who had been prosecuted and convicted under the Espionage Act for allegedly inciting insubordination, disloyalty, or mutiny within the United States military. According to Justice Brandeis, the United States Supreme Court could gain jurisdiction over the case only if the ruling of the trial court implicated a substantive constitutional question. Finding that the trial judge's instructions to the jury were proper and hence that no constitutional violation had occurred, Brandeis dismissed the case. Holmes's concurrence in *Sugarman* does not reveal a substantive position on free speech because the Court declined to hear the case on its merits. On the same day, however, the Court decided *Schenck v. United States* (1919),[88] which also involved the Espionage

Act and the conviction of a socialist who had printed and mailed leaflets or circulars urging men to defy the draft during a time of war. Holmes authored the unanimous opinion from which the popular sayings "clear and present danger" and "shouting fire in a crowded theater" originated. "We admit that in many places and in ordinary times," Holmes intoned, "the defendants in saying all that was said in the circular would have been within their constitutional rights. But the character of every act depends upon the circumstances in which it is done."[89] The meaning of an utterance, Holmes seems to suggest, is not only in the words in which it is couched but also in the context in which it is issued. "The most stringent protection of free speech," Holmes continues by way of example, "would not protect a man in falsely shouting fire in a theatre and causing a panic. It does not even protect a man from an injunction against uttering words that may have all the effect of force."[90] So the leaflets or circulars distributed by the socialists during wartime were not protected speech: they were used "in such circumstances" and were "of such as nature as to create a clear and present danger that they [would] bring about the substantive evils that Congress has a right to prevent."[91] Holmes's *Schenck* opinion represents his characteristic if programmatic deference to local legislatures and not his later embrace of free speech and expression.

Holmes's opinions in *Frohwerk v. United States* (1919)[92] and *Debs v. United States* (1919),[93] which, like *Schenck*, were joined by all of the justices on the Court, were released one week after *Sugarman* and *Schenck*. *Frohwerk* involved an appeal of the conviction of Jacob Frohwerk, a journalist in Missouri who had authored 12 newspaper editorials criticizing the involvement of the United States in World War One. The trial court fined and sentenced Frohwerk to 10 years' imprisonment for each of the 12 counts of which he was convicted; the later counts were, the trial court indicated, to run concurrently with the first count. Faced with the issue of whether Frohwerk's conviction under the Espionage Act violated his speech rights under the First Amendment, Holmes answered in the negative, stating that the First Amendment was not "intended to give immunity for every possible use of language."[94] Returning to his fire metaphor, Holmes wrote that, based on the record before the Court, "it is impossible to say that it might not have been found that the circulation of the paper was in quarters where a little breath would be enough to kindle a flame and that the fact was known and relied upon by those who sent the paper out."[95]

His holding in *Debs*, which involved the conviction and sentencing of Eugene Debs, a prominent leader of the Socialist Party of America, was similar. It had "nothing to do," Holmes qualified, with "the main theme of the speech," which "was socialism, its growth, and a prophecy of its ultimate success," but "if a part or the manifest intent of the more general

utterances was to encourage those present to obstruct the recruiting
service and if in the passages such encouragement was directly given,
the immunity of the general theme may not be enough to protect the
speech."[96] These words were directed at the charge that Debs had deliberately interfered with the military recruitment of service-members; the
other charge at issue was that Debs had incited "insubordination, disloyalty, mutiny, and refusal of duty in the military and naval forces of the
United States and with intent so to do delivered, to an assembly of people,
a public speech."[97] Holmes's words effectively upheld Debs's sentence,
and Debs entered prison shortly thereafter.

This series of rulings seems to contradict Holmes's dissent in *Abrams*
(discussed in detail in Chapter 2). The majority holding in *Abrams*
merely tracks Holmes's own prior reasoning on freedom of speech and
the First Amendment. Holmes's position on freedom of speech and the
First Amendment, however, changed considerably. The historical narrative about Holmes's evolved views on the First Amendment has already
received a great deal of scholarly treatment. Of concern to this chapter
are the philosophical ramifications of the First Amendment jurisprudence on which Holmes finally settled. In his book about Holmes's First
Amendment jurisprudence, Thomas Healy describes Holmes's ultimate
stance on the First Amendment, as represented by his *Abrams* dissent,
as a synthesis of Holmes's pragmatism: "[I]t incorporated nearly all the
major themes of his life—his belief in the supremacy of experience over
logic, his strange combination of confidence and doubt, his commitment to Darwinism, his bettabilitarianism, [and] his taste for battle."[98]
Holmes's evolving view of freedom of speech was a reflection of his
pragmatic belief about the manner in which the common-law system,
which accommodated change, already worked. Holmes was "primarily
concerned with a process" that served as the basis for the evolutionary
common-law system "in which those who hold minority views are given
a fighting chance to win over a critical mass and grow into a dominant
force."[99] Holmes's desire to protect freedom of speech stemmed from his
desire to allow dissenting rhetoric to lead to dissenting decision-making
in governments and courts.[100]

Some, like Heyman, have portrayed Holmes's freedom of speech paradigm as bleak and ominous, calling it a "darker vision" that "rejects the
values of human freedom and dignity on which the liberal humanist view
rests" and adding that it "is best understood as part of the struggle for
power between different social groups—a struggle that ultimately can
be resolved only by force."[101] I propose that something emphatically different is true: as long as the inevitable and perpetual battle for power or
leverage remains dialogic and argumentative, and as long as it remains
in the realm of rhetoric and argumentation, it is less likely to succumb to
an unthinking brute force and more likely to marginalize or disempower

extreme, violent positions that cannot thrive or gain momentum amid relentless competition; those who acknowledge and propel the natural processes of sustaining perpetual counterpoints through competitive discourse are more likely to practice and encourage tolerance of different ideas because they are more aware that a variety of viewpoints and rivaling theories brings about, not deadlock or gridlock, but progress—and because such people are more likely to doubt the certainty of their own convictions.

This is the reasoning I believe Holmes to have adopted with regard to freedom of speech. Others agree to varying extent and for similar reasons. Consider the following passages by scholars and jurists about Holmes and freedom of speech. I quote at length because the language of these impressions is as suggestive as the impressions themselves:

Different persons attach differing degrees of importance to matters of politics, religion, art, ethics, and so forth, depending on their individual temperament and the circumstances under which the convictions were initially acquired. [. . .] [I]f we accepted Holmes's proposition that other people's preferences are based on grounds as good as ours, it is hard to justify why they would not have the same entitlement to express them.[102]

[Holmes's] invocation of the market metaphor in the *Abrams* peroration may have been to make the point that truth reduces to choice. Perhaps the imagery that we should take from Holmes's figure of speech is not that of a highly structured price-determining *market* such as a stock exchange, a mechanism designed to achieve plebiscitary and transactional precision, but rather a choice-proliferating market*place*, a site for spontaneous and promiscuous browsing, comparing, tasting, and wishing, a paean to peripatetic subjectivity amid abundance. Applied to ideas, the image evokes intellectual serendipity.[103]

These, then, were the elements of Holmes's argument [in *Abrams*] for tolerance: an acknowledgment, based on experience, that human judgment is fallible; a recognition, thanks to [John Stuart] Mill, that free speech is the necessary predicate on which our bets about the universe must be based; and a conviction, inherited from [Adam] Smith, about the power of free trade and competition to promote the greater good.[104]

[The marketplace of ideas] is the metaphor of probabilistic thinking: the more arrows you shoot at the target, the better sense you will have of the bull's-eye. The more individual variations, the greater the chances that the group will survive. We do not (on Holmes's reasoning) permit the free expression of ideas because some individual may have the right one. We permit free expression because we need the resources of the whole group to get us the ideas we need. Thinking is a social activity. I tolerate your thought because it is part of my thought—even when my thought defines itself in opposition to yours.[105]

These bases for freedom of speech are also the reasons why Holmes contributed dissents to a common-law system that was constitutionally predisposed to vary and adapt: only by introducing diversity among judicial viewpoints can an efficient pattern of social coordination arise. Such diversity minimizes the power of any one judge or group of judges and keeps in check any legal theories that fly in the face of the guiding principles of society. The more viable legal options that are accessible for the legal community in a common-law system, the harder it becomes for any one judge or group of judges to assign values or to impose unwanted rules on their supposed subordinates, and the more feasible it becomes for the corporate needs and demands of society to be met by judicial decisions that are agreeable to most people.

BETTABILITARIANISM AND CIVILIZATION

Counterintuitively, Holmes's call for tolerance complements rather than contradicts his infatuation with military rhetoric. It would be wrong to associate Holmes's glorification of the soldier and his frequent use of martial metaphors with the promotion of violence or death. Holmes reviled the Civil War,[106] which he considered "a hideous human waste."[107] His rejection of certitude as a legitimate or a desirable goal was a reaction to the bloodshed he witnessed firsthand as a first lieutenant in the 20th Massachusetts Volunteer Infantry, a regiment that included his close friend Henry Abbott, who despised Abraham Lincoln and the Emancipation Proclamation, claimed to be a Copperhead, and praised Southern racial ideologies but who nevertheless gave his life in battle for the Union. Men like Abbott taught Holmes to appreciate the strange, irreducible complexity of political and philosophical struggle and to cultivate a legal methodology in which "[c]ertitude is not the test of certainty."[108] "We have," Holmes cautioned elsewhere, "been cocksure of many things that were not so."[109] Although he was famously dedicated to attending the funerals of soldiers, the dedications of war monuments, and the gatherings of veterans,[110] his recollection of the Civil War occasioned not triumphalism or fearsome approval but the skeptical disinterestedness that he believed was essential to the work of a good judge and to the peaceful resolution of conflicts via the common law.[111]

Holmes portrayed the evolution of the Anglo-American legal system in *The Common Law* as progressing from a primitive state in which tribal interests sought to institutionalize revenge through authorized violence to a more mature system that recognized private property rights and the validity and enforcement of contracts as mechanisms for minimizing conflict and for facilitating cooperation; conflict was inevitable even in the mature system, but the way in which it was diffused and mediated reflected the degree of civilization that society had attained. "The degree of civilization which a people has reached, no doubt," he said in a reformulation of the Golden Rule, "is marked by their anxiety to do as they would be done by."[112] Doubt rather than certitude characterized a civilization in which such relationships were common and widespread. "To have doubted one's own first principles," Holmes opined, "is the mark of a civilized man."[113] The certainty of both Southerners and Northerners in their respective causes during the Civil War brought about what Holmes considered to be avoidable death. The law suited Holmes because it could mitigate conflict in a flawed universe where "the *ultimate ratio*, not only *regum*, but of private persons, is force," and where "at the bottom of all private relations, however tempered by sympathy and all the social feelings, is a justifiable self-preference."[114] The law curtailed hostility by guaranteeing that "a man is answerable for all the consequences of his acts, or, in other words, that he acts at his peril always, and wholly irrespective of the state of his consciousness upon the matter."[115]

Louis Menand characterizes Holmes's reaction to the Civil War as follows:

> The moment Holmes returned home from the war, he seems to have fast-frozen his experience, and to have sealed its meaning off from future revision. He told the stories of his wounds for the rest of his life, he recalled former comrades with emotion, and he alluded frequently to the experience of battle in his writings and speeches. But although he read almost every other kind of book imaginable, he could not bear to read histories of the Civil War. He rarely mentioned the issues that had been the reason for the fighting or expressed a political opinion about the outcome. The war had burned a hole, so to speak, in his life. It was a hole he had paid a high price for, and he had no interest in rethinking its significance.[116]

One of Holmes's most famous speeches is his 1884 Memorial Day Address, in which he displays an apparent enthusiasm for the warlike spirit and seems to celebrate the carnage of the sectional conflict that wounded him three times and took the lives of many of his comrades. In the context of his entire *oeuvre*, however, this speech reads less like an apology for violence and more like a demonstration of what he referred to as "enlightened skepticism,"[117] a feature of his "bettabilitarianism" that made him appear agonistically to hold both certainty and uncertainty in his mind at the same time.[118]

Emerson's approach shared this sort of balance between faith and skepticism, and Holmes, like Emerson, was simultaneously a man of conviction and an enthusiastic doubter of certainties.[119] Both men were focused more on the experiences and habits of seeking truth and finding error in daily life than in formal designs or demonstrations of final certainties or even uncompromising skepticisms.[120]

Bettabilitarianism, a play on the word *utilitarianism,* is Holmes's term for the creed that probability and statistical inference narrow our range of guesses about the possible outcomes of actions and events that transpire in this vast and mysterious cosmos. Holmes wrote these clarifying lines about bettabilitarianism in a letter to Sir Frederick Pollock dated August 30, 1919: "Chauncey Wright, a nearly forgotten philosopher of real merit, taught me when young that I must not say *necessary* about the universe, that we don't know whether anything is necessary or not. So I describe myself as a *bet*tabilitarian. I believe that we can *bet* on the behavior of the universe in its contact with us. We bet we can know what it will be."[121] A bettabilitarian is therefore someone who believes that there is no final certainty, only probability, regarding what will happen if we make this choice or that one, take this road or another one.[122] This description recalls Holmes's searching remark in "Natural law" that the "universe has in it more than we understand" so that we are all, with our limited perspective and selective, partial knowledge, like "private soldiers" who "have not been told the plan of campaign, or even that there is one."[123]

The distinction between faith and doubt is discernable in Holmes's exaltation of the soldier as against the politicians and proselytizers who controlled the soldier's fate. Holmes revered the faith of the soldier but doubted the ideological certainty of those who used the soldier for personal gain or to chase an abstract cause.[124] Holmes romanticized Abbott's death in his Memorial Day Address, not to praise fighting and killing but to lament that in war the "boldest were the likeliest to die."[125] He rebuked those "who believe that their idea of civilization is a justification for killing those who decline to share it" and maintained that civilizations "sacrifice their moral advantage" when they "take up arms in order to impose their conception of civility on others." When Holmes crooned in his Memorial Day Address that "the faith is true and adorable which leads a soldier to throw away his life in obedience to a blindly accepted duty, in a cause which he little understands, in a plan of campaign of which he has no notion, under tactics of which he does not see the use," he undoubtedly had in mind Abbott.[126]

Evidence of Holmes's doubt or skepticism is abundant in his many writings. Evidence of his faith is more subtle but still perceptible in his paeans to the virtues of courage, ambition, and soldierly perseverance. Holmes believed that faith and doubt depended on each other and that humans must seek to attain their ideals even though we are doomed to fail.[127] He also considered our philosophies and desires to be products of our environment that cannot be trusted to correspond with absolute truth or moral rightness. "What we most love and revere," he explained, "generally is determined by early associations."[128] "I love granite rocks and barberry bushes," he persisted, "no doubt because with them were my earliest joys that reach back through the past eternity of my life. But while one's experience thus makes certain preferences dogmatic for oneself, recognition of how they came to be leaves one able to see that others [. . .] may be equally dogmatic about something else. And this again means skepticism."[129]

The coexistence of faith and doubt in Holmes's philosophy came in large part from his from experiences in the Civil War.[130] That foundation led him to believe that although one can never be certain that one's ideals are always and everywhere final and true, one must live life with an ardent conviction in those ideals.[131] Holmes summarized this position as follows: "Not that we would not fight and die for [our belief or love] if important—we all, whether we know it or not, are fighting to make the kind of world that we should like—but that we have learned to recognize that others will fight and die to make a different world, with equal sincerity or belief."[132] Society in this view is rife with conflict that necessitates eusociality, a behavioral condition in which members of a civilization learn to work together to secure healthier, safer lives for themselves and their posterity regardless of their divergent principles and fundamental disagreements. Nonviolent resolution guided by laws confers competitive advantages to those societies that pursue and practice it. Nonviolence is a precondition for a society to graduate into a civilization. The devastation of the Civil War was, in Holmes's imagination, a lesson about the fragility of civilization.

His memory of the Civil War led him to promote a fluctuating legal system of predictable and consensus-based rules that restrained violence and engendered tolerance. According to Holmes's common-law paradigm, a person cannot help but have convictions, which can and ought to be pursued, but civilization depends upon the collective awareness that such convictions may not be right. Each individual is an indispensable part of the overall process of social development; if each individual acts on his or her own convictions and pursues his or her own motivations, then the sum of our combined activity will reveal which individual preferences and beliefs yield profitable dividends and which should be abandoned. It follows *a fortiori* that any "sound body of law" should "correspond with the actual feelings and demands of the community, whether right or wrong."[133] Only the common-law system could produce this body of law "based upon a morality which is generally accepted" within a given jurisdiction.[134] This was the system in which Holmes's commitment to nonviolence converged with his views about dissent, agonism, creative expression, freedom of speech, the evolutionary nature of the law, and the need for society to mature into a more advanced and civilized state.

The gradual working out and occasional overturning of judicial precedent in a common-law system depends on free expression and ongoing
conflict between different points of view—expressed most iconically
in the majority and dissenting opinions of the United States Supreme
Court.[135] This agonistic or antithetical method of jurisprudence depends
on present judges rereading, reinterpreting, and thus necessarily mis-
reading the decisions of the past.[136] This fact extends Bloom's theory of
the anxiety of influence beyond any context that he himself has explored.

CONCLUSION

Over time creative misreadings become incorporated in the legal canon
and vested with authority by judges or justices who wish to supplant the
temporary authority of some decisions (soon to become part of the anti-
canon) with updated or superior rules and reasoning. Because freedom
of speech in a common-law system entrusts to the community the power
to formulate the rhetorical antagonisms to which the judiciary must respond, it is also what enables judges and justices to exercise their creative
faculties, at least to the degree that judges and justices may consider
competing binaries against one another dialectically and in furtherance
of binding decisions. Judges and justices are like poets struggling against
the anxiety of influence: they "are sometimes strong, creative misread-
ers of prior texts, and their strength can reroute the path of precedent,
change the meaning of the Constitution or federal law, and become a new
source of anxiety for their descendants."[137] The idea that the interaction of
contending theories and beliefs is socially advantageous can lead a judge
or justice to dissent; the anxiety of influence can cause judges or justices
like Holmes to experiment with superfluities of language, which increase
the probability that the dissent will be reconsidered by others and canonized in textbooks, hornbooks, and treatises—and eventually redeemed by
some future majority.

L'Heureux-Dubé acknowledges John Locke as the source of the observation that "new opinions in law are often suspect and are opposed
for the sole reason that they are not already shared by a majority of the
profession."[138] She agrees with Locke that because of technological, economic, and cultural developments, society is constantly changing and jurisprudence must adapt to fit the new form of the social order.[139] The rules
and principles prevailing in a common-law system are mostly imparted
to judges and justices through the innumerable influences of culture and
training. Obligated by institutional design and sworn duty to uphold and
sustain the precedents that obtain as law within the community, judges
and justices in a common-law system tend to transmit by mechanical

repetition the values and priorities of one age to the next. The law in this sense is little more than an official affirmation of the beliefs and normative character of the jurisdiction in a particular time and place.

Not all times and places are the same, however. Some are chaotic; some are revolutionary; and some so nearly destructive that any attempt to coordinate human action by judicial imperative could result in backlash and organized disobedience. Therefore, to preserve an orthodoxy in times of transition is not always tenable or desirable, especially when exigencies demand adaptation. Dissents can supply fitful alternatives for achieving social coordination and for redirecting society toward a state of relative harmony and cooperation. Dissents represent the sort of constructive competition that enables judges and justices to facilitate profitable collaboration among acting agents within circumstances of unrest. Judicial dissents are themselves forms of unrest that preserve an anticipated response to *potential* unrest; conflict and contention are thus conditions for their own perpetuation. Their exercise within a common-law framework permits the system to grow alongside the changing standards and practices of the social unit. In this respect, dissents can be prophetic. I have argued that Holmes's aesthetic dissents yield appreciable results because of their form and qualities as much as for their reasoning. They are prophetic in that they anticipate future results predicated upon projected changes in values.

The underlying ideal of pragmatism is the recognition that thought is never perfect, final, and permanent but must grow, decay, and transform just as all life must.[140] To the extent that this is true and that Holmes's dissents incorporated this Emersonian approach, we can say that Holmes sought to preserve the welter of differences and alternatives in American common law, seeing in the confused multitudes of jurisdictions and precedents the fecund ground from which new ways of living and lawyering might emerge; thus, the canonization of Holmes's dissents and of Emerson's writings are themselves subject to similar processes of natural selection and creative destruction. Holmes and Emerson represent the type of critics who, even when they "do not modify or revise the Canon," at least "ratify the true work of canonization, which is carried on by the perpetual agon between past and present."[141] Perhaps this judgment is premature. Regardless, Holmes's dissents were instrumental to the emergence of freedom of speech and expression as those concepts are understood today.

Holmes's dissents were seeds planted for future growth. Whether they will continue to hold a place in the legal canon as it develops in the future is not as important as the fact that they have increased the number of variables requisite for the survival of certain legal theories and for the resilience of the common-law system writ large. What matters, in short, is that he was an indispensable part of the process, superfluous as his writing may have been, and that he kept the system moving forward, cycling on, descending by modification, as he elaborately constructed, in his several dissents, alternative forms of logic and reasoning in response to external conditions about which he had little control. For that the American constitutional structure owes to him its very essence.

NOTES

1. Claire L'Heureux-Dubé, "The Dissenting Opinion: Voice of the Future," *Osgoode Hall Law Journal* 38 (2000): 504-9.

2. L'Heureux-Dubé, "Dissenting Opinion," 496.

3. L'Heureux-Dubé, "Dissenting Opinion," 516.

4. L'Heureux-Dubé, "Dissenting Opinion," 496. Legal historian Harold J. Berman makes this very analogy in *Law and Revolution: The Formation of the Western Legal Tradition*: "From the eleventh and twelfth centuries on, monophonic music, reflected chiefly in the Gregorian chant, was gradually supplanted by polyphonic style" (Harold J. Berman, *Law and Revolution: The Formation of the Western Legal Tradition* [Cambridge, MA: Harvard University Press, 1983], 7). Of significance to Holmes's use of sound is Berman's observation that early Germanic and Irish law was written as poetry or in proverbs so that the illiterate public, drawn by the sound of the law, could memorize the rules governing society (Berman, *Law and Revolution*, 59).

5. *Tyson* 273 U.S. 418 (1927) at 446.

6. L'Heureux-Dubé, "Dissenting Opinion," 496.

7. Harold Bloom, *The Western Canon* (New York: Riverhead Books, 1994), 7.

8. Danisch, "Aphorism," 220.

9. Bloom, *Western Canon*, 7.

10. Bloom, *Western Canon*, 8.

11. Ibid.

12. Bloom, *Western Canon*, 63.

13. Holmes's writings on the First Amendment, discussed later in the chapter, substantiate the peacefulness at the core of his jurisprudence of competition.

14. L'Heureux-Dubé, "Dissenting Opinion," 506.

15. Benjamin Cardozo, "Mr. Justice Holmes," *Harvard Law Review* 44 (1931): 684.

16. White, "Canonization," 577.

17. Ibid.

18. White, "Canonization," 578. White uses these labels to refer to both Holmes and Brandeis and in the context of describing the shifting views of Holmes and Brandeis since their time on the bench.

19. Harold R. McKinnon, "The Secret of Mr. Justice Holmes: An Analysis," *American Bar Association Journal* 36 (1950): 345.

20. Scott E. Sundby and Lucy B. Ricca, "The Majestic and the Mundane: The Two Creation Stories of the Exclusionary Rule." *Texas Tech Law Review* 43 (2010): 394.

21. Cornel West, *The American Evasion of Philosophy: A Genealogy of Pragmatism* (Madison, WI: University of Wisconsin Press, 1989), 5.

22. Allan C. Hutchinson, *Evolution and the Common Law* (New York: Cambridge University Press, 2005), 127.

23. Hutchinson, *Evolution*, 126.

24. Hutchinson, *Evolution*, 125.

25. Holmes, "Path of the Law," 461; emphasis added.

26. Holmes, "Path of the Law," 457.

27. Harold Bloom, *Agon: Towards a Theory of Revisionism* (New York: Oxford University Press, 1982), 148; emphasis in original.

28. Bloom, *Agon*, 39.

29. Ibid.

30. Hutchinson, *Evolution*, 128.

31. Posner, *Law and Literature*, 15.

32. Posner, *Law and Literature*, 18.

33. Hutchinson, *Evolution*, 131.

34. See Hutchinson, *Evolution*, 134.

35. Hutchinson, *Evolution*, 139, 145.

36. White, "Canonization," 576-77.

37. Brad Snyder, "The House That Built Holmes," *Law and History Review* 30 (2012): 720.

38. See ibid.

39. White, "Canonization," 576.

40. Mathias Reimann, "Why Holmes?" *Michigan Law Review* 88 (1990): 1916.

41. Ibid.

42. Krishnakumar, "Evolution," 793.

43. Former President of the United States and Chief Justice of the United States Supreme Court William Howard Taft reportedly complained that Holmes "gives more attention to [. . .] his dissents than he does to the opinions he writes for the court, which are very short and not very helpful" (quoted in Lerner, *Mind and Faith*, 132). See also the mention of Taft in the introduction to this book.

Richard Posner has likewise said the following about Holmes's dissent in *Lochner*: "Would the dissent in *Lochner* have received a high grade in a law school examination in 1905? I think not. It is not logically organized, does not join issue sharply with the majority, is not scrupulous in its treatment of the majority opinion or of precedent, is not thoroughly researched, does not exploit the factual record, and is highly unfair to Herbert Spencer, of whom most Americans nowadays know no more than what Holmes told them in the *Lochner* dissent. The dissent also misses an opportunity to take issue with the fundamental premise of the majority opinion, which is that unreasonable statutes violate the due process clause of the Fourteenth Amendment; the dissent is silent on the origin and purpose of the amendment. Indeed, at the end Holmes seems to concede the majority's fundamental (and contestable) premise that the due process clause outlaws unreasonable legislation and to disagree merely with the conclusion that New York's maximum-hours law is unreasonable. The sweeping assertions at the beginning of the dissent are thus discordant with its conclusion. Read as a whole, the opinion does not clearly challenge Lochnerism but just the abuses of Lochnerism.

It is not, in short, a good judicial opinion. It is merely the greatest judicial opinion of the last hundred years" (*Law and Literature*, 271). See also the mention of this passage of Posner in the introduction to this book.

44. Primus, "Canon," 243.

45. Compare J.M. Balkin and Sanford Levinson on legal canons with Bloom on literary canons: Jack M. Balkin and Sanford Levinson, "The Canons of Constitutional Law," *Harvard Law Review* 111 (1998): 968, 983; Bloom, *Western Canon*, 19. The correlation between the legal and literary canons ultimately collapses, but the hermeneutical, conceptual, and analogical benefits of comparing and modeling the two canons justify further investigation into their likeness.

46. Jamal Greene, "The Anticanon," *Harvard Law Review* 125 (2011): 380.

47. Greene, "Anticanon," 380.

48. Primus, "Canon," 245.

49. Ibid.

50. Greene, "Anticanon," 381.

51. "The canonicity of a dissent is not a function of the dissent itself but of the later court or courts that redeem it and make it canonical" (Primus "Canon," 247).

52. Primus, "Canon," 247.

53. Primus, "Canon," 251-52.

54. Primus, "Canon," 252.

55. Ibid.

56. Primus, "Canon," 254.

57. Primus, "Canon," 259.

58. Harold Bloom, *Genius* (New York: Warner Books, 2002), 4.

59. Bloom, *Genius*, 7.

60. Ross Posnock, *The Trial of Curiosity: Henry James, William James, and the Challenge of Modernity* (New York: Oxford University Press, 1991), 5.

61. Posnock, *Trial*, 10.

62. Posnock, *Trial*, 8.

63. Posnock, *Trial*, 16.

64. Ibid.

65. Posnock, *Trial*, 17.

66. Ibid.

67. Primus, "Canon," 259.

68. Primus, "Canon," 284.

69. Primus, "Canon," 267.

70. Primus, "Canon," 268.

71. Primus, "Canon," 269.

72. Cole, *Agon*, 866.

73. Bloom, *Genius*, 6.

74. Harold Bloom, *How to Read and Why* (New York. Simon & Schuster, 2001), 23.

75. Cole, *Agon*, 860.

76. Ibid.

77. Ibid.

78. Cole, *Agon*, 861.

79. Norton v. Discipline Committee of East Tennessee State University, 399 U.S. 906 (1970) at 907; emphasis added.

80. Craig v. Harney, 331 U.S. 367 (1947) at 386.

81. The literature on this subject is so vast that it could not be summarized here. Those interested in the topic might read the account presented by Thomas Healy (2013) in *The Great Dissent: How Oliver Wendell Holmes Changed His Mind—And Changed the History of Free Speech in America.*

82. Toledo Newspaper Company v. United States, 247 U.S. 402 (1918).

83. *Toledo* 247 U.S. 402 (1918) at 419.

84. *Toledo* 247 U.S. 402 (1918) at 423.

85. *Toledo* 247 U.S. 402 (1918) at 425.

86. The *Toledo* majority was overruled by Nye et. al v. U.S., 313 U.S. 33 (1941), which cites Holmes's *Toledo* dissent from which it draws some of its reasoning. The following cases have expressly recognized the overruling of the *Toledo* majority: Atlanta Newspapers, Inc. v. State, 101 Ga. App. 105, 113 S.E. 2d 148 (Ga. App. 1960); In re Grogan, 972 F. Supp. 992 (E.D. Vir. 1997); U.S. v. Rangolan, 464 F. 3d 321 (2nd Cir. 2006); and Weidt v. State, 312 P. 3d 1035 (Wyo. 2013). Of these, *Rangolan* and *Weidt* discuss Holmes's dissent.

87. Sugarman v. United States, 249 U.S. 182 (1919).

88. Schenck v. United States, 249 U.S. 47 (1919).

89. *Schenck* 249 U.S. 47 (1919) at 52.

90. Ibid.

91. Ibid.

92. Frohwerk v. United States, 249 U.S. 204 (1919).

93. Debs v. United States, 249 U.S. 211 (1919).

94. *Frohwerk* 249 U.S. 204 (1919) at 206.

95. *Frohwerk* 249 U.S. 204 (1919) at 209.

96. *Debs* 249 U.S. 211 (1919) at 212-13.

97. *Debs* 249 U.S. 211 (1919) at 212.

98. Healy, *Great Dissent*, 210.

99. Irene M. Ten Cate, "Speech, Truth, and Freedom: An Examination of John Stuart Mill's and Justice Oliver Wendell Holmes's Free Speech Defenses," *Yale Journal of Law & the Humanities* 22 (2010): 40.

100. Ibid.

101. Steven J. Heyman, "The Dark Side of the Force: The Legacy of Justice Holmes for First Amendment Jurisprudence," *William and Mary Bill of Rights Journal* 19 (2011): 664.

102. Cate, "Speech," 48.

103. Blasi, "Holmes," 13.

104. Healy, *Great Dissent*, 206.

105. Louis Menand, *The Metaphysical Club* (New York: Farrar, Straus, Giroux, 2001), 431.

106. Menand, *Metaphysical Club*, 3.

107. Menand, *Metaphysical Club*, 43.

108. Oliver Wendell Holmes Jr., "Natural Law," *Harvard Law Review* 32 (1918-19): 40.

109. Ibid.

110. Baker, *Justice*, 156.
111. Baker, *Justice*, 158.
112. Holmes, *Common Law*, 30.
113. Oliver Wendell Holmes Jr., "Ideals and Doubts," *Illinois Law Review* 10 (1915): 1.
114. Holmes, *Common Law*, 30.
115. Holmes, *Common Law*, 54-55.
116. Menand, *Metaphysical Club*, 61.
117. Holmes, "Path of the Law," 469.
118. Reimann, "Why Holmes?" 1916.
119. Levin, *Poetics*, 18.
120. Ibid.
121. Howe, *Holmes-Pollock Letters*, 2:252.
122. Louis Menand, *American Studies* (New York: Farrar, Straus, and Giroux, 2002), 45.
123. Holmes, "Natural Law," 43.
124. Holmes "rate[d] the professionalism and discipline of the soldier higher than the merits of any particular cause" (Menand, *Metaphysical Club*, 43-44).
125. Menand, *Metaphysical Club*, 43.
126. Oliver Wendell Holmes Jr., "Memorial Day Address," in *The Essential Holmes: Selections from the Letters, Speeches, Judicial Opinions, and Other Writings of Oliver Wendell Holmes, Jr.*, edited by Richard Posner (Chicago: University of Chicago Press, 1992), 89.
127. Reimann, "Why Holmes?" 1917.
128. Holmes, "Natural Law," 41.
129. Ibid.
130. Reimann, "Why Holmes?" 1917, 1919.
131. Ibid.
132. Holmes, "Natural Law," 41.
133. Holmes, *Common Law*, 28.
134. Holmes, *Common Law*, 30.
135. Cole, "Agon," 861.
136. Cole, "Agon," 869.
137. Cole, "Agon," 866.
138. L'Heureux-Dubé, "Dissenting Opinion," 504.
139. Ibid.
140. Richardson, *Natural History*, 1, 8.
141. Bloom, *Western Canon*, 486.

4

Holmes and the Differential Reproduction of Emersonian Ideas in a Transitional Era

This book has pointed out that among the operative paradigms for the common law within the American constitutional framework, two take prominence: one that treats the common law as a settled and complete canon of rules unchanged over time, and the other that treats the common law as a process for deciphering malleable and adaptive rules within a fluctuating canon.[1] Although these paradigms of the common law track similar, related debates about whether the United States Constitution should be interpreted as a "living" document or according to its original meaning,[2] they involve a different subject and inquiry: the role of the judge or justice with regard to case precedent derived from custom and practice and the assimilation of cultural norms and standards into the body of rules that governs society. A constitution fixes the parameters within which a judge or justice may interpret rules and precedents, but the methodology of following or revising precedent is still resolved by common-law traditions and hermeneutics to a great extent, even in the United States.[3] The two paradigms for the common law—static and fluid—seem like an irresolvable dichotomy, but they are permeable: in theory both necessarily exclude the other, but in practice the separation is not total and the difference not obvious.

Throughout his legal writing and in his book *The Common Law*, Holmes presented the common law as evolutionary rather than static.[4] In the third paragraph of *The Common Law* he cautioned against the error of "supposing, because an idea seems familiar and natural to us, that it has always been so."[5] His notion of the common law was rooted in "historicism and Darwinian natural selection,"[6] which ground the methods and practices of pragmatism as well.[7] Holmes admired Sir Frederick Pollock, his British pen pal and a popular jurist, and Pollock admired Darwin and modeled his jurisprudence on evolutionary theories. Pollock once stated in a letter to Holmes that "I have been turning over the life of a much greater man, C. Darwin. His letters are about the most fair-minded and charitable a much attached man ever wrote."[8] Harold Laski seemed to be reading Darwin regularly and dashing off missives to Holmes that praised Darwin as a great, brilliant, and gentle man. Frederic R. Kellogg's *Oliver Wendell Holmes, Jr., Legal Theory, and Judicial Restraint* picks up on Holmes's connections to Darwinism and calls attention to the pragmatic qualities of Holmes's evolutionary common-law theories. Kellogg suggests that the common law was for Holmes the instantiation of Darwinian pragmatism. Affirming Kellogg, the present volume has demonstrated that Holmes's stylish and superfluous mode of dissenting revealed, as H. L. A. Hart observed of Holmes's judicial writings, that what is "taken to be settled and stable is really always on the move."[9] Holmes concretized in dissents his conviction that the fittest rules in the common-law system adapt and evolve and that animated, memorable, and sonorous iterations of legal principles facilitate such adaptation and evolution.

The term "pragmatism" was not in wide circulation during the early years of Holmes's long career. Holmes did not declare himself a pragmatist. Nevertheless, the term *pragmatism* gained purchase over the course of the early twentieth century because of such pragmatist thinkers as C.S. Peirce, William James, John Dewey, Chauncey Wright, Jane Addams, George Santayana, and George Herbert Mead. Holmes's pragmatism resounds in his belief that the meaning of law inheres in the practical effects of applying certain rules, that rules are preeminently settled by the observable consequences of their exercise, that abstract pieties and epistemological pretensions are not useful guides for jurists, and that received practices and customs reveal the normative, synthetic cultural patterns to which the common law responds.

Over the years, many writers on Holmes have described his legal methodology as *pragmatist*. In 1943, Paul L. Gregg called attention to Holmes's "delightful literary style"[10] and placed him in the tradition of Peirce and James insofar as Holmes "refers to majority vote as the test of truth."[11] In the 1940s, Holmes's pragmatism underwent pointed reproach and was even accused of sharing the positivist themes and goals of Nazism.[12] But such tendentious exaggerations were counterbalanced by more reasonable and levelheaded assessments just a few years later.[13] Attention to Holmes's pragmatism fell away as general attention to pragmatism fell away during the 1950s, '60s, and '70s. With the explosion of studies on pragmatism in the 1980s and 1990s, scholarship on Holmes began to reconsider his relationship to pragmatism and the pragmatists. In 1990,

Southern California Law Review held a symposium entitled "The Renaissance of Pragmatism in American Legal Thought." Holmes was the catalyst for this renaissance. Six years later a conference on Holmes and pragmatism took place at Brooklyn Law School to commemorate the 100th anniversary of "The Path of the Law." Posner was the keynote speaker. Other speakers included Grey, Catharine Pierce Wells, G. Edward White, and Gary Minda. A flurry of articles on Holmes and legal pragmatism pursued the arguments put forth at the conference.[14] The sudden attention to Holmes led many legal scholars to contemplate the relationship between pragmatism and the American legal system.

But Richard Rorty, seemingly dismissive of the growing interest in pragmatism among legal academics, declared, "I think it is true that by now pragmatism is banal in its application to law."[15] Legal pragmatism seemed banal because, according to Rorty, who was borrowing from Thomas Grey, pragmatism was simply what lawyers and judges do: the school of legal realism that separated law from morals and broke down the "is/ought" distinction in the nature of the law had prevailed, rendering legal formalism and natural-law theory relics of the past. Rorty inveighed that even Ronald Dworkin, who purported to extend natural law theory, or the teachings of neonatural law, committed himself (despite himself) to the pragmatic methods of legal realism. Although judges reach different conclusions using different approaches, Rorty alleged, their methodology is mostly the same or at least substantially similar. What differs is their political vision: They deduce and formulate unlike rules only because they are visionaries of unlike causes.

Louis Menand was the first popular writer to recognize an Emersonian streak in Holmes's pragmatism. Emerson's role as a pragmatist or proto-pragmatist is highly contested, but this book has shown that Holmes more than anyone bears out the pragmatic elements of Emerson's thought. Menand's Pulitzer Prize winning *The Metaphysical Club* generated attention to Holmes's pragmatism as a response to the trauma and suffering of the Civil War and to the burgeoning ideas of Darwinian evolution. Menand also attended to the ways in which Holmes's boyhood "enthusiasm for Emerson never faded" and explained how Holmes's "posture of intellectual isolation" was "essentially Emersonian."[16]

Holmes's position as the originator of legal pragmatism is now well established. Susan Haack[17] has announced that in the disciplines of law and the history of philosophy, Holmes is acknowledged as the first legal pragmatist. And Kellogg has argued persuasively that Holmes's notion of the common law, influenced by such philosophical pragmatists as Chauncey Wright and by the ideas of Darwinian evolution, was new in scholarly writing about the common law—and Holmes himself was aware that what he was doing was new.[18]

It has been said that "it is quite impossible to understand and appreciate the judicial method of Justice Holmes without taking into account the
fact that he was steeped in the tradition of the common law."[19] Holmes's
career spanned some of the most transitional eras of American history;
widely accepted notions of the common law changed during various
periods of his life. Many of those changes are attributable to him.[20] He
pushed American jurisprudence away from the Blackstonian conception
of the common law that had appealed to the founding generation[21] and
that had been dealt a heavy blow by the Civil War and Reconstruction.

Kellogg summarizes Blackstone's conception of the common law as
a fixed entity that is universal,[22] continuous,[23] valid because of its long
standing,[24] and customary.[25] Like Sir Edward Coke and Sir Matthew Hale,
Blackstone envisioned the common law as the institutional perfection of
human reason that was separated from codified legislation.[26,27] Against
statutory commands, Blackstone referred to the common law as "unwrit-
ten" law, dispersed among different courts, and rooted in binding oral
traditions.[28] He submitted that "[o]ur ancient lawyers [. . .] insist with
abundance of warmth, that these customs are as old as the primitive Brit-
ons, and continued down, through the several mutations of government
and inhabitants, to the present time, unchanged and unadulterated."[29]
Blackstone's insistence upon the "unchanged" and "unadulterated"
aspect of the common law contrasts with Holmes's conception of the
common law as a spontaneously ordered system of growth that adapts
and evolves over time. Blackstone viewed the common law as divorced
from legislation,[30] as a "judicial prerogative" set against "a transformative
tide toward majoritarian legislation and central government."[31] Holmes
more than Blackstone took into account the manifold rules and regulations that were not judicially made: the countless acts of parliaments or
legislatures.[32] Also more than Blackstone, Holmes accounted for the role
of the sovereign through its legislature to confer rights and duties upon
its citizens. In Blackstone's paradigm the sovereign was the king, who
shared his power with the legislature or Parliament, but in Holmes's it
was an executive and legislative branch in a maturing American republic.

For Holmes, the judge did not divine pure law or right reason by con-
sulting the wisdom of the ages as embodied in enduring case precedent
but considered also the new and unprecedented elements of each case,
while engaging with lawyers and fellow judges to resolve disputes over
time and work out general principles "through progressive abstraction
from specific cases."[33] As Holmes put it in a line that has already been
quoted in this book: "The substance of the law at any given time pretty
nearly corresponds, so far as it goes, with what is then understood to be
convenient; but its form and machinery, and the degree to which it is able
to work out desired results, depend very much upon its past."[34]

Although Holmes went beyond Blackstone in acknowledging the plain historical fact that codification was on the rise and increasingly displacing the common-law tradition, he remained enamored with the common law. The irony of *The Common Law* is that it describes the processes of the common law and the courts in isolation, at a time just before the common law actually began to retreat in importance—and legislation by the sovereign began to advance to the forefront of social decision-making.[35] *The Common Law* was published when "legislation had become the acknowledged and central means by which the state pursued social ends."[36] Holmes sought to incorporate the latest science into his jurisprudence "by using the new biological and anthropological materials on evolution that the Darwinian revolution in thought was providing."[37] Robert Gordon has called Holmes's jurisprudence "evolutionary pragmatism."[38] Gordon means by this that Holmes regarded laws and legal processes as constantly changing, taking on new meanings and new purposes as generation after generation makes use of them for new ends. The primary difference between Blackstone and Holmes is that the former embraces a common-law paradigm consisting of fixed rules rooted in ancient custom whereas the latter embraces a common-law paradigm consisting of fluid rules responsive to changing social conditions.

Haack lists the following features of Holmes's jurisprudence that are compatible with traditional common-law theory that flies in the face of legal positivism and that underplays the role of legislatures in transmitting laws to the public: the prediction theory of law;[39] the growth and adaptation of legal concepts;[40] the evolution of legal systems;[41] the past and the future of the law;[42] the relevance of the sciences, and especially the social sciences, to the law;[43] and moral fallibilism.[44] Each of these features participates with one another; none exists to the exclusion of the others. For instance, Holmes's dogged insistence that law and morality were separate or only incidentally aligned brought about his reasonable man theory of negligence that turned on the foreseeable consequences of a given human action.[45] This theory captures his signature concept of law as prediction,[46] grows out of his prior theories of negligence,[47] and incorporates moral fallibilism insofar as it proposes that a tortfeasor is not judged according to his particular state of mind but according to an objective standard about how reasonable people in general ought to behave in light of their circumstances.[48]

Kellogg suggests that insofar as Holmes's conception of the law offers a model of an "ongoing community exploring common problems," it is similar to ideas expressed by Holmes's friend, Charles S. Peirce, who was describing the social process of scientific inquiry.[49] Holmes's "underlying conception of society" reflects his "exposure to the struggle of Darwinian evolution."[50] This conception was "much discussed in the Metaphysical

Club and confirmed in some respects by the American Civil War, both of which reinforced doubts concerning the prospects for [the] law-based liberal or utilitarian reform."[51] Kellogg argues that Holmes thought of the common law as a system of decentralized problem solving, tending toward stability and uniformity in the long run, but also constantly adapting to unforeseeable changes and local variations.[52] To this end Holmes viewed the judge's role as receptive to existing cultures at local levels and considered order itself to be "decentralized, supple, [. . .] unfinished, [and] constantly under construction and revision."[53] He was unlikely to deem as unconstitutional any enacted legislation and in fact did so only once during his twenty-year career (1882-1902) on the Massachusetts Supreme Judicial Court. He disapproved of legislation only if it abridged freedom of speech and came to be committed to the notion that a marketplace of ideas was necessary for the best theories to outdo competitors and to prove their practical worth.[54] Holmes's jurisprudence commemorates judges who interpret and adapt the customs of their place and time—those customs themselves being derived from the past. In his view, judges should neither create policy nor merely cling dogmatically to interpretations of the past. Instead, they "could and should update the reasoning" about how to apply old concepts in the current environment.[55]

What sets Holmes apart from the other classical pragmatists is not just his station as a Supreme Court justice but also his commitment to Emersonian thought and aesthetics. Emerson thought of the forms of the past as a "faded wardrobe" with which to "put the living generation into masquerade."[56] And Holmes wrote that the "form of continuity" is "nothing but the evening dress which the new-comer puts on to make itself presentable according to conventional requirements."[57] Like Emerson, Holmes appreciated the joy of illustrating the connections between present praxis and past traditions, but he also warned that "the present has a right to govern itself so far as it can; and it ought always to be remembered that historic continuity with the past is not a duty, it is only a necessity."[58]

TRANSITION AND REPRODUCTION

Holmes published *The Common Law* in 1881. In 1882, Emerson died. The year between 1881 and 1882 represents the passing of a baton as Holmes preserved Emerson's ideas and aesthetics but stripped them of the characteristics and qualities that were no longer suited for the postwar era.[59] In 1881 America was in transition. Reconstruction was coming to a close in the South. Immigration, urbanization, and industrialization continued apace; the federal government expanded its power over the states. Everything, it seemed, was changing; the quotidian habits and practices of individuals in all areas of the country seemed to have transformed after the Civil War. Gone was the transcendental optimism in New England; gone were the feudal ways of the Old South. Gone were the defining characteristics of American culture with which the founding generation would have been familiar. America was taking shape, growing, waking up from its post-war slumber and reaching out for fresh ideas. Menand suggests that "the Civil War discredited the beliefs and assumptions of the era that preceded it."[60] He submits that those "beliefs had not prevented the country from going to war; they had not prepared it for the astonishing violence the war unleashed; they seemed absurdly obsolete in the new, postwar world."[61] And then there was the publication, in Boston, of a curious little book called *The Common Law*, a compilation of essays by Holmes, who had enjoyed intimate connections with traditional, Protestant New England families and traditions but was striking a new course. Holmes turned forty in 1881. The publication of *The Common Law* that year gave him a chance to express his jurisprudence to a wide audience. This marked a turning point in his career. Over the next year, he would become a professor at Harvard Law School and then, a few months later, an associate justice of the Massachusetts Supreme Judicial Court.

The trauma of the Civil War had affected Holmes's thinking and would eventually impact his jurisprudence. Leading up to the Civil War, he had been an Emersonian idealist who associated with such abolitionists as Wendell Phillips. Holmes emerged from the Civil War a different man. He was colder now, and more sober-minded. "Holmes believed," Menand says, "that it was no longer possible to think the way he had as a young man before the war, that the world was more resistant than he had imagined. But he did not forget what it felt like to *be* a young man before the war."[62] And he learned that forms of resistance were necessary and natural in the constant struggle of humans to organize their societies and to discover what practices and activities ought to govern their conduct. The Civil War made him both wiser and more disillusioned. His disillusionment reflected the general attitudes of many men his age. But not all men his age shared his penetrating intellect or his exhilarating facility with words; nor did they have his wartime experience. Most men who experienced what he had during the Civil War did not live to tell about it. Certainly no one besides Holmes could claim to have experienced such intimate and privileged access to the Brahmin, Emersonian culture of New England before the Civil War, and he more than anyone was equipped to see the continued relevance of that culture to the present. He knew there were things the Civil War could not destroy and varieties of thought that could endure.

It is not too much to say that only Holmes could have served as an intellectual link between the old and new ethos of New England; he was a carryover, a lively and sometimes bombastic highbrow whose ideas and methodologies retained qualities of Emersonian transcendentalism. But Emersonian transcendentalism was maladapted to the current climate. It could not survive the turmoil of the preceding era, at least not in the form in which Emerson had articulated it. Philosophy and idealism had advanced in slow degrees since the Revolution, and Emerson seemed to have been the culmination of American optimism. The Civil War undermined Emerson; its massive slaughter and economic tumult suggested there was no heritable advantage to embracing transcendentalism and that Emerson, brilliant though he was, had not produced the particular combination of aesthetics and knowledge necessary to outlast the selective elimination of unfit ideas.

Yet Emerson's ideas were not destroyed; they descended by modification. They survived in part because of thinkers like Holmes. Holmes revised them and in so doing endowed them with the variation necessary for their subsequent existence. He also realized their poetic vision in the most improbable of fields: the law. The hard and mechanical features of the law enabled Emersonian thought to change in the critical ways necessary to remain fit in the new American climate. Holmes, like his father and Emerson, was a poet, indeed had been the class poet at Harvard, and he discovered that poetry could be effective and powerful when it was clothed in legal lexica and preserved in legal canons. Holmes did not think like his father or his father's friends, but he knew how they thought, and he employed what features of their thought were worth preserving and discarded what features he knew to be unsuited for the challenges of the day. Holmes carved out a legacy by finding room for old principles, including Emersonian aesthetics and propheticism, in his rapidly transitioning society. Although he was more skeptical and realistic after the Civil War, he did not lose the joy he had felt since boyhood in exploring and building on the ideas of Emerson.[63] Holmes recognized, in short, the significance of Emerson to the index of modern thought.

It is no coincidence that Holmes admired both the common law and Emersonian pragmatics and treated them as paired enterprises; the two have much in common. Holmes was historically conscious; he revered the past from which he sought to break; he felt that the new necessarily derived from what came before, that nothing was without an antecedent, and that ideas did not spring from a vacuum outside of time. He agreed with Emerson that "the inventor only knows how to borrow."[64] Just as Emerson held that "the artist must employ the symbols in use in his day and nation"[65] or that "the new in art is always formed out of the old,"[66] so Holmes believed that the law is "forever adopting principles from life at one end" while "retain[ing] old ones from history at the other, which have not yet been absorbed or sloughed off."[67] Holmes thus did not view the artist and the judge as working in mutually exclusive fields; he demonstrated with his own writings that Emersonian aesthetics had a place in the otherwise dull and doctrinal prose of the law.

Emerson had in mind an aesthetic canon of ingenious inventors, himself among them, building upon the works of one another. This notion carried over into Holmes's conception of the common law: "When we find that in large and important branches of the law the various grounds of policy on which the various rules have been justified are later inventions to account for what are in fact survivals from more primitive times, we have a right to reconsider the popular reasons, and, taking a broader view of the field, to decide anew whether those reasons are satisfactory."[68] Like Emerson, Holmes considered extensive knowledge of the past empowering; also like Emerson, he was willing to attribute invention and insight to genius. For Emerson as for Holmes, genius could be realized in the course of studying ordinary social conditions prevailing at various points in history. Genius, then, did not arise without some effort on the part of the person possessing it, and Holmes was inclined to view that effort as a search for the clarity needed to apprehend the complex instrumentalities of legal institutions. This clarity motivated prudent judges in their search for the desirable directions for the law to take and for the useful categories for the law to assume. "[W]hen ancient rules maintain themselves," Holmes explained, "new reasons more fitted to the time have been found for them, and [. . .] they gradually receive a new content, and at last a new form, from the grounds to which they have been transplanted."[69] Inferred in these lines and in Holmes's treatment of the common law is the idea that it is personal knowledge that makes one aware of the impersonal mechanisms driving the law toward some imperfectly realized ideal.

To come to Holmes's understanding of the law as a system of growth rooted in human knowledge requires an initiation into the field of history. The more comprehensive one's knowledge of history, especially as it pertains to the law, the greater facility one has to contextualize any fleeting standard within the operative paradigms that influence ongoing conversations about human conduct. "However much we may codify the law into a series of seemingly self-sufficient propositions," Holmes maintained to this end, "those propositions will be but a phase in a continuous growth."[70] Analyzing such propositions in light of the standards, values, and tastes with which various communities have experimented is itself a test of the validity of those standards, values, and tastes. In other words, such analyses can reveal the practical consequences of certain legal rules. Such analyses are, therefore, indispensable guides for judges considering how to rule in new cases. A judge determining whether a seemingly unfair or deceptive label on a product should qualify as false advertising or mere puffery would consult the decisions of past judges and compare whether and to what extent the facts before the past judges are analogous to the facts at present. If the comparison suggests that a similar ruling in this case would lead to a bad result, then the present judge modifies the rule by highlighting the facts that are readily or obviously distinguishable from those of the past. But if the present judge thinks a past decision would apply to the circumstances at hand, he downplays or disregards the distinguishable facts and highlights their family resemblances. Hence when judges and jurists study the history of the law they must bear in mind their own historical position in relation to those older propositions that shaped the current content of the law: "To understand [the propositions'] scope fully, to know how they will be dealt with by judges trained in the past which the law embodies, we must ourselves know something of that past. The history of what the law has been is necessary to the knowledge of what the law is."[71] On this score, Holmes echoes Emerson:

> No man can quite emancipate himself from his age and country, or produce a model in which the education, the religion, the politics, usages, and arts, of his times shall have no share. Though he were never so original, never so wilful and fantastic, he cannot wipe out of his work every trace of the thoughts amidst which it grew. The very avoidance betrays the usage he avoids. Above his will, and out of his sight, he is necessitated, by the air he breathes, and the idea on which he and his contemporaries live and toil, to share the manner of his times, without knowing what that manner is.[72]

The difference between Holmes and Emerson in this regard is that Holmes suggests we can, in fact, know what the manner is, at least to some degree, if we understand how and from where it developed. The function of the common law is to supply us with this understanding.

The common law describes a body of rules that develop as literary canons develop. Works of literature become canonized just as rules become settled through the endless processes of the common law. Only the test of time shows whether a work of literature will remain in the canon after extraordinary content has been filtered from content unable to speak meaningfully to future generations. Literary works of enduring appeal are able to outlast the embedded prejudices, pressing issues, and prevailing tastes of an age. On the other hand, works that cannot remain relevant do not survive the onslaught of competition that must be overcome to procure a place in the canon. This is what Emerson meant when he described the eternal process of transmuting life into truth through texts as a "distillation" of "process," none of which is "quite perfect."[73] He goes on to say, in furtherance of this theme, "As no air-pump can by any means make a perfect vacuum, so neither can any artist entirely exclude the conventional, the local, the perishable from his book, or write a book of pure thought, that shall be as efficient, in all respects, to a remote posterity, as to cotemporaries, or rather to the second age. Each age, it is found, must write its own books; or rather, each generation for the next succeeding. The books of an older period will not fit this."[74] So it is with the common law: the decisions issued by various judges speak to their present audience but with an eye toward an imagined future consisting of rational citizens to whom earlier principles remain valid and by whom those principles advance in subsequent increments. The principle that perennial truths must be restated in the vocabularies of successive generations has been embodied in the common law since time immemorial. Indeed, that principle defines the common law.

INTEGRATING HOLMES WITH PEIRCE, DEWEY, AND JAMES

To know why pragmatism was such a natural fit for an Emersonian Holmes, one needs only to consider what the common law is and why it appealed to him. Doing so shows that pragmatism is not "The American Philosophy," as it is so often proclaimed to be, for the common law is, in effect, pragmatism by another name, and its characteristics and methodologies gradually have developed, hand in hand with evolving mores, for centuries. Kellogg suggests that insofar as Holmes's conception of the law offers a model of an "ongoing community exploring common problems," it bears "remarkable similarities to the model of scientific inquiry emerging at roughly the same historical period in the writings of Holmes's controversial friend Charles S. Peirce, a model later adopted by John Dewey."[75] Kellogg could have also mentioned Holmes's affinity for the ideas of William James, who advocated for the "experimental method" to guard against error, and for the "comparative method" to supplement the experimental method.[76] The mark of these methods was their starting point of "introspective observation"[77] for the process of discerning the relation of individual consciousness to external objects.[78] Peirce wished to model philosophy off the consensus-based practices and protocols of the scientific community. His essay "Some Consequences of Four Incapacities"[79] proposed that a single, fallible mind cannot be the absolute arbiter of truth because truth is established by a lack of doubt, which occurs when several individuals agree about some state of existence. A corollary is the inverse notion that we should doubt whatever is rejected by a collection of intelligent and disciplined minds. These premises are strikingly resonant in Holmes's recognition that a single judge or small group of judges ought to have reason to doubt their logic and inferences that conflict with the legislative process. That rigorous process represents the end result of painstaking negotiations, compromises, and experiments among lawmakers receiving direction from their constituents, and it should not be undone by the convictions of a judge altogether dislocated from popular representation and electoral accountability.

Holmes considered good law to be the product of a method similar to the scientific method, which, according to Peirce in "The Fixation of Belief," stands in contradistinction to the method of authority; the former prizes inquiry and practices the drawing of inferences from sustained observation, whereas the latter assumes without challenge the validity and viability of an allegedly right or unassailable premise. The former is like the common law with its inherent positivism; the latter is like natural law theories about origins preceding posited laws. The scientific method of the common law is always about experimentation; the theory of our Constitution, with its adoption of the common law within a covenantal framework, is "an experiment, as all life is an experiment."[80] What motivates experimentation, according to Peirce, is the irritation of doubt, the vexing insecurity that we are not right about what we believe. Inquiry is the means by which we seek to pacify or eradicate that irritation. The sole object of inquiry for the scientific philosopher was the settlement of an opinion.[81] For the common law judge, who is not unlike the scientific philosopher, the sole object of inquiry is the settlement of rules, which, remarkably, is called an "opinion" in the legal vocabulary. The civil law method of codification operates by force or imposition and short-circuits inquiry: it directs others to conform to it and threatens to visit consequences upon those who fail to comply. Peirce and Holmes did not see this method as likely to generate good beliefs, whether in phenomena generally or in supposedly moral principles guiding legal rules. As Peirce declared,

> The willful adherence to a belief, and the arbitrary forcing of it upon others, must, therefore, both be given up, and a new method of settling opinions must be adopted, which shall not only produce an impulse to believe, but shall also decide what proposition it is which is to be believed. Let the action of *natural preferences* be unimpeded, then, and under their influence let men, conversing together and regarding matters in different lights, gradually develop beliefs in harmony with natural causes.[82]

By way of analogy, Peirce seems to be advocating a common-law approach to the settling of opinions and rules as against the ritual of executive or sovereign command. The common law advances by accommodating the natural preferences of society and by facilitating their constant articulation in the superintending rulings of judges and justices. Like the "machinery of the mind" that transforms knowledge "but never originate[s] it,"[83] the common law never purports to have an identifiable origin or a fixed point of entry. It registers indirect dialogues between judges about the rules of the jurisdiction and establishes case precedents to ensure that the conversation remains ongoing. Some precedents are preserved and passed down in their entirety; others persist in residual form only. Precedents are improved or diminished by their utility; the effort to integrate the differentiated elements of experience within a system of rules tends to neutralize or eliminate bad and inexpedient practices. The corrective processes of the common law and of Peirce's scientific method (or method of inquiry) enable the incremental development of consistent and predictable guidelines; they provide the legal or scientific community with an element of certainty and stability. They also establish a comprehensive and comprehensible record of the continual adaptations of human behavior.

Despite its capacity for growth, or perhaps because of it, the common law never attains some fixed, transcendental unity that allows us to predict all of the legal outcomes of any specified action; the rules in a common-law system are constantly being remade and thus cannot accomplish perfect uniformity. "The truth is," Holmes remarked, "the law is always approaching, and never reaching, consistency."[84] So it must be that the prudent judge determines the laws of social interaction as Peirce suggests that scientists and philosophers determine the natural laws of the universe: by the study of probabilities and chance. Holmes knew the law would never attain perfect consistency because, to borrow from Peirce (who, again, was referring to the natural laws of the universe and not the laws of human government, but whose comments are nevertheless germane), they "developed out of pure chance, irregularity, and indeterminacy."[85] "For every conceivable object," Peirce adds, "there is a greater probability of acting as on a former like occasion than otherwise. This tendency itself constitutes a regularity, and is continually on the increase."[86] The nature of a tendency in the common law matures in a similar manner; the difference, if there is one, is that in the common law tendencies reflect what judges determine will resolve a dispute between litigants in a manner that can be replicated under like circumstances. Laws for both Holmes and Peirce resolve themselves into probabilities about the soundness and workability of some rule or set of rules. Such probability is derived from experience and observation that have varying degrees of reliability in proportion to the extent to which they have been tested. When the rule of a case yields profitable dividends, confidence in the rule grows and spreads until it achieves general assent within the jurisdiction, at which point it becomes the authority until such time as changed circumstances in society challenge its worth. Judges seek out the tendencies of human behavior to determine what tendencies in the law will suffice to keep the peace, compensate victims, punish wrongdoers, and maintain order. The law is an exercise in probability, developed according to a growing assurance in the viability of binding rules.

In "The Path of the Law," Holmes put forth the bad man theory or prediction theory of law, which holds that we should not view the law as an abstract statement about morals but as those consequences that a bad man predicts will obtain if he chooses one course of action instead of another. The law is, accordingly, a prediction about what will happen if one performs certain acts. Informed and calculated guesses about outcomes are what most of us turn to before choosing any particular course of action. Most of us do not, when we stop at a traffic light, for example, consider the morality of the action we are performing, but instead consider the ramifications of our potential act should we actually carry it out. Therefore, determining in advance what the law is or might be involves determining the probability that certain social ramifications will result from choosing to perform the act under consideration. But judges do not guess in advance what the law will be, at least not in their capacity as judges; other people do. Judges sort through facts already given to determine which general principles will apply, and then, in Menand's words, "what judges say *is* law."[87] Put another way, judges decide what the law is only after the facts of the case, however sanitized, reach the court; or maybe it is more accurate to say that judges decide whether and how precedent squares with those facts, since general principles are passed to judges through prior cases, and judges must categorize the facts in line with the general principles previously established. Once a general principle is made to fit a set of facts, the facts are just as dispositive as the general principles in illustrating what the law is. The general principle of trespass—for the purposes of this example, trespass is a wrongful entry onto another's property—is only a principle and not an effective law until the judge determines to which situations the principle pertains: a person's front yard may be property, but what about his poetry or his ideas or his children? Once the judge determines whether and how the general principles attach to the concrete facts before him, he announces the rule and thereby supplies the population with a guiding illustration. Now the population, bad men and all, can predict, with a little more certainty, whether taking actions in relation to, say, a man's poetry or ideas or children will trigger a legal analysis regarding trespass or whether a different law—or no law at all—will obtain. It is in light of this process that Holmes proclaimed, "General propositions do not decide concrete cases."[88] The decision is not in the principle but in the method in which the facts are shaped to fulfill the principle.

This process resembles the very method that Dewey considered necessary for the examination of society: the search for "the interrelations of observable acts and their results."[89] Dewey, like Holmes, considered facts to come from method and technique and to provide the basis for knowing the import of theories, which are like the general principles guiding the common law.[90] Dewey's entire method of social inquiry is in fact comparable to the common law inasmuch as it rejects the search for causal origins[91] and evaluates theories in terms of their perceived consequences[92] in the environment of a specific time. Dewey's introduction to Sidney Hook's *The Metaphysics of Pragmatism* reformulates Emerson's concept of the new arising out of the old through dialectical refutation and assimilation.[93] Dewey demonstrates his consequentialism this way: "Conditions are stated in reference to consequences which may be incurred if they are infringed or transgressed."[94] What Dewey calls a "theory" might well have been a "law" for Holmes. Both entities reveal themselves in the concerted actions of others—bad men, if you will—and can be quantified as a series of predictions; the growth of that series of predictions is tantamount to the operation of the common law, namely, to the process of following and simultaneously establishing precedents to direct social inquiry and order social relations. The common law is, in this respect, a system of probabilities about human action and its consequences. The implication is that in one case after another rules build upon rules and then eventually abstract into general principles to which facts about human action are made to conform; the resultant laws are therefore not legislative commands[95] but an aggregation of dialectical developments.

The sheer weight of precedent may mean that seemingly archaic taxonomies remain in force. Master-servant law, for instance, continues in full operation today in terms of principals and their agents under the doctrine of *respondeat superior*. It does not follow, however, that because such vocabulary and principles remain, the facts giving rise to the present cases reflect the facts that would have borne out at earlier times. Like the Peircean scientist who relies upon community consensus or the Holmesian judge who defers to the legislature, Dewey acknowledged that no thought or scheme of organization springs from an individual mind deliberating in isolation. Generating knowledge by testing ideas within a community of thinkers enables the proliferation of democracy, which is, for Dewey, the ultimate ideal; and even if an ideal "is not a fact" and "never can be"[96]—in other words, an ideal cannot be perfectly realized—it nevertheless inspires or motivates people to assemble bodies of knowledge (like the canons of literature or the precedents of the common law) and facilitate communication between groups. The associated ties of an intellectual community thus strengthen, not weaken, the individual minds within it. "There is no limit," Dewey intones, "to the liberal expansion and confirmation of limited personal intellectual endowment which proceed from the flow of social intelligence when that circulates by word of mouth from one to another in the communications of the local community."[97] Accordingly, the judge or justice divorced from the local community and withdrawn from the processes of deliberation that brought about habits of mind and conduct within the community cannot himself deduce the optimal legal conditions for the community; he must defer to the judgment of the community as embodied in enacted legislation. The term "majoritarianism" as ascribed to both Holmes and Dewey derives from this proposition. The judge must also leave factfinding to juries in cases demonstrating genuine issues of material fact because a judge's province in such cases is to charge or instruct juries regarding the pertinent laws whereas the role of juries—the litigants' peers—is to determine the truthfulness or probability of truthfulness of the narratives presented by the litigants and substantiated or unsubstantiated by the evidence.

Of the so-called "classical pragmatists," Dewey was the person Holmes claimed to admire most. Max Harold Fisch[98] describes this admiration as follows:

> Holmes did not discover Dewey until the latter's *Experience and Nature* was recommended to him by a young Chinese friend. He began it skeptically; it seemed to be so badly written. But he read it twice in the winter of 1926-27, and wrote his impressions in five letters over a period of a year and a half. "He seems to me," Holmes said, "to have more of our cosmos in his head than any philosopher I have read." Holmes reread the book in 1929 when a second edition appeared, and recommended it to Sir Frederick Pollock. The only clearly intelligible sentences Pollock professed to find in it were the two pages Dewey had quoted from Holmes.

It is possible, in light of Holmes's late arrival to Dewey's writings, that Dewey benefited from Holmes's influence more than Holmes benefited from Dewey's, but at any rate their ideas were sufficiently similar to have attracted each man to the other. It is possible that Holmes, who rarely liked to give credit where credit was due, did not wish to draw attention to the similarities of his jurisprudence with the thinking of Peirce and James and thereby to detract from his reputed originality, but found Dewey to be different enough to warrant praise safe from public speculation about the two men's shared premises.

Holmes's ideas shared more with those of Peirce and James than Holmes liked to acknowledge. Holmes's jurisprudence smacked of Peircean theories about probability, prediction, and communicative consensus. And it had much to do with the philosophical musings of William James, whose version of pragmatism Holmes disingenuously dismissed as an "amusing humbug."[99] In fact, Holmes agreed with much of what James wrote about "truth." "Truth then, as one, I agree with you," Holmes wrote to James in 1907, "is only an ideal—an assumption that if everyone was as educated and clever as I he would feel the same compulsions that I do."[100] James was a pluralist. So was Holmes. James's salutary stand against monism and deference to the practices and beliefs of different communities correspond with Holmes's judicial restraint and enthusiasm for the common law. His description of how the mind forms impressions and chooses between options seems to have influenced Holmes's theories about intentional torts and quantitative prediction:

> [T]he mind is at every stage a theatre of simultaneous possibilities. Consciousness consists in the comparison of these with each other, the selection of some, and the suppression of the rest by the reinforcing and inhibiting agency of attention. The highest and most elaborated mental products are filtered from the data chosen by the faculty below that, which mass in turn was sifted from a still larger amount of yet simpler material, and so on.[101]

The psychological fundamentals of Holmes's bad man theory consist in these lines by James. The bad man considers the legal possibilities of his various actions and the consequences he suspects will flow from them. In other words, this bad man holds in his mind the simultaneous possibilities of deeds that are probably criminal or tortious, and those that are probably not; then he selects one of the options before him for action and suppresses the others.

James likened a pluralistic world to a "federal republic" rather than an "empire or kingdom."[102] A federal republic depends upon checks and balances not only between competing branches of government but also between competing cultures. A federal republic is pluralist to the extent that its constituent parts "hitch up" but do not mirror one another or correspond absolutely. Pluralism is the opposite of monism. Monism holds that all the parts of the world must connect to one another simultaneously and without intermediation. Nothing is separate. Everything connects with and interpenetrates everything else.[103] Holmes noticed such totalism or monism in natural law theories, the uncompromising supporters of which believed their jurisprudence was universally binding and unconditionally true and therefore innately superior to anyone else's. Holmes by contrast did not view judges as Platonic guardians and was loath to intrude upon the local intelligence of distant communities. "Constitutions," he said, "are intended to preserve practical and substantial rights, not to maintain theories" that any particular judge or justice might entertain.[104] Holmes maintained that the personal preferences of judges or justices should not govern the outcome of cases by standing in the way of the natural orders that arise apart from the design or plan of any one judge. "I can't help preferring champagne to ditchwater—I doubt if the universe does," he wrote to William James.[105] Echoing James's claims about truth, Holmes speculated that "there are as many truths as there are men" and that "if we all agreed, we should only have formulated our limitations and the conditions of life and the kind of world we wanted to make."[106] Holmes believed that the inevitable differences and disagreements among people required a legal system that was flexible and accommodating and that minimized violent conflict.

Adhering to the notion that "the attempt to make [our] limitations compulsory on anything outside our dream—to demand significance, etc., of *the* universe—[is] absurd,"[107] Holmes adopted a position of skepticism about the ability of a judge or justice to reason on behalf of a community. The utility of this skeptical position was to leave it to the people and their representatives to risk their own well-being in determining what they thought was best for themselves. "I always say, as you know," Holmes wrote to Harold J. Laski, "that if my fellow citizens want to go to Hell I will help them. It's my job."[108] Related to this constructive skepticism is the principle that one who is honest about the probable limitations of his ingrained convictions must acknowledge the danger of carrying those convictions to their logical end in an illogical world full of people with different convictions. The trouble is when hostile ideas, unlike in kind but not in degree, bring their adherents into irreconcilable conflict. Productive antagonisms and dissents are one thing; stalemate and destruction are quite another. The quickest way to retard growth and upset social harmony is unreservedly to embrace militant and extreme ideas.

Militant and extreme ideas are comprised of such particles as to become combustible when brought into contact with other ideas having similarly combustible properties. The collision of these ideational forces results in their total annihilation, along with the people who cling to them. Holmes, extending the alcoholic-beverage analogy to weightier subjects, puts it this way: "Deep-seated preferences cannot be argued about—you cannot argue a man into liking a glass of beer—and therefore, when differences are sufficiently far reaching, we try to kill the other man rather than let him have his way. But that is perfectly consistent with admitting that, so far as appears, his grounds are just as good as ours."[109] For Holmes, then, the simple recognition of our possible error is enough to generate healthy opposition. It is when opposition shuts down all communication and disregards all awareness of probable error that it becomes violent and destructive. That, Holmes believed, is what happened during the Civil War. Holmes took it to be his duty as a judge to ensure that other civil wars would not happen, that antagonisms remained constructive, and that totalizing worldviews would not result in the obliteration of good ideas or in complete intellectual stasis. The common law demonstrated that parties came into conflict all the time, yet their conflicts led not to devastation but to clarity and growth in the legal system. Although it was acceptable for unfit ideas to become extinct, as it were, through natural processes, it was not acceptable to eliminate fit ideas by means of overpowering force. Opposition and dissent were necessary, of course, to facilitate competition among people and principles; in turn, competition was necessary to prevent militant people and principles from gathering such force that they would bring about violence. Imposition of rules from the top down distorted the bottom-up flow of rules from person to person and group to group.

Accordingly, it was not relativism that Holmes welcomed. It was a method of debate and exchange; the coordination of human action toward dispute resolution; the distillation and dispersal of power; and the arrangement of practical rules, derived from common experience, into an articulable classification that could guide judges and lawyers to the benefit of society writ large. This combination of traits enabled an evaluation of ideas based upon the well-substantiated belief that free thinking and open, critical dialogue would in the long run contribute to the advancement of knowledge.[110] Posner argues that Holmes's belief in this "marketplace of ideas" implies that there really is an objective truth in the universe—objectively discoverable by humans—and that therefore the "market," not the judge, ought "to be the arbiter."[111] Let the people experiment with their own communicative standards and prescriptions, Holmes maintained, for an obligation is not enjoined on the courts to sit in ultimate judgment over the solemn acts and decent politics of reasonable people. Courts were not designed to referee or legislate moral tendencies but to ensure that the consequences of human action are reasonable and practicable in the workaday social sphere.

The confluence of Emerson, Peirce, Dewey, and James in the jurisprudence of Holmes gave rise to what Richard Posner has dubbed *legal pragmatism*. The features of legal pragmatism retain the influence of each of these thinkers. The classical pragmatists sought to strip philosophy—in Holmes's case, the philosophy of law—of its extraneous modes of reasoning and its abstract or dogmatic moralizing and to avoid attenuated lines of thinking that did not comport with commonsense empiricism. They viewed social communities as composite unities replete with differing opinions and motivations. They examined ideas in light of human expectations concerning causes and effects, actions and consequences. They expressed these expectations in terms of probability. And whatever meaning they took from these expectations depended upon what practical difference it made to interpret the expectations in one manner as opposed to another.

Holmes's non-identitarian, unaffiliated disposition makes him difficult to categorize politically. He was neither a political naïf nor an impartial observer of congressional activity, but he was largely indifferent to current events. He refused to read newspapers, and he did not take sides in partisan games or ideological movements, at least not consistently. His position as a judge required him to maintain an appearance of neutrality and to avoid overtly political pronouncements or risk seeming partial on matters that might come before him on the bench. Although he became a darling of the progressives like Harold Laski, Herbert Croly, Walter Lippmann, and Felix Frankfurter who published in the *The New Republic*,[112] his personal views were mostly antagonistic to progressivism and his legal opinions were characteristically reticent about *any* sort of crusading political mobilization, left or right.[113]

Progressives were not a uniform or homogeneous group; neither were the classical pragmatists or their progeny. Progressivism as a movement and progressives as a class stretched from the late nineteenth century to the early 1930s and included individuals with different backgrounds and beliefs. Richard Hofstadter described the progressive movement as "the complaint of the unorganized against the consequences of organization"[114] and posited a serviceable definition for *progressivism* as "that broader impulse toward criticism and change that was everywhere so conspicuous after 1900, when the already forceful stream of agrarian discontent was enlarged and redirected by the growing enthusiasm of middle-class people for social and economic reform."[115] Under this definition Holmes was not a progressive, yet his evolutionary paradigm of the common-law and of civilization more generally led inexorably toward a worldview in which progress was always possible but never inevitable.

Theodore Roosevelt, whose presidential administration prioritized antitrust litigation and "trustbusting," nominated Holmes to the United States Supreme Court to fill the seat vacated upon Justice Horace Gray's retirement. Holmes's sprightly dissent in *Northern Securities Company v. United States* (1904)[116] contradicted Roosevelt's allegation that the Northern Securities Company had violated the Sherman Antitrust Act. Holmes's dissent permanently damaged his relationship with Roosevelt. He began his criticism of the majority opinion in *Northern Securities Company* with the maxim that "[g]reat cases, like hard cases, make bad law."[117] Despite disappointing progressives in *Northern Securities Company*, Holmes endeared himself to progressives a year later when he dissented in *Lochner*. He ruled in favor of Southern progressive efforts to disenfranchise black voters in Alabama in *Giles v. Harris*,[118] and appealed to Northern progressives with his vigorous defense of free speech in *Abrams*. As a result, progressives began to lionize Holmes for upholding regulatory labor laws and for preserving civil liberties.[119]

A war veteran with an academic pedigree, Holmes was a fitting symbol for the progressives who advocated for military intervention and imperialism in the pages of the *The New Republic*. It is against the backdrop of progressivist militarism that we must understand the progressive valorization of Holmes as well as Holmes's resort to martial metaphors and military language in his writings and speeches. President Roosevelt had nominated Holmes for a seat on the United States Supreme Court in part because he was impressed with Holmes's Memorial Day Speech and admired Holmes's service as a soldier in the Union Army.[120] The progressives "canonized Holmes partly because his Civil War service reinforced his heroic image,"[121] which squared with progressive narratives about military might that were articulated by such leaders as Woodrow Wilson. A year before Holmes was elevated to the High Court, Wilson published "The Ideals of America" (1902)[122] in *The Atlantic Monthly*. The piece was adopted from a speech Wilson had given in 1901 and represented a rallying cry for military power and American exceptionalism, likening opponents of such things to the opponents of the American Revolution. A decade later in *The Promise of American Life*, Herbert Croly wrote that "[w]ar may be and has been a useful and justifiable engine of national policy."[123] Even William James, who identified as a pacifist, wrote in 1910 that "war has been the only force that can discipline a whole community."[124] "[U]ntil an equivalent discipline is organized," he said, "war must have its way."[125] James praised virtues he associated with war, such as discipline, valor, glory, and honor and speculated that "[i]f war had ever stopped, we should have to reinvent it [. . .] to redeem life from flat degeneration."[126]

The reality is that Holmes eluded pure, unmediated, essentialized political groupings, measures, and types. He was not an ordinary politician but a political and legal theorist whose thought encompassed an enormous, even a planetary scale, and who envisioned the known cosmos as a measureless likeness of the common law, expanding by endogenous, continual processes of modification by descent and dissent. Dewey himself wrote that Holmes "has no social panacea to dole out, no fixed social programs, no code of fixed ends to be realized. His social and legal philosophy derives from a philosophy of life and of thought as a part of life, and can be understood only in this larger connection."[127] Holmes's philosophy, according to Dewey, is "free, growing, ever learning, never giving up the battle for truth, or coming to rest in alleged certainties, or reposing a formula in a slumber that means death."[128] Dewey was as prophetic as Holmes when he predicted that "the day will come when the principles set forth by Justice Holmes, even in minority dissent, will be accepted commonplaces."[129]

LEGAL PRAGMATISM

It is difficult to imagine the emergence of legal pragmatism as a named discipline or a celebrated method apart from the contributions of Peirce, Dewey, or James. The jurisprudence of Benjamin Cardozo and Posner, among others, seems to have cobbled together its substance from these pragmatists who inspired Holmes. Nevertheless, Posner notes a difference between philosophical and legal pragmatism. *Contra* philosophical pragmatism, which Posner deems "orthodox" pragmatism, legal pragmatism focuses on the everyday. "Everyday pragmatists," Posner clarifies, "tend to be 'dry,' no-nonsense types."[130] More often than formalist judges, judges who are pragmatic implement anti-foundational and precedent-based techniques to transform the useful or the convenient into the legal or operative. "An everyday-pragmatist judge," Posner submits, "wants to know what is at stake in a practical sense in deciding a case one way or another. . . . [He] does not deny the standard rule-of-law virtues of generality, predictability, and impartiality, which generally favor a stand-pat approach to novel legal disputes. He just refuses to reify or sacralize those virtues. He dares to balance them against the adaptationist virtues of deciding the case at hand in a way that produces the best consequences for the parties and those similarly circumstanced."[131]

A pragmatist judge might therefore dissent on the grounds that the majority opinion abstracts into airy flourishes about "justice," "rights," and "equity." Opinions that turn on such loaded terminology, the pragmatist judge might say, reveal more about judges' personal ideologies than about the meaning of the terminology. Legal pragmatism would seem to be, in this respect, both common sense and no-nonsense. Certainly that is how Holmes thought of the law. "[T]he only definition of law for a lawyer's purpose," the English jurist Sir Frederick Pollock wrote to Holmes, "is something which the Court will enforce."[132] Holmes agreed with his friend and pen pal. It was not that he considered the law to be without philosophical substance or that he delighted in its inevitable malleability; it was that he had it out for jurists who overstated the ontology of the law and glorified the law as the earthly manifestation of divine purpose or as a majestic surrogate for morality.

Law did not work this way; it was not divorced from the mundane social sphere or autonomous from ordinary, routine human interactions. Indeed, it derived from those things. Lawsuits with specific facts and murky issues came before the courts, which assessed the arguments of both sides and extracted a general rule based on the evidence and consistent with the principles expressed in patterns of established precedent. The actions of a few people were thereby plugged into a vast network of human relations spanning different times and places; what linked the people and places was the general rule, which had been in circulation long before the parties disputed. When they initiated suit, the parties did not know which general rule the judge would apply to their case, but their aim was to present the facts in such a way as to implicate the general rule that would allow them to prevail. In essence, the parties knew the facts of their case and had an assortment of general rules to choose from, and based on the precedents related to their claim, they predicted what the judge or jury would need to hear in order to find or rule in their favor. Legal pragmatism looks at this process and does not see anything ontologically or epistemologically magnificent. It looks at this process and sees, rather, a plain representation of the way things are and a possible prophecy about the way things might be.

As a link between the old and the new, Holmes appreciated the ways in which the law, like history itself, unfolds in stages and in accordance with community consensus. He had witnessed firsthand the stark cultural transitions in New England before, during, and after the war, and he understood the importance of adjusting to change, or rather of accommodating it. He neither liked nor disliked the concept of change; he simply recognized that it was what it was and would happen despite anyone's preferences for or against it. That became his take on the law as well: it was neither good nor bad; it just was. Some people sought to remake it—they were supposed to be the legislators and their constituents—but whatever passed as law at any given moment was just a temporary placemarker until something different came along. This does not mean that he did not welcome certain changes, only that he did not see those changes as steps towards realizing an abstract teleology. When other justices or jurists seemed to champion an absolute or teleological position about the law, Holmes knew he had to dissent, and to dissent well, lest the law itself become fixed in a maladapted state from which it could not recover.

Holmes's opinion in *Buck v. Bell* (1927)[133] has undergone warranted and extensive criticism for upholding Virginia's eugenics law of compulsory sterilization for the mentally disabled. It is tempting to dismiss *Buck* as an outlier case, as an aberration, or as just another example of Holmes's programmatic deference to state legislatures that have passed unpalatable laws.[134] However, Holmes upheld the Virginia law with apparent enthusiasm, stating, "It is better for all the world if instead of waiting to execute degenerate offspring for crime, or to let them starve for their imbecility, society can prevent those who are manifestly unfit from continuing their kind."[135] He added, "Three generations of imbeciles are enough."[136]

Two points of qualification place these remarks within a legal and historical context that explains their motivation without diminishing their horror. The first is that, stripped of his gratuitous asides about the merits of eugenics, Holmes's legal position is simply that the appellants made weak constitutional arguments for voiding Virginia's statute under the Fourteenth Amendment, which had yet to undergo the jurisprudential shifts caused by *Brown v. Board of Education* (1954), *Griswold v. Connecticut* (1965),[137] *Roe v. Wade* (1973), *Planned Parenthood v. Casey* (1992),[138] and *Lawrence v. Texas* (2003),[139] among other cases. Holmes technically was not wrong when he called equal protection "the usual last resort of constitutional arguments" because, as of his writing, the Equal Protection Clause of the Fourteenth Amendment had yet to be utilized as it was after *Brown v. Board of Education* (1954) and its progeny.[140] In Holmes's day only the right wing of the United States Supreme Court was open to expansive, activist readings of the Fourteenth Amendment that would overturn state laws as violating the Fourteenth Amendment. The right wing of the United States Supreme Court, for instance, invoked the Fourteenth Amendment to strike down state legislation prohibiting foreign companies from transacting business in a state (*Allgeyer v. Louisiana*, 1897), state legislation restricting weekly working hours (*Lochner v. New York*, 1905), federal legislation prohibiting companies from banning union membership among employees (*Adair v. United States*, 1908, and *Coppage v. Kansas*, 1915), federal regulations of child labor (*Hammer v. Dagenhart*, 1918), federal legislation potentially exempting labor unions from antitrust litigation (*Duplex Printing Press Co. v. Deering*, 1921), federal taxation of companies with goods in interstate commerce if those companies hired underage children (*Bailey v. Drexel Furniture Company*, 1922), federal legislation setting a minimum wage for woman- and child-workers in the District of Columbia (*Adkins v. Children's Hospital*, 1923), and federal legislation regulating the coal industry (*Carter v. Carter Coal Company*, 1936). Striking down Virginia's eugenics law would have required Holmes to adopt the Fourteenth-Amendment jurisprudence of the justices on the right wing of the United States Supreme Court. Holmes, however, shared with progressives the view that it was wrong to invoke the Fourteenth Amendment beyond the purpose for which it was ratified: to confer citizenship on former slaves, guarantee the privileges and immunities of that citizenship to all qualified individuals irrespective of race, and to guarantee due process and equal protection of the laws to all citizens, again irrespective of race. Articulating what was then the progressive view that the federal courts had a limited role to play in constitutional adjudication, Holmes once explained that "a state legislature can do whatever it sees fit to do unless it is restrained by some express prohibition in the Constitution of the United States or of the State, and that Courts should be careful not to extend such prohibitions beyond their obvious meaning by reading into them conceptions of public policy that the particular Court may happen to entertain."[141]

The second qualification is that Holmes was not alone in his opinion; only one justice—Justice Pierce Butler—dissented and without writing. Although enthusiasm for eugenics was widespread in the 1920s, it is unlikely that the concurring justices were all ardent eugenicists. The fact of the matter is that judges and justices in a common-law system lack the authority to raise arguments *ex mero motu* or *sua sponte* except under certain conditions subject to strict rules. Judges and justices are supposed to remain impartial and thus cannot supply arguments that one party or another has failed or refused to raise. Proffering legal arguments on one party's behalf would bring a judge or justice into the realm of advocacy and partiality. Therefore, judges and justices, against their hopes and desires, are often required to rule in favor of parties whose argument is based on deplorable laws and against parties who wish to strike down deplorable laws. Even if Holmes had despised Virginia's mandatory sterilization law—and the language of his opinion suggests that he did not—he could not have raised constitutional arguments that the parties did not raise unless he could support doing so under extant, precedential grounds. In light of these two qualifications, Holmes's opinion in *Buck* cannot be attributed exclusively to apocalyptic eugenics, yet the seeming endorsement of eugenics in the opinion also cannot be ignored or downplayed. It is possible that this endorsement reflects Holmes's overcommitment to Darwinism and science at the expense of traditional humanism and the precepts of natural law that tended to proclaim the basic dignity and bodily integrity of every human person.

By the time 1881 came to a close, Holmes had made his mark. *The Common Law* had been favorably received; it earned him the reputation of an accomplished jurisprudent and guaranteed his continued friendship with such renowned legal figures as Pollock. It also made him a discussion point among important political figures and public intellectuals. The year 1882 ushered in a new phase of his life. He began to adjust to the duties and responsibilities of life on the bench. His lifelong hero Emerson died that year, and as a novice justice on the highest court in Massachusetts Holmes was faced with rare opportunities to give Emersonian expression to pragmatic principles that would obtain to the people of that state. Emerson's ideas remained persuasive to Holmes and others inasmuch as they addressed theories that had not gone away. But Emerson's language no longer conveyed the convictions of the age and no longer registered a perspective familiar to the younger generation. The country was asking questions, and the answers were not to be found in pure transcendentalism. Holmes realized this and so sought to repackage Emerson in pragmatic idioms and ideas that the current era could recognize and through a medium that would have a direct impact on the problems concerning ordinary Americans.

Eventually he would sit on the United States Supreme Court, and from that revered post he would begin to promulgate and preserve his lively variety of pragmatism—which synthesized Emerson, Peirce, Dewey, and James—in the legal canons of the country. Holmes availed himself of Emersonian superfluity in his dissents to vest the legal canon with the agon and variety necessary for the common-law system to flourish. He couched his dissents in memorable style and sound to make them more competitive among their peers. He thereby instantiated in his legal writing his belief that "free competition is worth more to society than it costs."[142] Rather than imposing his personal convictions on communities not his own, shutting down the free flow of ideas within some distant jurisdiction, or rendering judgments with the potential to incite strife and violence among those who disagree, he indicated that "I simply infer that my biggest is inadequate" and that, therefore, he would keep his preferences to himself and "leave to the universe the care of deciding how much it cares about them."[143] Enough time has passed to proffer the conclusion that the universe of American constitutional law cares a great deal about Holmes's jurisprudence. Without his sparkling dissents, the laws of the land would be very different from what they are. The American constitutional canon would not have been shaped as it has if Holmes had not dissented in the vein of his mentor, Emerson. Perhaps, after all, the fourteen-year-old Holmes was right: Holmes would one day owe his accomplishments to Emerson. If that is the case, as I believe it is, then all of us within the common-law tradition in the United States are to some extent governed by the unintended consequences of Emerson's superfluity that inspired Holmes to "write like the devil."[144]

NOTES

1. The dichotomy can be expressed as the difference between a static and dynamic view. Consider this passage, which is not strictly about the common law but about two interpretative modes: "Static and dynamic modes have in common that the lawyer appeals to history for *authority*; to the authority of an original text or tradition or founding moment, or to the authority of the course of history itself, that is to the changing circumstances or long-run evolutionary trends that dictate the need for a new rule or new interpretation. The past is *read* as if it were a legal text with binding force, even if what is being cited is not exactly a text, but a body of intentions or a collection of practices. The premise is that if we decipher the signs correctly, we can read out of them principles and precedents that ought to control current interpretations. The past can control the present because it is continuously connected with the present through narratives of stasis or tradition, or of progress and decline.

"The *critical* modes by contrast are used to destroy, or anyway to question, the authority of the past. They assert discontinuous breaks between past and present. In ordinary legal arguments perhaps the most familiar of these critical modes is the argument from obsolescence or changed circumstances; the argument that the original reasons or purposes of a rule have ceased to exist, or that the rule sprang from motives or a context that are no longer acceptable to modern eyes, are rooted in ugly, barbaric, primitive conceptions or practices" (Robert W. Gordon, "The Struggle Over the Past," *Cleveland State Law Review* 44 [1996]: 125).

C.f., Jeffrey G. Miller's "Evolutionary Statutory Interpretation," which "examines the seeming contrast between the legal doctrines that the interpretation of statutes can evolve over time and that the interpretation of statutes must be grounded only in their texts, which never change unless amended by Congress" (Jeffrey G. Miller, "Evolutionary Statutory Interpretation: Mr. Justice Scalia Meets Darwin," *Pace Law Review* 20 [2000]: 409).

Bernadette Meyler has explained that "Originalists' invocations of the common law posit a fixed, stable, and unified eighteenth-century content, largely encapsulated in William Blackstone's *Commentaries on the Laws of England*" (Bernadette Meyler, "Towards a Common Law Originalism," *Stanford Law Review* 59 [2006]: 553).

On evolutionary common law within a constitutional context, see Jack M. Balkin, "The Roots of the Living Constitution," *Boston University Law Review* 92 (2012): 1129-60.

2. "One of the most important contemporary constitutional debates is whether the meaning of the Constitution may evolve in light of current circumstances, or whether the Constitution should be interpreted in accordance with how the text was originally understood by the public that ratified it" (Miguel Schor, "Contextualizing the Debate between Originalism and the Living Constitution," *Drake Law Review* 59 [2010-11]: 961).

"The Constitution and the common law had a core of 'principle,' of fundamental unchanging meanings. But principles had to be adapted to changing circumstances, and above all, to the modernizing dynamic of historical evolution. The static and dynamic modes were ultimately reconciled through eleology: The assertion that basic legal principles were 'working themselves pure,' were gradually evolving from primitive, obscure or cluttered forms to the highest and best realization of themselves. The 'Classical' liberals who dominated legal thought at the end of the 19th century needed a dynamic view of history because they knew perfectly well that the economic and political liberalism they espoused had not existed in any pure form at the Nation's founding" (Gordon, "Struggle," 128).

[. . .]

"In their insistence that the 'rule of law is a law of rules,' the originalist-traditionalist jurists are, ironically, swimming against the main current of *traditional* American historical jurisprudence, that is common-law dynamic adaptationism, given content and direction by liberal modernization theory" (Gordon, "Struggle," 132).

"[T]extualism and originalism remain inadequate models for understanding American constitutional law. They owe their preeminence not to their plausibility but to the lack of a coherently formulated competitor. The fear is that the alternative to some form of textualism or originalism is 'anything goes[.]' [. . .]

"In fact, however, the alternative view is at hand, and has been for many centuries, in the common law. The common law approach restrains judges more effectively, is more justifiable in abstract terms than textualism or originalism, and provides a far better account of our practices. The emphasis on text, or on the original understanding, reflects an implicit adherence to the postulate that law must ultimately be connected to some authoritative source: either the Framers, or 'we the people' of some crucial era. Historically the common law has been the great opponent of this authoritarian approach. The common law tradition rejects the notion that law must be derived from some authoritative source and finds it instead in understandings that evolve over time. And it is the common law approach, not the approach that connects law to an authoritative text, or an authoritative decision by the Framers or by 'we the people,' that best explains, and best justifies, American constitutional law today" (David Strauss, "Common Law Constitutional Interpretation," *University of Chicago Law Review* 63 [1996]: 879).

3. "The common law method has not gained currency as a theoretical approach to constitutional interpretation because it is not an approach we usually associate with a written constitution, or indeed with codified law of any kind. But our written constitution has, by now, become part of an evolutionary common law system, and the common law—rather than any model based on the interpretation of codified law—provides the best way to understand the practices of American constitutional law" (Strauss, "Common Law," 885).

[. . .]

[. . .] "Constitutional law in the United States today represents a flowering of the common law tradition and an implicit rejection of any command theory.

"In a sense this should not be surprising. The common law is the most distinctive feature of our legal system and of the English system from which it is descended. We should expect that the common law would be the most natural model for understanding something as central to our legal and political culture as the Constitution" (Strauss, "Common Law," 887).

[. . .]

"Properly understood, then, the common law provides the best model for both understanding and justifying how we interpret the Constitution. The common law approach captures the central features of our practices as a descriptive matter. At the same time, it justifies our current practices, in reflective equilibrium, to anyone who considers our current practices to be generally acceptable—either as an original matter or because they are the best practices that can be achieved for society. The common law approach makes sense of our current practices in their broad outlines; but at the same time, it suggests other ways in which our practices should be modified" (Strauss, "Common Law," 888).

4. "Holmes considered himself a Darwinist and concentrated his scholarly energies on the question of how law evolves. When Holmes was attending the meetings of the Metaphysical Club during the early 1870s, Chauncey Wright, the group's leader who Holmes treated as a mentor, was in the midst of an extended, mutually supportive correspondence with Darwin" (Vincent Blasi, "Holmes and the Marketplace of Ideas," *Supreme Court Review* (2004): 25).

5. Holmes, *Common Law*, 1.

6. Alschuler, "Rediscovering," 87.

7. Joan Richardson, *Pragmatism and American Experience: An Introduction* (Cambridge: Cambridge University Press, 2014), 2.

8. Frederick Pollock to Oliver Wendell Holmes, Jr., November 14, 1923, Harvard University Holmes Digital Suite, Mark DeWolfe Howe's research materials on Holmes, 1858-1968: Finding Aid, Complete set of typescripts, interfiled, 1923-1924, online.

9. Henry M. Hart Jr., "Holmes' Positivism—An Addendum," *Harvard Law Review* 64 (1951): 593.

10. Paul L. Gregg, "The Pragmatism of Mr. Justice Holmes," *Georgetown Law Journal* 31 (1942-43): 263.

11. Gregg, "Pragmatism," 267.

12. E.g., Ben W. Palmer, "Hobbes, Holmes, and Hitler," *American Bar Journal* 31 (1945): 569-73; Ben W. Palmer, "Defense against Leviathan," *American Bar Journal* 32 (1946): 328-32; Ben W. Palmer, Ben W. "The Totalitarianism of Mr. Justice Holmes: Another Chapter in the Controversy," *American Bar Journal* 37 (1951): 809-11.

13. E.g., Mark DeWolfe Howe, "The Positivism of Mr. Justice Holmes," *Harvard Law Review* 64 (1951): 529-46; Hart, "Holmes' Positivism," 929-37; Mark DeWolfe Howe, "Holmes's Positivism—A Brief Rejoinder," *Harvard Law Review* 64 (1950-51): 937-39.

14. E.g., Alschuler, "Rediscovering," 353-420; Linda E. Fisher, "Pragmatism Is as Pragmatism Does: Of Posner, Public Policy, and Empirical Reality," 31 (2001): 455-92; R. Blake Brown and Bruce A. Kimball, "When Holmes Borrowed from Langdell: The Ultra Legal Formalism and Public Policy of Northern Securities (1904)," *American Journal of Legal History* 45 (2001): 278-321; Barry Friedman, "History of the Countermajoritarian Difficulty, Part Three: The Lesson of Lochner," *New York University Law Review* 76 (2001): 1383-455; David E. Bernstein, "Lochner's Legacy's Legacy," *Texas Law Review* 82 (2003): 1-64; Mark Strasser, "Why Theories of Law Have Little or Nothing to Do with Judicial Restraint," *Colorado Law Review* 74 (2003): 1379-408.

15. Richard Rorty, "The Banality of Pragmatism and the Poetry of Justice," *Southern California Law Review* 63 (1989-90): 1811.

16. Menand, *Metaphysical Club*, 68.

17. Susan Haack, "Pragmatism, Law, and Morality: The Lessons of Buck v. Bell," *European Journal of Pragmatism and American Philosophy* 3 (2011): 67-68.

18. Kellogg, *Oliver Wendell Holmes, Jr.*, 14, 47.

19. John C. H. Wu, "Justice Holmes and the Common-Law Tradition," *Vanderbilt Law Review* 14 (1960-61): 222.

20. "He is one of the few jurists in American history whose career was long enough, and whose impact pervasive enough, to have functioned as a kind of repository of changing juristic attitudes. Holmes's role as a repository has in part been a function of the seminality of his thought and the memorable quality of his style, but it has also been a function of the deeply ambivalent character of his jurisprudence and the cryptic nature of his expressions" (G. Edward White, "Looking at Holmes in the Mirror," *Law and History Review* 4 [1986]: 440).

21. "It was in thinly settled colonial America that the Commentaries received most acclaim. By 1776 nearly twenty-five hundred copies were in use here, one thousand five hundred of which were the American edition of 1772; a sale which Burke in 1775 in his speech on 'Conciliation with the American Colonies' said rivaled that in England" (Julian S. Waterman, "Thomas Jefferson and Blackstone's Commentaries," *Illinois Law Review* 27 [1932-33]: 629-59, 629-59). "It is part of the accepted wisdom of American history that Sir William Blackstone and his

Commentaries on the Laws of England (*Commentaries*) have exercised a dominant and pervasive influence on America's political thought and legal development" (Nolan 1976, 731-68). "Before the Revolution one thousand English sets [of Blackstone's *Commentaries*] at ten pounds a set were sold in American and many more American editions sold at the bargain price of three pounds a set. In fact, before the war broke out almost as many sets were sold in the American colonies as in England. The work had an enormous effect in America not because of the 'social consistency' of Blackstone's thinking, but because it was the only general treatise available in a land where well-trained lawyers were almost non-existent" (Joseph W. McKnight, "Blackstone, Quasi-Jurisprudent," *Southwestern Law Journal* 13 [1959]: 401). Moreover, "during the period from 1789 to 1915, the authority of the *Commentaries* was cited ten thousand times in reported American cases" (McKnight, "Blackstone," 401). Americans' reverence toward Blackstone was not reciprocated: "While in Parliament from 1761 to 1770, he went along with all those restrictive measures which first enraged and then estranged the American colonists. Actually, he was very extreme in his anti-American bias, and he appeared among the most vociferous advocates of a harsh and uncompromising attitude towards America. It might be said that he definitely delighted in showing the colonists the rod" (Anton-Hermann Chroust, "Blackstone Revisited," *University of Kansas City Law Review* 17 [1949]: 28-29).

22. Kellogg, *Oliver Wendell Holmes, Jr.*, 48.

23. Ibid.

24. Ibid.

25. Kellogg, *Oliver Wendell Holmes, Jr.*, 49.

26. Kellogg, *Oliver Wendell Holmes, Jr.*, 48-49.

27. Coke stated, "And it appeareth in our Books, that in many Cases, the Common Law doth controll Acts of Parliament, and somtimes shall adjudge them to be void: for when an Act of Parliament is against Common right and reason, or repugnant, or impossible to be performed, the Common Law will controll it, and adjudge such Act to be void" (Coke, *The Selected Speeches and Writings of Sir Edward Coke*, edited by Steve Sheppard [Indianapolis, IN: Liberty Fund, 2003], 275).

Cf. Hale's statement: "I come now to that other Branch of our Laws, the common Municipal law of this Kingdom, which has the Superintendency of all those other particular Laws used in the before-mentioned Courts, and is the common Rule for the Administration of common Justice in this great Kingdom; of which it has been always tender, and there is great Reason for it; for it is not only a very just and excellent Law in itself, but it is singularly accommodated to the Frame of the English Government, and to the Disposition of the English Nation, and such as by a long Experience and Use is at it were incorporated into their very Temperament, and, in a manner, become this Complexion and Constitution of the English Commonwealth" (Matthew Hale, *The History of the Common Law of England* [Stafford, England: J. Nutt, assignee of Edw. Sayer for J. Walthoe, 1713], 45).

28. Blackstone, *Commentaries*, 62-63. To say that Blackstone was categorically opposed to legislation is hyperbolic. The mistake is understandable given Blackstone's celebration of the common law. However, Blackstone notoriously declared that, "if the parliament will positively enact a thing to be done which is unreasonable, I know of no power in the ordinary forms [. . .] that is vested to

with authority to control it" (Blackstone [1765] 1966, 91). Blackstone would seem to suggest here that a statute could be valid even if it does not correspond with divine or natural law, a position that contradicts his willingness to overturn any prior cases that do not comport with reason or divine law: "For it is established rule to abide by former precedents, where the same points come again in litigation; [. . .] [y]et this rule admits of exception, where the former determination is most evidently contrary to reason, much more if it be contrary to the divine law" (Blackstone [1765] 1966, 69-70). Michael Lobban explains that "Blackstone seems to have adopted [his] notion of parliamentary without fully realizing its difficulties for his natural-law arguments and his belief in the primacy of the common law" ("Blackstone," 326).

29. Blackstone, *Commentaries*, 64.
30. Kellogg, *Oliver Wendell Holmes, Jr.*, 54-55.
31. Kellogg, *Oliver Wendell Holmes, Jr.*, 55.
32. Kellogg, *Oliver Wendell Holmes, Jr.*, 56.
33. Ibid.
34. Holmes, *Common Law*, 1.
35. Touster, "Holmes," 693.
36. Ibid.
37. Touster, "Holmes," 684.
38. Gordon, "Holmes's *Common Law*," 721.
39. Haack, "Pragmatism," 68.
40. Haack, "Pragmatism," 69.
41. Haack, "Pragmatism," 70.
42. Haack, "Pragmatism," 71.
43. Ibid.
44. Haack, "Pragmatism," 72.
45. See generally Holmes's (1897) "bad man theory" in "The Path of the Law."
46. "[A] legal duty so called is nothing but a prediction that if a man does or omits certain things he will be made to suffer in this or that way by judgment of the court;—and so of a legal right" (Holmes, "Path of the Law," 458). Here Holmes calls the law a "body of dogma or systemized prediction" (ibid.).
47. "The law talks about rights, and duties, and malice, and intent, and negligence, and so forth, and nothing is easier, or, I may say, more common in legal reasoning, than to take these words in their moral sense, at some stage of the argument, and so to drop into fallacy. For instance, when we speak of the rights of man in a moral sense, we mean to mark the limits of interference with individual freedom which we think are prescribed by conscience, or by our ideal, however reached. Yet it is certain that many laws have been enforced in the past, and it is likely that some are enforced now, which are condemned by the most enlightened opinion of the time, or which at all events pass the limit of interference as many consciences would draw it. Manifestly, therefore, nothing but confusion of thought can result from assuming that the rights of man in a moral sense are equally rights in the sense of the Constitution and the law. No doubt simple and extreme cases can be put of imaginable laws which the statute making power would not dare to enact, even in the absence of written constitutional prohibitions, because the community would rise in rebellion and fight; and this gives some plausibility to the

proposition that the law, if not a part of morality, is limited by it. But this limit of power is not coextensive with any system of morals. For the most part it falls far within the lines of any such system, and in some cases may extend beyond them, for reasons drawn from the habits of a particular people at a particular time. I once heard the late Professor Agassiz say that a German population would rise if you added two cents to the price of a glass of beer. A statute in such a case would be empty words, not because it was wrong, but because it could not be enforced. No one will deny that wrong statutes can be and are enforced, and we should not all agree as to which were the wrong ones" (Holmes, "Path of the Law," 460).

48. "[N]owadays no one doubts that a man may be liable, without any malevolent motive at all, for false statements manifestly calculated to inflict temporal damage. In stating the case in pleading, we still should call the defendant's conduct malicious; but, in my opinion at least, the word means nothing about motives, or even about the defendant's attitude toward the future, but only signifies that the tendency of his conduct under the known circumstances was very plainly to cause the plaintiff temporal harm" (Holmes, "Path of the Law," 463).

49. Kellogg, *Oliver Wendell Holmes, Jr.*, 34.

50. Kellogg, *Oliver Wendell Holmes, Jr.*, 94.

51. Ibid.

52. Kellogg, *Oliver Wendell Holmes, Jr.*, 95.

53. Ibid.

54. See Chapter 3 of this book.

55. Kellogg, *Oliver Wendell Holmes, Jr.*, 122.

56. Ralph Waldo Emerson, "Nature," in *Emerson: Essays & Lecture*, edited by Joel Porte (New York: Library of America, 1983), 7.

57. Oliver Wendell Holmes Jr., "Book Notices," *American Law Review* 14 (1880): 234.

58. Oliver Wendell Holmes, Jr., "Learning and Science," speech at a dinner of the Harvard Law School Association in Honor of Professor C. C. Langdell, June 25, 1895, Harvard University Holmes Digital Suite, Mark DeWolfe Howe's research materials on Holmes, 1858-1968: Finding Aid, Learning and Science, p. 68, online.

59. "[T]he North [. . .] was anxious to leave transcendentalism behind. The generational shift from transcendentalism to pragmatism is well known. [. . .] A classic example is Oliver Wendell Holmes Jr., the son of Emerson's good friend Oliver Wendell Holmes Sr. The younger Holmes left for a war he called 'a crusade in the cause of the whole civilized world,' but returned to announce, 'I do not know what is true.' Higher law lost its allure among the young men who fought a bloody war on its behalf" (Alan M. Levine and Daniel S. Malachuk, *A Political Companion to Ralph Waldo Emerson* [Lexington, KN: University of Kentucky Press, 2011], 15-16).

60. Menand, *Metaphysical Club*, x.

61. Ibid.

62. Menand, *Metaphysical Club*, 68.

63. Ibid.

64. Ralph Waldo Emerson, "Plato, or the Philosopher," in *Emerson: Essays & Lectures*, edited by Joel Porte (New York: Library of America, 1983), 634.

65. Emerson, "Art," 431.

66. Ibid.

67. Holmes, *Common Law*, 25.

68. Ibid.

69. Holmes, *Common Law*, 24.

70. Holmes, *Common Law*, 25.

71. Ibid.

72. Emerson, "Art," 432.

73. Emerson, "American Scholar," 56.

74. Emerson, "American Scholar," 56–57.

75. Kellogg, *Oliver Wendell Holmes, Jr.*, 34.

76. James, *Principles*, 192-94.

77. James, *Principles*, 185.

78. James, *Principles*, 187.

79. C.S. Peirce, "Some Consequences of Four Incapacities," *Journal of Speculative Philosophy* 2, no. 3 (1868): 140-57.

80. *Abrams* 250 U.S. 616 (1919) at 630.

81. C.S. Peirce, "The Fixation of Belief," *Popular Science Monthly* 12, no. 1 (1877): 6, Philpapers.

82. Peirce, "Fixation," 10.

83. C.S. Peirce, "How to Make Our Ideas Clear," *Popular Science Monthly* 12 (1887): 287, Philpapers.

84. Holmes, *Common Law*, 25.

85. C.S. Peirce, "A Guess at a Riddle," in *The Collected Papers of Charles Sanders Peirce*, edited by Charles Hartshorne and Paul Weis (Cambridge, MA: Harvard University Press, [1932] 1974), 223.

86. Peirce, "Guess," 224.

87. Menand, *Metaphysical Club*, 343.

88. *Lochner* 198 U.S. 45 (1905) at 79.

89. John Dewey, *The Public and its Problems*, edited by Melvin L. Rogers (University Park, PA: The Pennsylvania State University Press, [1927] 2012).

90. Dewey, *Public*, 86-89.

91. Dewey, *Public*, 44, 60.

92. Dewey, *Public*, 51.

93. John Dewey, "An Introductory Word," introduction to *The Metaphysics of Pragmatism*, by Sidney Hook (Chicago: Open Court Publishing Company, 1927), 1-5.

94. Dewey, *Public*, 70.

95. Dewey, *Public*, 69, 167.

96. Dewey, *Public*, 119-20.

97. Dewey, *Public*, 159-60.

98. Max Harold Fisch, *Classic American Philosophers: Peirce, James, Royce, Santayana, Dewey, Whitehead, 2nd ed* (New York: Fordham University Press, 1951), 8.

99. Oliver Wendell Holmes, Jr., Letter from Holmes to Lewis Einstein, June 17, 1908, Harvard University Holmes Digital Suite, Mark DeWolfe Howe's research materials on Holmes, 1858-1968: Finding Aid, Major Correspondence: Einstein, Lewis, Correspondent, March 22, 1908-July 23, 1910, online.

100. Oliver Wendell Holmes, Jr. to William James, March 24, 1907, Harvard University Holmes Digital Suite, Mark DeWolfe Howe's research materials on Holmes, 1858-1968: Finding Aid, James, William, 1867-1907, online.

101. James, *Principles*, 288.

102. William James, *A Pluralistic Universe* (New York: Longmans, Green & Co, 1909), 321-22.

103. James, *A Pluralistic Universe*, 322.

104. Davis v. Mills, 194 U.S. 451, 457 (1904) at 1904.

105. Holmes to James, March 24, 1907.

106. Ibid.

107. Ibid.

108. Oliver Wendell Holmes, Jr. to Harold Laski, March 4, 1920, Harvard University Holmes Digital Suite, Mark DeWolfe Howe's research materials on Holmes, 1858-1968: Finding Aid, Major Correspondence: Laski, Harold, correspondent, March-April 1920, online.

109. Holmes, Jr., "Natural Law," 41.

110. Posner, "What Has Pragmatism," 1661.

111. Posner, "What Has Pragmatism," 1662.

112. White, *Justice Oliver Wendell Holmes*, 359-60; Snyder, "House," 664-65, 673-74, 690-96, 702, 704-8, 713, 715, 717-19, 720.

113. Snyder, "House," 665-66, 671-74.

114. Richard Hofstadter, *The Age of Reform* (New York: Vintage Books, 1955), 216.

115. Hofstadter, *Age*, 5.

116. Northern Securities Co. v. United States, 193 U.S. 197 (1904).

117. *Northern Securities Company* 193 U.S. at 400.

118. For more on progressive efforts to disenfranchise black voters, see Michael Perman, *Struggle for Mastery: Disenfranchisement in the South, 1888-1908* (Chapel Hill, NC: University of North Carolina Press 2001); Jack Temple Kirby, *Darkness at the Dawning: Race and Reform in the Progressive South* (Philadelphia, PA: Lippincott, 1972); and Dewey W. Grantham, *Southern Progressivism: The Reconciliation of Progress and Tradition* (Knoxville, TN: University of Tennessee Press, 1983.

119. Snyder, "House," 678-87.

120. Snyder, "House," 697.

121. Snyder, "House," 696.

122. Woodrow Wilson, "The Ideals of America," *Atlantic Monthly* 90 (1902): 721-34, accessed May 8, 2015, http://www.theatlantic.com/magazine/archive/1902/12/the-ideals-of-america/376192.

123. Herbert David Croly, *The Promise of American Life* (New York: Macmillan Company, 1911), 255.

124. William James, *William James: Writings 1902-1910* (New York: Library of America, 1987), 1292.

125. Ibid.

126. James, *William James*, 1284.

127. John Dewey, *The Public and Its Problems*, edited by Melvin L. Rogers (University Park, PA: Pennsylvania State University Press, [1984] 2008), 178.

128. Dewey, *Public*, 179.

129. Dewey, *Public*, 183.

130. Richard Posner, *Law, Pragmatism, and Democracy* (Harvard University Press, 2003), 12.

131. Posner, *Law, Pragmatism*, 12.

132. Letter from Pollock to Holmes, July 3, 1874, in Howe, *Holmes-Pollock Letters*, 3.

133. Buck v. Bell, 274 U.S. 200 (1927).

134. Consider Giles v. Harris, 189 U.S. 475 (1903) in which Holmes refused to grant relief from an Alabama law disqualifying many blacks from voting.

135. *Buck* 274 U.S. at 207.

136. *Buck* 274 U.S. at 207.

137. Griswold v. Connecticut, 381 U.S. 479 (1965).

138. *Casey* 505 U.S. at 833-74.

139. Lawrence v. Texas, 539 U.S. 558 (2003).

140. *Buck* 274 U.S. at 208.

141. *Tyson* 273 U.S. 418 at 446.

142. *Vegelahn v. Guntner*, 167 Mass. at 104.

143. Holmes to James, March 24, 1907.

144. Touster, "Holmes," 679.

Bibliography

"The Supreme Court, 1967 Term: The Statistics." *Harvard Law Review* 82: 301.
"The Supreme Court, 1968 Term: The Statistics." *Harvard Law Review* 83: 277.
"The Supreme Court, 1969 Term: The Statistics." *Harvard Law Review* 84: 247.
"The Supreme Court, 1970 Term: The Statistics." *Harvard Law Review* 85: 344.
"The Supreme Court, 1971 Term: The Statistics." *Harvard Law Review* 86: 297.
"The Supreme Court, 1972 Term: The Statistics." *Harvard Law Review* 87: 303.
"The Supreme Court, 1973 Term: The Statistics." *Harvard Law Review* 88: 274.
"The Supreme Court, 1974 Term: The Statistics." *Harvard Law Review* 89: 275.
"The Supreme Court, 1975 Term: The Statistics." *Harvard Law Review* 90: 276.
"The Supreme Court, 1976 Term: The Statistics." *Harvard Law Review* 91: 295.
"The Supreme Court, 1977 Term: The Statistics." *Harvard Law Review* 92: 339.
"The Supreme Court, 1978 Term: The Statistics." *Harvard Law Review* 93: 275.
"The Supreme Court, 1979 Term: The Statistics." *Harvard Law Review* 94: 289.
"The Supreme Court, 1980 Term: The Statistics." *Harvard Law Review* 95: 339.
"The Supreme Court, 1981 Term: The Statistics." *Harvard Law Review* 96: 304.
"The Supreme Court, 1982 Term: The Statistics." *Harvard Law Review* 97: 295.
"The Supreme Court, 1983 Term: The Statistics." *Harvard Law Review* 98: 307.
"The Supreme Court, 1984 Term: The Statistics." *Harvard Law Review* 99: 322.
"The Supreme Court, 1985 Term: The Statistics." *Harvard Law Review* 100: 304.
"The Supreme Court, 1986 Term: The Statistics." *Harvard Law Review* 101: 362.
"The Supreme Court, 1987 Term: The Statistics." *Harvard Law Review* 102: 350.
"The Supreme Court, 1988 Term: The Statistics." *Harvard Law Review* 103: 394.
"The Supreme Court, 1989 Term: The Statistics." *Harvard Law Review* 104: 359.
"The Supreme Court, 1990 Term: The Statistics." *Harvard Law Review* 105: 419.
"The Supreme Court, 1991 Term: The Statistics." *Harvard Law Review* 106: 378.
"The Supreme Court, 1992 Term: The Statistics." *Harvard Law Review* 107: 372.
"The Supreme Court, 1993 Term: The Statistics." *Harvard Law Review* 108: 372.

"The Supreme Court, 1994 Term: The Statistics." *Harvard Law Review* 109: 340.

"The Supreme Court, 1995 Term: The Statistics." *Harvard Law Review* 110: 367.

"The Supreme Court, 1996 Term: The Statistics." *Harvard Law Review* 111: 431.

"The Supreme Court, 1997 Term: The Statistics." *Harvard Law Review* 112: 366.

"The Supreme Court, 1998 Term: The Statistics." *Harvard Law Review* 113: 400.

"The Supreme Court, 1999 Term: The Statistics." *Harvard Law Review* 114: 390.

"The Supreme Court, 2000 Term: The Statistics." *Harvard Law Review* 115: 539.

"The Supreme Court, 2001 Term: The Statistics." *Harvard Law Review* 116: 453.

"The Supreme Court, 2002 Term: The Statistics." *Harvard Law Review* 117: 480.

"The Supreme Court, 2003 Term: The Statistics." *Harvard Law Review* 118: 497.

"The Supreme Court, 2004 Term: The Statistics." *Harvard Law Review* 119: 420.

"The Supreme Court, 2005 Term: The Statistics." *Harvard Law Review* 120: 372.

"The Supreme Court, 2006 Term: The Statistics." *Harvard Law Review* 121: 436.

"The Supreme Court, 2007 Term: The Statistics." *Harvard Law Review* 122: 516.

"The Supreme Court, 2008 Term: The Statistics." *Harvard Law Review* 123: 382.

"The Supreme Court, 2009 Term: The Statistics." *Harvard Law Review* 124: 411.

Abrams, Paula. *Cross Purposes: Peirce v. Society of Good Sisters and the Struggle Over Compulsory Public Education.* Ann Arbor: University of Michigan Press, 2009.

Aichele, Gary J. *Oliver Wendell Holmes, Jr.: Soldier, Scholar, Judge.* Boston, MA: Twayne Publishers, 1989.

Albrecht, James M. *Reconstructing Individualism: A Pragmatic Tradition from Emerson to Ellison.* New York: Fordham University Press, 2009.

Alschuler, Albert W. "Rediscovering Blackstone." *University of Pennsylvania Law Review* 145-97 (1996-97): 1-55.

Alschuler, Albert W. "Descending Trail: Holmes' Path of the Law One Hundred Years Later." *Florida Law Review* 49 (1997): 353-420.

Alschuler, Albert W. "From Blackstone to Holmes: Revolt against Natural Law." *Pepperdine Law Review* 36 (2000-2001): 491-506.

Alschuler, Albert W. *Law without Values: The Life, Work, and Legacy of Justice Holmes.* Chicago: University of Chicago Press, 2000.

Anagnost, George T. "Trial by Jury and 'Common Law' Antecedents." *Arizona Attorney* 43 (2006): 38-42.

Bader, William D. "Some Thoughts on Blackstone, Precedent, and Originalism." *Vermont Law Review* 19: 5-18.

Baker, Liva. *The Justice from Beacon Hill: The Life and Times of Oliver Wendell Holmes.* New York: HarperCollins, 1991.

Balkin, Jack M. "Wrong the Day It Was Decided: *Lochner* and Constitutional Historicism." *Boston University Law Review* 85 (2005): 677-725.

Balkin, Jack M. "The Roots of the Living Constitution." *Boston University Law Review* 92 (2012): 1129-60.

Balkin, Jack M., and Sanford Levinson. "The Canons of Constitutional Law." *Harvard Law Review* 111 (1998): 964-1024.

Bartrum, Ian. "Constitutional Canon as Argumentative Metonymy." *William and Mary Bill of Rights Journal* 18 (2009): 327-93.

Berman, Harold J. *Law and Revolution: The Formation of the Western Legal Tradition.* Cambridge, MA: Harvard University Press, 1983.

Bernstein, David E. "Lochner's Legacy's Legacy." *Texas Law Review* 82 (2003): 1-64.

Bernstein, David. *Rehabilitating Lochner: Defending Individual Rights against Progressive Reform.* Chicago: University of Chicago Press, 2011.

Biddle, Francis. *Mr. Justice Holmes.* New York: Charles Scribner's Sons, 1943.

Blackstone, William. *Commentaries on the Laws of England, Book the First.* London: Dawsons of Pall Mall, (1765) 1966.

Blasi, Vincent. "Reading Holmes through the Lens of Schauer: The Abrams Dissent." *Notre Dame Law Review* 72 (1997): 1343-59.

Blasi, Vincent. "Holmes and the Marketplace of Ideas." *Supreme Court Review.* 2004: 1-46.

Bloom, Harold. *Agon: Towards a Theory of Revisionism.* New York: Oxford University Press, 1982.

Bloom, Harold. *The Western Canon.* New York: Riverhead Books, 1994.

Bloom, Harold. *How to Read and Why.* New York. Simon & Schuster, 2001.

Bloom, Harold. *Genius.* New York: Warner Books, 2002.

Bork, Robert H. *The Tempting of America: The Political Seduction of Law.* New York: Free Press, 1990.

Brown, R. Blake, and Bruce A. Kimball. "When Holmes Borrowed from Langdell: The Ultra Legal Formalism and Public Policy of Northern Securities (1904)." *American Journal of Legal History* 45 (2001): 278-321.

Cardozo, Benjamin. "Mr. Justice Holmes." *Harvard Law Review* 44 (1931): 682-92.

Cairns, John W. "Blackstone, an English Institutist: Legal Literature and the Rise of the Nation State." *Oxford Journal of Legal Studies* 4, no. 3 (1984): 318-360.

Cate, Irene M. Ten. "Speech, Truth, and Freedom: An Examination of John Stuart Mill's and Justice Oliver Wendell Holmes's Free Speech Defenses." *Yale Journal of Law & the Humanities* 22 (2010): 35-81.

Chroust, Anton-Hermann. "Blackstone Revisited." *University of Kansas City Law Review* 17 (1949): 24-34.

Coke, Edward. *The Reports of Sir Edward Coke in Thirteen Parts,* 1572-1617. London: Joseph Butterworth and Son, (1777) 1826.

Coke, Edward. *The Selected Speeches and Writings of Sir Edward Coke,* edited by Steve Sheppard. Indianapolis, IN: Liberty Fund, 2003.

Cole, David. "Agon at Agora: Creative Misreadings in the First Amendment Tradition." *Yale Law Journal* 95 (1986): 857-905.

Collins, Ronald. "Prologue." In *The Essential Holmes: A Free Speech Chronicle and Reader,* edited by Ronald Collins. New York: Cambridge University Press, 2010.

Cover, Robert. "The Left, the Right, and the First Amendment: 1918-1928." *Maryland Law Review* 95 (1981): 349-88.

Croly, Herbert David. *The Promise of American Life.* New York: Macmillan Company, 1911.

Crosskey, William W. *Politics and the Constitution in the History of the United States.* Chicago: University of Chicago Press, 1953.

Currie, David P. *The Constitution in the Supreme Court.* Chicago: University of Chicago Press, 1990.

Danisch, Robert. "Aphorism, Enthymemes, and Oliver Wendell Holmes, Jr. on the First Amendment." *Rhetoric Review* 27 (2008): 219-35.

Dewey, John. "An Introductory Word." In *The Metaphysics of Pragmatism,* by Sidney Hook. Chicago: Open Court Publishing Company, 1927.

Dewey, John. *The Public and Its Problems*, edited by Melvin L. Rogers. University Park, PA: Pennsylvania State University Press, (1927) 2012.

Dewey, John. "Justice Holmes and the Liberal Mind." In *John Dewey: The Later Works, Vol. 3: 1927-28*, edited by Ann Boydston. Carbondale: Southern Illinois University Press, (1984) 2008.

Dickinson, Emily. *The Selected Poems of Emily Dickinson*. Hertfordshire, United Kingdom: Worsdsworth Editions, Ltd., 1994. See esp. "Void."

Dudley, Earl C. "Federalism and Federal Rule of Evidence 501: Privilege and Vertical Choice of Law." *Georgetown Law Journal* 82 (1994): 1781-843.

Duggan, Michael F. "The Municipal Ideal and the Unknown End: A Resolution of Oliver Wendell Holmes." *North Dakota Law Review* 83 (2007): 463-546.

Eastman, John. "Reflections on Justice Thomas's Twenty Years on the Bench." *University of Detroit Mercy Law Review* 88 (2011): 691-705.

Emerson, Ralph Waldo. "The American Scholar." In *Emerson: Essays & Lectures*, edited by Joel Porte. New York: Library of America, 1983.

Emerson, Ralph Waldo. "Art." In *Emerson: Essays & Lectures*, edited by Joel Porte. New York: Library of America, 1983.

Emerson, Ralph Waldo. "Nature." In *Emerson: Essays & Lecture*, edited by Joel Porte. New York: Library of America, 1983.

Emerson, Ralph Waldo. "Plato, or the Philosopher." In *Emerson: Essays & Lectures*, edited by Joel Porte. New York: Library of America, 1983.

Emerson, Ralph Waldo. "Spiritual Laws." In *Emerson: Essays and Lectures*, edited by Joel Porte. New York: Library of America, 1983.

Emerson, Ralph Waldo. "The Visit." In *Emerson: Collected Poems and Translations*, edited by Harold Bloom and Paul Kane. New York: Library of America, 1994.

Emerson, Ralph Waldo. "The American Scholar." In *Emerson: Essays & Poems*. New York: Library of America, 1996.

Emerson, Ralph Waldo. "Circles." In *Emerson: Essays & Poems*. New York: Library of America, 1996.

Emerson, Ralph Waldo. "Divinity School Address." In *Emerson: Essays & Poems*. New York: Library of America, 1996.

Emerson, Ralph Waldo. "Literary Ethics." In *Emerson: Essays & Poems*. New York: Library of America, 1996.

Emerson, Ralph Waldo. "Plato, or the Philosopher." In *Emerson: Essays & Poems*. New York: Library of America, 1996.

Emerson, Ralph Waldo. "The Poet." In *Emerson: Essays & Poems*. New York: Library of America, 1996.

Emerson, Ralph Waldo. "Politics." In *Emerson: Essays & Poems*. New York: Library of America, 1996.

Emerson, Ralph Waldo. "Self-Reliance." In *Emerson: Essays & Poems*. New York: Library of America, 1996.

Emerson, Ralph Waldo. "The Transcendentalist." In *Emerson: Essays & Poems*. New York: Library of America, 1996.

Emerson, Ralph Waldo. "The Young American." In *Emerson: Essays & Poems*. New York: Library of America, 1996.

Epstein, Lee, William M. Landes, and Richard Posner. "Why (and When) Judges Dissent: A Theoretical and Empirical Analysis." *Journal of Legal Analysis* 3 (2011): 101-37.

Fagan, Jr., James F. "*Abrams v. United States*: Remembering the Authors of Both Opinions." *Touro Law Review* 8 (1992): 453-520.

Fairman, Charles. *American Constitutional Decisions*. New York: Holt, 1950.

Feldman, Stephen M. "Free Speech, World War I, and Republican Democracy: The Internal and External Holmes." *First Amendment Law Review* 6 (2008): 192-251.

Fisch, Max Harold. *Classic American Philosophers: Peirce, James, Royce, Santayana, Dewey, Whitehead, 2nd ed.* New York: Fordham University Press, 1951.

Fisher, Linda E. "Pragmatism Is as Pragmatism Does: Of Posner, Public Policy, and Empirical Reality." *New Mexico Law Review* 31 (2001): 455-92.

Frankfurter, Felix. *Mr. Justice Holmes and the Supreme Court*. Cambridge, MA: Harvard University Press, 1938.

Frankfurter, Felix. *Mr. Justice Holmes and the Supreme Court*. Cambridge, MA: Harvard University Press, 1939.

Friedman, Barry. "History of the Countermajoritarian Difficulty, Part Three: The Lesson of Lochner." *New York University Law Review* 76 (2001): 1383-455.

Frost, Robert. *The Poetry of Robert Frost*, edited by Edward Connery Lathem. New York: Henry Holt and Company, 1975.

Gamso, Jeffrey M. "Sex Discrimination and the First Amendment." *Texas Tech Law Review* 17 (1986): 1577-603.

Garrow, David J. "'The Lowest Form of Animal Life?': Supreme Court Clerks and Supreme Court History." *Cornell Law Review* 84 (1999): 855-94.

Gillies, Paul S. "Dissents and Deceptions." *Vermont Bar Journal and Law Digest* 25 (1999): 9-10.

Gillmore, Howard. "De-Lochnerizing Lochner." *Boston University Law Review* 85 (2005): 859-65.

Ginsburg, Ruth Bader. "Remarks on Writing Separately." *Washington Law Review* 65 (1990): 133-50.

Goodnight, David. "Chaos on Appeal: The Tenth Circuit's Local Judge Rule." *Denver University Law Review* 67 (1990): 515-44.

Gordon, Robert W. "Holmes's *Common Law* as Legal and Social Science." *Hofstra Law Review* 10 (1981-82): 719-46.

Gordon, Robert W. "Introduction." In *The Legacy of Oliver Wendell Holmes Jr.*, edited by Robert W. Gordon. Stanford, CA: Stanford University Press, 1992.

Gordon, Robert W. "The Struggle Over the Past." *Cleveland State Law Review* 44 (1996): 123-44.

Grantham, Dewey W. *Southern Progressivism: The Reconciliation of Progress and Tradition*. Knoxville, TN: University of Tennessee Press, 1983.

Greene, Jamal. "The Anticanon." *Harvard Law Review* 125 (2011): 380-475.

Gregg, Paul L. "The Pragmatism of Mr. Justice Holmes." *Georgetown Law Journal* 31 (1942-43): 262-95.

Grey, Thomas C. "Holmes and Legal Pragmatism." *Stanford Law Review* 41 (1989): 787-870.

Grey, Thomas. "Hear the Other Side: Wallace Stevens and Pragmatist Legal Theory." *Southern California Law Review* 63 (1990): 1569-596.

Grey, Thomas. *The Wallace Stevens Case: Law and the Practice of Poetry*. Cambridge, MA: Harvard University Press, 1991.

Grey, Thomas. "Holmes and Legal Pragmatism." *Stanford Law Review* 41 (1989): 787-870.

Gross, Daniel. "An Empirical Study of the Vindicated Dissents of the New York Appellate Division, Fourth Department, From 2000 to 2010." *Albany Law Review* 74 (2010-11): 931-949.

Gunther, Gerald. "Learned Hand and the Origins of Modern First Amendment Doctrine: Some Fragments of History." *Stanford Law Review* 27 (1975): 719-73.

Gunther, Gerald. *Learned Hand: The Man and the Judge, 2nd Ed* (New York: Oxford University Press, 2011.

Haack, Susan. "Pragmatism, Law, and Morality: The Lessons of Buck v. Bell." *European Journal of Pragmatism and American Philosophy* 3 (2011): 65-87.

Hale, Matthew. *The History of the Common Law of England.* Stafford, England: J. Nutt, assignee of Edw. Sayer for J. Walthoe, 1713.

Hart, Jr., Henry M. "Holmes' Positivism—An Addendum." *Harvard Law Review* 64 (1951): 929-37.

Healy, Thomas. *The Great Dissent: How Oliver Wendell Holmes Changed His Mind—and Changed the History of Free Speech in America.* New York: Metropolitan Books, 2013.

Henderson, M. Todd. "From Seriatim to Consensus and Back Again: A Theory of Dissent." *Supreme Court Review* (2007): 283-344.

Heyman, Steven J. "The Dark Side of the Force: The Legacy of Justice Holmes for First Amendment Jurisprudence." *William and Mary Bill of Rights Journal* 19 (2011): 661-723.

Hofstadter, Richard. *The Age of Reform.* New York: Vintage Books, 1955.

Holmes, Jr., Oliver Wendell. "Learning and Science." Speech at a dinner of the Harvard Law School Association in Honor of Professor C. C. Langdell, June 25. Harvard University Holmes Digital Suite. Mark DeWolfe Howe's research materials on Holmes, 1858-1968: Finding Aid, Learning and Science. Online.

Holmes, Jr., Oliver Wendell. Oliver Wendell Holmes, Jr. to Ellen A. Curtis, April 26, 1908. Harvard University Holmes Digital Suite. Mark DeWolfe Howe's research materials on Holmes, 1858-1968: Finding Aid, Curtis, Ellen A., 1900-1933. Online.

Holmes, Jr., Oliver Wendell. Oliver Wendell Holmes, Jr. to James Bradley Thayer, December 11, 1898. Harvard University Holmes Digital Suite. Mark DeWolfe Howe's research materials on Holmes, 1858-1968: Finding Aid, Thayer, James Bradley, 1890-1900. Online.

Holmes, Jr., Oliver Wendell. Oliver Wendell Holmes, Jr. to Lady Pollock, July 2, 1895. Harvard University Holmes Digital Suite. Mark DeWolfe Howe's research materials on Holmes, 1858-1968: Finding Aid, Typescripts with footnotes, 1874-1895. Online.

Holmes, Jr., Oliver Wendell. Oliver Wendell Holmes, Jr. to Lady Pollock, July 20, 1897. Harvard University Holmes Digital Suite. Mark DeWolfe Howe's research materials on Holmes, 1858-1968: Finding Aid, Complete set of typescripts, in-terfiled, 1896-1902. Online.

Holmes, Jr., Oliver Wendell. Oliver Wendell Holmes, Jr. to Nina L. Grey. Harvard University Holmes Digital Suite. Mark DeWolfe Howe's research materials on Holmes, 1858-1968: Finding Aid, Major Correspondence: Gray, Nina L., corre-spondent, September 1, 1928-December 30, 1928. Online.

Holmes, Jr., Oliver Wendell. Oliver Wendell Holmes, Jr. to Sir Frederic Pollock, August 27, 1883. Harvard University Holmes Digital Suite. Mark DeWolfe Howe's research materials on Holmes, 1858-1968: Finding Aid, Typescripts with footnotes, 1874-1895. Online.

Holmes, Jr., Oliver Wendell. Oliver Wendell Holmes, Jr. to Sir Frederick Pollock, May 13, 1898. Harvard University Holmes Digital Suite. Mark DeWolfe Howe's research materials on Holmes, 1858-1968: Finding Aid, Typescripts with footnotes, 1896-1909. Online.

Holmes, Jr., Oliver Wendell. Oliver Wendell Holmes, Jr. to William James, April 19, 1868. Harvard University Holmes Digital Suite. Mark DeWolfe Howe's research materials on Holmes, 1858-1968: Finding Aid, James, William, 1867-1907. Online.

Holmes, Jr., Oliver Wendell. Letter from Holmes to Lewis Einstein, June 17, 1908. Harvard University Holmes Digital Suite. Mark DeWolfe Howe's research materials on Holmes, 1858-1968: Finding Aid, Major Correspondence: Einstein, Lewis, Correspondent, March 22, 1908-July 23, 1910. Online.

Holmes, Jr., Oliver Wendell. Letter from Leland B. Duer to Justice Frankfurter, February 16, 1938. Harvard University Holmes Digital Suite. John G. Palfrey (1875-1945), collection of Oliver Wendell Holmes, Jr. Papers, 1715-1938: Finding Aid, Secretaries (OHW's law clerks), 1912-1938. Online.

Holmes, Jr., Oliver Wendell. Letter to A.G. Sedgwick, 12 July 1879. Quoted in Robert W. Gordon, "Holmes' *Common Law* as Legal and Social Science." *Hofstra Law Review* 10: 719-46.

Holmes, Jr., Oliver Wendell. "Book Notices." *American Law Review* 14 (1880): 232-35.

Holmes, Jr., Oliver Wendell. *The Common Law*. Chicago: American Bar Association, 1881.

Holmes, Jr., Oliver Wendell. "The Path of the Law." *Harvard Law Review* 10 (1897): 457-78.

Holmes, Jr., Oliver Wendell. "The Theory of Legal Interpretation." *Harvard Law Review* 12 (1898-99): 417-20.

Holmes, Jr., Oliver Wendell. "Law in Science and Science in Law." *Harvard Law Review* 12 (1899): 443-63.

Holmes, Jr., Oliver Wendell. "Ideals and Doubts." *Illinois Law Review* 10 (1915): 1-4.

Holmes, Jr., Oliver Wendell. "Ideals and Doubts." *Law Student's Helper* 23 (1915): 4-5.

Holmes, Jr., Oliver Wendell. "Natural Law." *Harvard Law Review* 32 (1918-19): 40-44.

Holmes, Jr., Oliver Wendell. "Memorial Day Address." In *The Essential Holmes: Selections from the Letters, Speeches, Judicial Opinions, and Other Writings of Oliver Wendell Holmes, Jr.*, edited by Richard Posner. Chicago: University of Chicago Press, 1992.

Holmes, Jr., Oliver Wendell. Oliver Wendell Holmes, Jr. to Albert J. Beveridge. July 11, 1926. Harvard University Holmes Digital Suite. Mark DeWolfe Howe's research materials on Holmes, 1858-1968: Finding Aid, Beveridge, Albert J., 1915-1917. Online.

Holmes, Jr., Oliver Wendell. Oliver Wendell Holmes, Jr. to Baroness Marie Moncheur, July 16, 1910. Harvard University Holmes Digital Suite. Mark DeWolfe Howe's research materials on Holmes, 1858-1968: Finding Aid, October 1909-1910. Online.

Holmes, Jr., Oliver Wendell. Oliver Wendell Holmes, Jr. to Ellen A. Curtis, February 9, 1926. Harvard University Holmes Digital Suite. Mark DeWolfe Howe's research materials on Holmes, 1858-1968: Finding Aid, Curtis, Ellen A. 1900-1933. Online.

Holmes, Jr., Oliver Wendell. Oliver Wendell Holmes, Jr. to Ellen A. Curtis, January 12, 1913. Harvard University Holmes Digital Suite. Mark DeWolfe Howe's research materials on Holmes, 1858-1968: Finding Aid, Curtis, Ellen A. 1900-1933. Online.

Holmes, Jr., Oliver Wendell. Oliver Wendell Holmes, Jr. to Ellen A. Curtis, November 16, 1926. Harvard University Holmes Digital Suite. Mark DeWolfe Howe's research materials on Holmes, 1858-1968: Finding Aid, Curtis, Ellen A. 1900-1933. Online.

Holmes, Jr., Oliver Wendell. Oliver Wendell Holmes, Jr. to Ethel Scott, February 18, 1910. Harvard University Holmes Digital Suite. Mark DeWolfe Howe's research materials on Holmes, 1858-1968: Finding Aid, 1908-1912. Online.

Holmes, Jr., Oliver Wendell. Oliver Wendell Holmes, Jr. to Harold Laski, April 12, 1931. Harvard University Holmes Digital Suite. Mark DeWolfe Howe's research materials on Holmes, 1858-1968: Finding Aid, Major Correspondence: Laski, Harold, correspondent, January-April 1931. Online.

Holmes, Jr., Oliver Wendell. Oliver Wendell Holmes, Jr. to Harold Laski, May 12, 1922. Harvard University Holmes Digital Suite. Mark DeWolfe Howe's research materials on Holmes, 1858-1968: Finding Aid, Major Correspondence: Laski, Harold, correspondent, April-June 1922. Online.

Holmes, Jr., Oliver Wendell. Oliver Wendell Holmes, Jr. to Harold Laski, May 18, 1918. Harvard University Holmes Digital Suite. Mark DeWolfe Howe's research materials on Holmes, 1858-1968: Finding Aid, Major Correspondence: Laski, Harold, correspondent, March-May 1918. Online

Holmes, Jr., Oliver Wendell. Oliver Wendell Holmes, Jr. to Harold Laski, November 23, 1926. Harvard University Holmes Digital Suite. Mark DeWolfe Howe's research materials on Holmes, 1858-1968: Finding Aid, Major Correspondence: Laski, Harold, correspondent, October 16-November 21, 1926. Online.

Holmes, Jr., Oliver Wendell. Oliver Wendell Holmes, Jr. to Harold Laski, September 9, 1929. Harvard University Holmes Digital Suite. Mark DeWolfe Howe's research materials on Holmes, 1858-1968: Finding Aid: September 9 – November 3, 1929. Online.

Holmes, Jr., Oliver Wendell. Oliver Wendell Holmes, Jr. to Harold Laski, March 4, 1920. Harvard University Holmes Digital Suite. Mark DeWolfe Howe's research materials on Holmes, 1858-1968: Finding Aid, Major Correspondence: Laski, Harold, correspondent, March-April 1920. Online.

Holmes, Jr., Oliver Wendell. Oliver Wendell Holmes, Jr. to Joaquim Nabuco, July 2, 1908. Harvard University Holmes Digital Suite. Mark DeWolfe Howe's research materials on Holmes, 1858-1968: Finding Aid, Nabuco, Joaquim, 1907-1910. Online.

Holmes, Jr., Oliver Wendell. Oliver Wendell Holmes, Jr. to Laurence Curtis, November 18, 1926. Harvard University Holmes Digital Suite. Holmes, Oliver Wendell, Jr., Addenda, 1818-1978, Correspondence: Curtis, Laurence, correspondent, 1921-1929. Online.

Holmes, Jr., Oliver Wendell. Oliver Wendell Holmes, Jr. to Lewis Einstein, August 9, 1921. Harvard University Holmes Digital Suite. Mark DeWolfe Howe's research materials on Holmes, 1858-1968: Finding Aid, Major Correspondence: Einstein, Lewis, correspondent, October 10, 1920-March 31, 1922. Online.

Holmes, Jr., Oliver Wendell. Oliver Wendell Holmes, Jr. to Lewis Einstein." July 11, 1925. Harvard University Holmes Digital Suite. Mark DeWolfe Howe's research materials on Holmes, 1858-1968: Finding Aid, Einstein, Lewis, correspondent, June 4, 1924 – September 21, 1925. Online.

Holmes, Jr., Oliver Wendell. Oliver Wendell Holmes, Jr. to Margaret Bevan, August 19, 1913. Harvard University Holmes Digital Suite. Addenda, 1818-1978. Correspondence: Bevan, Margaret, correspondent, 1913-1915. Online.

Holmes, Jr., Oliver Wendell. Oliver Wendell Holmes, Jr. to Margaret Bevan, May 18, 1915. Harvard University Holmes Digital Suite. Addenda, 1818-1978. Correspondence: Bevan, Margaret, correspondent, 1913-1915. Online.

Holmes, Jr., Oliver Wendell. Oliver Wendell Holmes, Jr. to Margaret Bevan, November 6, 1913. Harvard University Holmes Digital Suite. Addenda, 1818-1978. Correspondence: Bevan, Margaret, correspondent, 1913-1915. Online.

Holmes, Jr., Oliver Wendell. Oliver Wendell Holmes, Jr. to Morris Cohen, November 29, 1926. Harvard University Holmes Digital Suite. Mark DeWolfe Howe's research materials on Holmes, 1858-1968: Finding Aid, Cohen, Morris Raphael, 1909-1934. Online.

Holmes, Jr., Oliver Wendell. Oliver Wendell Holmes, Jr. to Nina L. Grey, August 30, 1904. Harvard University Holmes Digital Suite. Mark DeWolfe Howe's research materials on Holmes, 1858-1968: Finding Aid, Major Correspondence: Gray, Nina L., correspondent, July 23, 1904-September 26, 1904. Online.

Holmes, Jr., Oliver Wendell. Oliver Wendell Holmes, Jr. to William James, March 24, 1907. Harvard University Holmes Digital Suite. Mark DeWolfe Howe's research materials on Holmes, 1858-1968: Finding Aid, James, William, 1867-1907. Online.

Horowitz, Irving Louis. *Persuasions & Prejudices: An Informal Compendium of Modern Social Science, 1953-1988.* New Brunswick, NJ: Transaction Publishers, 1989.

Howe, Mark DeWolfe, ed. *Holmes-Pollock Letters: The Correspondence of Mr. Justice Holmes and Sir Frederick Pollock 1874-1932, Volumes I and II.* Cambridge, MA: Harvard University Press, 1941.

Howe, Mark DeWolfe, ed. *Holmes-Laski Letters: The Correspondence of Mr. Justice Holmes and Harold J. Laski, 1916-1935, Volumes I and II.* Cambridge, MA: Harvard University Press, 1953.

Howe, Mark DeWolfe. "Holmes's Positivism—A Brief Rejoinder." *Harvard Law Review* 64 (1950-51): 937-39.

Howe, Mark DeWolfe. "The Positivism of Mr. Justice Holmes." *Harvard Law Review* 64 (1951): 529-46.

Hutchinson, Allan C. *Evolution and the Common Law.* New York: Cambridge University Press, 2005.

Hutchinson, Allan C. *Laughing at the Gods: Great Judges and How They Made the Common Law.* New York: Cambridge University Press, 2012.

Issacharoff, Samuel. "Federalized America: Reflections on *Erie v. Tompkins* and State-Based Regulation." *Journal of Law, Economics & Policy* 10 (2013): 199-224.

James, William. *The Principles of Psychology, Vol. 1.* New York: Henry Holt and Company, 1890.

James, William. *A Pluralistic Universe.* New York: Longmans, Green & Co, 1909.

James, William. *William James: Writings 1902-1910.* New York: Library of America, 1987. See esp. "The Moral Equivalent of War."

Jucewicz, Joseph, and Lawrence Baum. "Workload Influences on Supreme Court Acceptance Rates, 1975-1984." *Western Political Quarterly* 43 (1990): 123-35.

Kalven, Harry. *A Worthy Tradition: Freedom of Speech in America,* edited by Jamie Kalven. New York: Harper & Row, 1989.

Kellogg, Frederic R. *Oliver Wendell Holmes, Jr., Legal Theory, and Judicial Restraint.* Cambridge, UK: Cambridge University Press, 2007.

Kermode, Frank, and Joan Richardson, eds. *Stevens: Collected Poetry & Prose.* New York: The Library of America, 1997.

Kirby, Jack Temple. *Darkness at the Dawning: Race and Reform in the Progressive South.* Philadelphia, PA: Lippincott, 1972.

Koopman, Colin. *Pragmatism as Transition: Historicity and Hope in James, Dewey, and Rorty.* New York: Columbia University Press, 2009.

Koopman, Colin. "Genealogical Pragmatism: How History Matters for Foucault and Dewey." *Journal of the Philosophy of History* 5 (2011): 533-61.

Krishnakumar, Anita S. "On the Evolution of the Canonical Dissent." *Rutgers Law Review* 52 (2000): 781-826.

L'Heureux-Dubé, Claire. "The Dissenting Opinion: Voice of the Future." *Osgoode Hall Law Journal* 38 (2000): 496-517.

Leonard, Gerald. "Holmes on the Lochner Court." *Boston University Law Review* 85 (2005): 1001-15.

Lerner, Max. *The Mind and Faith of Justice Holmes: His Speeches, Essays, Letters, and Judicial Opinions.* New Brunswick, NJ: Transaction Publishers, 1989.

Levin, Jonathan. *The Poetics of Transition: Emerson, Pragmatism, & American Literary Modernism.* Durham, NC: Duke University Press, 1999.

Levine, Alan M., and Daniel S. Malachuk. *A Political Companion to Ralph Waldo Emerson.* Lexington, KY: University of Kentucky Press, 2011.

Levy, David W., and Bruce Allen Murphy. "Preserving the Progressive Spirit in a Conservative Time: The Joint Reform Efforts of Justice Brandeis and Professor Frankfurter, 1916-1933." *Michigan Law Review* 78 (1980): 1252-304.

Lewis, Anthony. *Make No Law: The Sullivan Case and the First Amendment.* New York: First Vintage Books Edition, (1991) 1992.

Litwiller, Lisa. "A SLAPP in the Face: Why Principles of Federalism Suggest That Federal District Courts Should Stop Turning the Other Cheek." *Journal of Court Innovation* 67 (2008): 67-96.

Lobban, Michael. "Blackstone and the Science of Law." *Historical Journal* 30 (1987): 311-35.

McKinnon, Harold R. "The Secret of Mr. Justice Holmes: An Analysis." *American Bar Association Journal* 36 (1950): 261-64, 342-46.

McKnight, Joseph W. "Blackstone, Quasi-Jurisprudent." *Southwestern Law Journal* 13 (1959): 399-411.

Menand, Louis. *The Metaphysical Club.* New York: Farrar, Straus, Giroux, 2001.

Menand, Louis. *American Studies.* New York: Farrar, Straus, and Giroux, 2002.

Mendenhall, Allen. "Oliver Wendell Holmes Jr. and the Darwinian Common Law Paradigm." *European Journal of Pragmatism and American Philosophy* 7 (2015), no. 2: 129-51.

Mendenhall, Allen. "Pragmatism on the Shoulders of Emerson: Oliver Wendell Holmes Jr.'s Jurisprudence as a Synthesis of Emerson, Peirce, James, and Dewey." *The South Carolina Review* 48, no. 1 (2015): 93–109.

Mendenhall, Allen. "Oliver Wendell Holmes Jr. Is the Use of Calling Emerson a Pragmatist: A Brief and Belated Response to Stanley Cavell." *Faulkner Law Review* 6, no. 1 (2014): 197–230.

Mendenhall, Allen. "Dissent as a Site of Aesthetic Adaptation in the Work of Oliver Wendell Holmes Jr." *British Journal of American Legal Studies* 1 (2012): 512–50.

Mendenhall, Allen. "Holmes and Dissent." *The Journal Jurisprudence* 12 (2011): 679–726.

Mendenhall, Allen. "The Power of Dissent." *The Alabama Lawyer* 77, no. 3 (2016): 170-71.

Mennel, Robert M., and Christine L. Compston, eds. *Holmes and Frankfurter: Their Correspondence, 1912-1934.* Hanover, NH: University Press of New England, 1996.

Meyler, Bernadette. "Towards a Common Law Originalism." *Stanford Law Review* 59 (2006): 551-600.

Miller, Jeffrey G. "Evolutionary Statutory Interpretation: Mr. Justice Scalia Meets Darwin." *Pace Law Review* 20 (2000): 409-32.

Minda, Gary. "Commentary: The Dragon in the Cave." *Brooklyn Law Review* 63 (1997): 129-44.

Monaghan, Henry Paul. "Supremacy Clause Textualism." *Columbia Law Review* 110 (2010): 731-96.

Nelson, William E., Harvey Rishikof, I. Scott Messinger, and Michael Jo. "The Liberal Tradition of the Supreme Court Clerkship: Its Rise, Fall, and Reincarnation?" *Vanderbilt Law Review* 62 (2009): 1749-814.

Nolan, Dennis R. "Sir William Blackstone and the New American Republic: A Study of Intellectual Impact." *New York University Law Review* 51 (1976): 731-68.

Oppenheim, Leonard. "Civil Liberties Doctrines of Mr. Justice Holmes and Mr. Justice Cardozo." *Tulane Law Review* 20 (1945): 177-219.

Palmer, Ben W. "Hobbes, Holmes, and Hitler." *American Bar Journal* 31 (1945): 569-73.

Palmer, Ben W. "Defense against Leviathan." *American Bar Journal* 32 (1946): 328-32.

Palmer, Ben W. "The Totalitarianism of Mr. Justice Holmes: Another Chapter in the Controversy." *American Bar Journal* 37 (1951): 809-11.

Peabody, James Bishop, ed. *The Holmes-Einstein Letters: Correspondence of Mr. Justice Holmes and Lewis Einstein, 1903-1935.* London: St. Martin's Press, 1964.

Peirce, C.S. "Some Consequences of Four Incapacities." *Journal of Speculative Philosophy* 2, no. 3 (1868): 140-57.

Peirce, C.S. "The Fixation of Belief." *Popular Science Monthly* 12, no. 1 (1877): 1-15, Philpapers.

Peirce, C.S. "How to Make Our Ideas Clear." *Popular Science Monthly* 12 (1887): 286-302, Philpapers.

Peirce, C.S. "A Guess at a Riddle." In *The Collected Papers of Charles Sanders Peirce*, edited by Charles Hartshorne and Paul Weis. Cambridge, MA: Harvard University Press, (1932) 1974.

Peppers, Todd C. *Courtiers of the Marble Palace: The Rise and Influence of the Supreme Court Law Clerk.* Stanford, CA: Stanford University Press, 2006.

Perman, Michael. *Struggle for Mastery: Disenfranchisement in the South, 1888-1908* Chapel Hill, NC: University of North Carolina Press, 2001.

Perry, Ralph Barton. *The Thought and Character of William James.* New York: George Braziller, 1954.

Plucknett, Theodore F. T. *A Concise History of the Common Law.* Indianapolis, IN: Liberty Fund, Inc., (1929) 2010.

Poirier, Richard. *Poetry and Pragmatism.* London: Faber and Faber, 1992.

Poirier, Richard. *Poetry and Pragmatism.* Boston and London: Faber and Faber, 1992.

Pollock, Frederick. Frederick Pollock to Oliver Wendell Holmes, Jr., November 14, 1923. Harvard University Holmes Digital Suite. Mark DeWolfe Howe's research materials on Holmes, 1858-1968: Finding Aid, Complete set of typescripts, interfiled, 1923-1924. Online.

Posner, Richard. "Blackstone and Bentham." *Journal of Law & Economics* 19 (1976): 569-606.

Posner, Richard. "What Has Pragmatism to Offer Law?" *Southern California Law Review* 63 (1990): 1653-70.

Posner, Richard, ed. *The Essential Holmes: Selections from the Letters, Speeches, Judicial Opinions, and Other Writings of Oliver Wendell Holmes, Jr.* Chicago: University of Chicago Press, 1992.

Posner, Richard. "Introduction." In *The Essential Holmes: Selections from the Letters, Speeches, Judicial Opinions, and Other Writings of Oliver Wendell Holmes, Jr.* Chicago: University of Chicago Press, 1992.

Posner, Richard. "Law and Literature: A Relation Reargued." In *Law and Literature: Text and Theory,* edited by Lenora Ledwon. New York: Garland Publishing, 1996.

Posner, Richard. *Law and Literature.* Cambridge, MA: Harvard University Press, 1998.

Posner, Richard. *Law, Pragmatism, and Democracy.* Cambridge, MA: Harvard University Press, 2003.

Posnock, Ross. *The Trial of Curiosity: Henry James, William James, and the Challenge of Modernity.* New York: Oxford University Press, 1991.

Post, Robert. "Federalism in the Taft Court Era: Can It Be 'Revived'?" *Duke Law Journal* 51 (2001-2): 1513-640.

Presser, Stephen B. "Some Thoughts on Our Present Discontents and Duties: The Cardinal, Oliver Wendell Holmes, Jr., the Unborn, the Senate, and Us." *Ave Maria Law Review* 1 (2003): 113-126.

Primus, Richard A. "Canon, Anti-Canon, and Judicial Dissent." *Duke Law Journal* 48 (1998): 243-303.

Ragan, Fred D. "Justice Oliver Wendell Holmes, Jr., Zechariah Chafee, Jr., and the Clear and Present Danger Test for Free Speech: The First Year, 1919." *Journal of American History* 58 (1971): 24-45.

Reimann, Mathias. "Why Holmes?" *Michigan Law Review* 88 (1990): 1908-924.

Richardson, Joan. *A Natural History of Pragmatism: The Fact of Feeling from Jonathan Edwards to Gertrude Stein.* Cambridge, UK: Cambridge University Press, 2007.

Richardson, Joan. *Pragmatism and American Experience: An Introduction.* Cambridge, UK: Cambridge University Press, 2014.

Richardson, Joan. *A Natural History of Pragmatism.* New York: Cambridge University Press, 2007.

Richardson, Robert D. *Emerson: The Mind on Fire.* Berkeley, CA: University of California Press, 1995.

Rogat, Yosal, and James M. O'Fallon. "Mr. Justice Holmes: A Dissenting Opinion—The Speech Cases." *Stanford Law Review* 36 (1984): 1349-406.

Rorty, Richard. "The Banality of Pragmatism and the Poetry of Justice." *Southern California Law Review* 63 (1989-90): 1811-819.

Schor, Miguel. "Contextualizing the Debate between Originalism and the Living Constitution." *Drake Law Review* 59 (2010-11): 961-72.

Schwartz, Bernard. "Holmes versus Hand: Clear and Present Danger or Advocacy of Unlawful Action?" *Supreme Court Review* (1994): 209-45.

Sears, Alan. "Preface." In *Sir William Blackstone and the Common Law: Blackstone's Legacy to America,* by Robert D. Stacey. Eugene, OR: ACW Press, 2003.

Snyder, Brad. "The House That Built Holmes." *Law and History Review* 30 (2012): 661-721.

Springer, James W. "Natural Selection or Natural Law: A Reconsideration of the Jurisprudence of Oliver Wendell Holmes." *Georgetown Journal of Law & Public Policy* 3 (2005): 53-82.

Starger, Colin. "Exile on Main Street: Competing Traditions and Due Process Dissent." *Marquette Law Review* 95 (2010): 1253-328.

Stein, Gertrude. *The Autobiography of Alice B. Toklas.* New York: Vintage Books, (1933) 1990.

Stein, Gertrude. "Three Portraits of Painters." In *Selected Writings of Gertrude Stein.* New York: Vintage Books, (1945) 1990.

Strasser, Mark. "Why Theories of Law Have Little or Nothing to Do with Judicial Restraint." *Colorado Law Review* 74 (2003): 1379-408.

Strauss, David. "Common Law Constitutional Interpretation." *University of Chicago Law Review* 63 (1996): 877-935.

Sundby, Scott E. and Lucy B. Ricca. "The Majestic and the Mundane: The Two Creation Stories of the Exclusionary Rule." *Texas Tech Law Review* 43 (2010): 391-434.

Titus, Herbert W. *God, Man, and Law: The Biblical Principles.* Oak Brook, IL: Institute in Basic Life Principles, 1994.

Titus, Herbert W. "God's Revelation: Foundation for the Common Law." *Regent University Law Review* 4 (1994): 1-38.

Touster, Saul. "Holmes a Hundred Years Ago: *The Common Law* and Legal Theory." *Hofstra Law Review* 10 (1981-82): 673-718.

Tsai, Robert L. "Fire, Metaphor, and Constitutional Myth Making." *Georgetown
Law Journal* 93 (2004): 181-239.

Urofsky, Melvin I. *Dissent and the Supreme Court: Its Role in the Court's History and
the Nation's Constitutional Dialogue.* New York: Pantheon Books, 2015.

Urofsky, Melvin I., and David W. Levy, eds. *Letters of Louis D. Brandeis, Vol. 5:
1921-1942: Elder Statesman.* Albany, NY: State University of New York Press,
1978.

Vannatta, Seth. *Conservatism and Pragmatism in Law, Politics, and Ethics.* New York:
Palgrave Macmillan, 2014.

Waldron, Jeremy. *"Partly Laws Common to All Mankind": Foreign Law in American
Courts.* New Haven, CT: Yale University Press, 2012.

Walker, Samuel. *In Defense of American Liberty: A History of the ACLU, Second Edition.* Carbondale: Southern Illinois University Press, 1999.

Waterman, Julian S. "Thomas Jefferson and Blackstone's Commentaries." *Illinois
Law Review* 27 (1932-33): 629-59.

Watson, Alan. "Structure of Blackstone's *Commentaries.*" *Yale Law Journal* 97
(1988): 795-822.

West, Cornel. *The American Evasion of Philosophy: A Genealogy of Pragmatism.* Madison: University of Wisconsin Press, 1989.

White, G. Edward. "Looking at Holmes in the Mirror." *Law and History Review* 4
(1986): 439-66.

White, G. Edward. *Justice Oliver Wendell Holmes: Law and the Inner Self.* New York:
Oxford University Press, 1993.

White, G. Edward. "The Canonization of Holmes and Brandeis: Epistemology and
Judicial Reputations." *New York University Law Review* 70 (1995): 576-621.

Willis, George. *The Philosophy of Language.* New York: MacMillan Company, n.d.
Original on file in the Cornell University Library, gifted to Cornell in 1891, Cornell University Library, Internet Archive. Online.

Wilson, Woodrow. "The Ideals of America." *Atlantic Monthly* 90 (1902): 721-34. Accessed May 8, 2015. http://www.theatlantic.com/magazine/archive/1902/12/
the-ideals-of-america/376192.

Wu, John C. H. "Justice Holmes and the Common-Law Tradition." *Vanderbilt Law
Review* 14 (1960-61): 221-38.

Young, William F. "The Federal Courts and the Federal System." *Texas Law Review*
32 (1954): 483-491.

Index

Abbott, Henry, 98, 100
Abrams v. United States, 61–66;
  influence on later rulings, 65;
  synopsis, 62
absolutes, 49, 50, 52
Adair v. U.S., 52
adaptability: and canonization of
  precedents, 85, 89, 92; of common
  law, 1, 53, 71, 81, 83, 102, 109–10,
  113; by decentralized problem
  solving, 114; Emersonians' view of,
  28; in response to cultural change,
  131; society's, xxi. *See also* evolution
aesthetic approach: Holmes's
  borrowing of Emerson's, xi; in
  jurisprudence, xi, 53; poetics of
  transition's, 46, 61; separation
  of powers and influence of, xxv;
  unique contribution to pragmatism,
  xxii. *See also* judicial aesthetics;
  literary writing
"After Apple-Picking" (Frost), 47–48
agonism, xviii–xxiii; canon formation
  through, xxi, xxii, 27, 86, 89, 123,
  134; and containment of conflict,
  98–99, 101–2; dissents' nature, xv, 2,
  29, 44, 65, 67, 71, 81–83, 89–90, 92;
  in social life, 90–91, 93, 96–97
alien peoples and cultures, 90–91
alliteration, 16, 56–57, 60, 64. *See also*
  sound
ambiguity. *See* clarity
antagonistic arguments. *See* agonism
anti-canon, constitutional, 88–89
anxiety of influence, 22, 25, 92, 102
aphorisms, 19, 56, 60, 61, 63, 65, 67,
  75n105
apostrophe, 59. *See also* sound
appellate courts, 43–44
Arizona v. Gant, 30n7
art, 51
artists, 116–17
asyndeton, 68. *See also* literary writing
authority, 119, 120
The Autobiography of Alice B. Toklas
  (Stein), 50–51
auxesis, 23–24, 68

Bacon, Francis, 57
bad-man theory of law, 122–23, 125
Baker, Liva, xviiin12
bakers, 54–56

159

transcendentalism: apostrophe in, 59;
    maladaptation of, 140n59, 115–16,
    133
transition: of Holmes's dissents, xxvi;
    in pragmatism, xxvi–xxvii. *See also*
    poetics of transition
trespass, principle of, 122
trial and error, xxiii, xxiv, 58, 103,
    109–10, 118, 126
trustbusting, 128
truth, 119–20, 124–25, 127
Tyson & Brother v. Banton, 26, 66–69;
    Holmes's dissent, 67–69; overruling
    of, 69; synopsis of, 67–68

uncertainty of speech, 24
United Kingdom, United States'
    common law *vs.*, xxiii
United States: common law in UK
    vs., xxiii; divine absolutes in, xviii;
    post–Civil War transition, 114–15
United States v. Chavez, 27
United States v. Schwimmer, 26

vindication. *See* judicial vindication
violence, prevention of, xxi–xxii,
    83–84, 96–97, 125–26

Waldron, Jeremy, 33n57
West, Cornel, 84
West Coast Hotel v. Parrish, 43–44
Western Canon, 82
White, Edward D., 94
White, G. Edward, 84
Whitman, Walt, 59
Whitney v. California, 21
*Williams v. Standard Oil Co. of
    Louisiana*, 3
Williams v. State of North Carolina, 26
Willis, George, 60
Wilson, Woodrow, 129
Wright, Chauncy, 100

yoked pairs, 89–90. *See also* anti-canon;
    canon
Youngstown Sheet & Tube Co. v. Sawyer,
    27

About the Author

Allen Mendenhall is Associate Dean and Executive Director of the Blackstone & Burke Center for Law & Liberty at Faulkner University Thomas Goode Jones School of Law. Visit his website at AllenMendenhall.com.